WITH WINSTON CHURCHILL AT THE FRONT
Winston in the Trenches 1916

WITH WINSTON CHURCHILL AT THE FRONT

Winston in the Trenches 1916

Major Dewar Gibb MBE, QC, LLD, MA, LLB

Introduced by Nigel Dewar Gibb

Foreword by Randolph Churchill

Frontline Books

WITH WINSTON CHURCHILL AT THE FRONT
Winston in the Trenches 1916

First published in 1924, under the pseudonym Captain X, by Gowans and Gray Ltd., London and Glasgow.

This extended edition published in 2016 and reprinted in this format in 2021 by Frontline Books,
an imprint of Pen & Sword Books Ltd,
47 Church Street, Barnsley, S. Yorkshire, S70 2AS.

Copyright © Major Andrew Dewar Gibb MBE, QC, LLD, MA, LLB

The right of Major Andrew Dewar Gibb to be identified as the author of this work has been asserted by him in accordance with the Copyright, Designs and Patents Act 1988.

ISBN: 9-781-39908-234-1

All rights reserved. No part of this publication may be reproduced, stored in or introduced into a retrieval system, or transmitted, in any form, or by any means (electronic, mechanical, photocopying, recording or otherwise) without the prior written permission of the publisher. Any person who does any unauthorized act in relation to this publication may be liable to criminal prosecution and civil claims for damages.

CIP data records for this title are available from the British Library

For more information on our books, please visit
www.frontline-books.com,
email info@frontline-books.com
or write to us at the above address.

Printed and bound by CPI Group (UK) Ltd, Croydon, CR0 4YY
Typeset in 11/13.25 Garamond Book

Foreword

In writing this foreword I must start by saying how delighted the Churchill family is that this remarkable book is being republished. There have been many books written about my great-grandfather, but this one is special. We hear and read so much about Churchill the statesman, the inspirational figure who led the nation and the Commonwealth to victory in the Second World War, but little is said about him during his brief spell away from politics in 1915/16 during the first 'World Crisis'. The author, Dewar Gibb, served with Churchill in the trenches during the First World War; his account shows that Churchill could practise what he preached and that, away from the public arena, was a brave and inspiring leader of men under fire.

I am often asked: 'What was the making of the man?' A large part of his unique character undoubtedly came from his remarkable and dynamic mother, the beautiful Jennie Jerome from Brooklyn, New York City. Another part was formed during Churchill's darkest hour: Gallipoli and the Dardanelles disaster. This project was brilliantly conceived from the noblest of motives, for Churchill had written to the Prime Minister, H.H. Asquith: 'Are there not other alternatives than sending our armies to chew barbed wire in Flanders?'

Churchill and the government planned to create a new front elsewhere, to alleviate the wholesale slaughter of a generation on the Western Front; this would lighten the load on the hard-pressed Russians fighting the Turks in the Caucasus, demonstrate to the wavering Balkan neutrals that they should not join the war on the enemy side, and – hopefully – knock Turkey out of the war. But the Navy could not force its way through the Strait, the military resources did not provide enough troops, and the Turkish resistance was strong. Churchill was obliged to give up his office as First Lord of the Admiralty, to allow the Conservative opposition party to join a Coalition government under Asquith (a Liberal). After six months in a minor cabinet post, he resigned from the government and, as a Territorial officer (he was a major in the Queen's Own Oxfordshire Hussars), he reported for duty at the front.

Churchill was made a scapegoat for the Gallipoli debacle. As political head of the Royal Navy, he had done his best to create the conditions needed to enable the fleet to force the Dardanelles. But he held no executive power over the landing of troops at Gallipoli; this was the responsibility of the Secretary-of-State at the War Office, Field Marshal the Earl Kitchener of Khartoum. The situation was Churchill's first real setback in a meteoric rise. His wife Clementine later said: 'I thought he would die of grief.'

When he arrived at the front in November 1915, Churchill presented himself to the Commander-in-Chief of the British Expeditionary Force, Field Marshal Sir John French, whom he knew well, telling him that he was 'the escaped scapegoat'. Churchill was delighted to be assigned by French, for a forty-day period of familiarisation, instruction and experience, to 2nd Battalion, Grenadier Guards: 'the best school of all'. It was not a coincidence that this was the regiment in which his ancestor, the first Duke of Marlborough, had served and later commanded. The commanding officer, Lieutenant Colonel 'Ma' Jeffreys, welcomed him by saying: 'I think I ought to tell you that we were not at all consulted in the matter of your coming to join us.' Charming! Churchill knew that nothing counted 'except military rank and behaviour'.

After his time with the Grenadiers, French had hoped to give Churchill command of a brigade (four battalions comprising around 5,000 men) and the rank of Brigadier General, which would have counted for a great deal. But when the time came, French had been replaced by Sir Douglas Haig and he and Asquith felt that 'perhaps he might have a battalion': not 5,000, but fewer than 800 men under command.

The 6th Battalion, Royal Scots Fusiliers had been mauled at the Battle of Loos and subsequent winter service on the Ypres Salient; its members were battered and demoralised. The troops distrusted him and were taken aback to have the politician whom they believed to have overseen the Gallipoli disaster as their commanding officer. Churchill's first words to the officers, after staring at each of them out of countenance during an uncomfortable welcome lunch, were: 'Gentlemen, I am now your commanding officer. Those who support me I will look after. Those who go against me I will break. Good afternoon, Gentlemen.' Yet he worked to earn their respect through his decency, hard work, humour and constant bravery. He inspired the devotion of his men in a remarkably short time. He overlooked nothing, taking great pains to gain their confidence: declaring war on lice, improvising baths out of brewery vats and bringing all his influence to bear in order to secure new equipment and clothing, improving the rations, and supervising the creation of a football pitch and arranging matches. He set about improving morale and conditions with customary dedication.

Churchill often led his platoons on sorties into No Man's Land and was nearly killed on several occasions. Shells were landing everywhere, and in one incident he was saved from almost certain injury by his trench torch which took the impact of flying shrapnel. Churchill demonstrated that here was a man who trusted in his own destiny.

Gibb's book is the story of a man who had fallen politically low and yet was not knocked down. I believe that, if not for the disaster at Gallipoli, the D-Day landings in 1944 would not have succeeded. As head of government in 1940 Churchill made sure that he had control and the resources for success – he was both Prime Minister and Minister of Defence – even as he privately acknowledged the risk it represented. On the night before D-Day he dined alone with Clementine and said to her: 'By the time you wake tomorrow there may be 20,000 young men dead.' The responsibility he bore was incredible, but he could not have achieved greatness without the failures.

What is perhaps most remarkable about Churchill's time at the front is how, in such a short space of time, he was able to win the respect and warm admiration of the men around him. Both with the Grenadier Guards and the Royal Scots Fusiliers he was able to turn his perceived public image of a remote politician into one of a kindly, almost father-like, compassionate comrade. This is revealed in Gibb's charming little book, which has been expanded to include much of the correspondence between Winston and Clementine during that period. As well as other accounts, it shows simply the relationship between a commanding officer and his men. Gibb could not know what a great man Churchill was to become. Indeed, after Gallipoli many assumed that Churchill's career was over. This book reveals only too clearly how a great man could be misunderstood and misrepresented by myth, before giving personal demonstration of great gifts for the benefit of all – for history.

It is also interesting to observe that, of the eight hundred soldiers in this small section of the line; three men were to become prominent, senior political leaders: Sir Archibald Sinclair, the second-in-command, would become leader of the Liberal Party; Dewar Gibb himself (disguised as Captain 'X') would become leader of the Scottish National Party; Churchill, as Prime Minister of a Coalition government, would become the saviour of his country in its darkest hour.

My great-grandfather was born on St Andrew's Day 1874; married the granddaughter of a Scottish nobleman in 1908; served as MP for Dundee in 1908-1922; and commanded a Scottish battalion at the front in 1916. So it is perhaps appropriate that his time in the trenches was chronicled by a future leader of the Scottish National party. Such are the comradeships formed in war!

FOREWORD

I shall end with Gibb's assessment of my great-grandfather after he had left the Royal Scots Fusiliers. 'Colonel Churchill,' he wrote, 'left behind him there men who will always be his loyal partisans and admirers, and who are proud of having served in the Great War under the leadership of one who is beyond question a great man.'

Randolph Churchill
February, 2016

Introduction

It is difficult to find words to describe my father. He was a serious academic with a good sense of humour and a passionate advocate of Scotland, its culture, history and identity. Many outside the legal profession knew him mainly for his political aspirations. He was born in Paisley on 13 February 1888. His father was Doctor William Fletcher Gibb who married Mary Jane Walker. He was educated at Paisley Grammar School, followed by a spell at a boarding school in Sutton in Surrey and then Trinity College Glenalmond in Perthshire. His life would be spent working in the legal profession and he studied law at Glasgow University, graduating with an MA in 1910 and a Bachelor of Laws (LLD) degree in 1913. Law classes began early, at 08.00 hours, and finished early to allow students to further their legal education in professional offices after lectures. Further to gaining his rugby cap at Glenalmond, he played full back for Glasgow University's 1st XV.

He became a member of the Scottish Bar in 1914 but decided to volunteer for the Army and was posted to France to join the 6th Battalion, Royal Scots Fusiliers. Here he was immediately faced with all the horrors of trench warfare. Like so many of his generation he spoke little of his wartime experiences. He had no wish to recount the terrible things he had witnessed, or to burden others with the pain he still felt. An indication of how he shielded his family from the realities of the war was revealed when he told me once that on one occasion when he was on leave his grandmother asked to be assured that there was never any fighting on Sundays!

Whilst he did not share his experiences with his family, we were all aware that he struggled with the memories of those difficult days throughout his life. The only exception to this self-imposed silence was when he was recounting tales of the time he spent with Winston Churchill, which prompted him to write his brief memoir.

My father was called to the English Bar in 1917 and after he was demobbed he decided to practise in England, which he did until 1929. By that time he had married my mother and, with a young family, he decided to return to his beloved Scotland. He became a member of the Bar in Edinburgh, at the same time gaining a visiting lectureship in English Law at Edinburgh University. He was also invited to start a course in Scots Law at Cambridge University. This dual role allowed him to make significant contributions to legal literature in the form of articles, papers and textbooks. He was appointed Regius Professor of Law at Glasgow University, where he remained until 1958. At Glasgow he served as Dean of the Law Faculty from 1937 to 1939 and again from 1945 to 1947 where he also made a substantial contribution as Assessor of the Senate and Assessor of the General Council. When he became an Honorary Sheriff of Lanarkshire he was appointed a King's Counsel in 1947. In 1959 he was capped with an honorary LLD from Aberdeen University. It is said that he trained an entire generation of Scottish lawyers.

Those are the basic fact of his working life, but they tell little about who my father really was. During the 1920s he stood twice for Parliament as a Unionist but increasingly he came to appreciate the history, culture and economic strength of the land of his birth and became convinced that Scotland should return to being an independent country within the Commonwealth. In 1930 he published *Scotland in Eclipse*, which argued that, whilst undertaken with the best of intentions, the Union benefited neither England nor Scotland. As a consequence he and a number of others from the Unionist Party founded the Scottish Party. This

INTRODUCTION

group later merged with the National Party of Scotland to form the Scottish National Party and my father became its leader from 1936 to 1940.

He stood unsuccessfully on three occasions as the SNP candidate for the Combined Scottish Universities, a parliamentary seat that no longer exists. He was also a founder member and Chairman of the Saltire Society which continues to recognise and reward excellence in literature, architecture and other cultural achievements in Scotland. In total he wrote fifteen books and monographs, principally on various aspects of law but also on the future of Scotland, which included *Scottish Empire* in 1937 and *Scotland Resurgent*, published in 1950. His memoir *With Winston Churchill at the Front* was his first book and was published anonymously in 1924, my father calling himself 'Captain X'. This book, which has been long out of print, forms the basis of this current publication.

He was somewhat austere and he was distinctly Victorian and old-fashioned in his habits, with a cold bath every morning in Glasgow, open razor shaving and dip pens, not fountain nor ballpoint pens. Before the Second World War we lived most of each year in Shandon, an area just outside Helensburgh on the Gareloch, Dunbartonshire. Almost every day, in all weathers, he would go down to the shore, and walk slowly into the freezing waters of the loch for a swim. This habit was followed by some of us but only in high summer!

He stopped eating out in protest at what he considered were the high prices charged in restaurants, and in around 1929 my father gave up his car. He did not enjoy driving, nor did he ever fully master the art. He was, though, a keen sailor. Both before and after the Second World War he owned a yacht which he moored in the Gareloch called *Sibylla*, which was succeeded by *Ripple*. Father always tried to take the yacht back to its mooring under sail and was disappointed if circumstances forced him to start the engine as he was not at all interested in things mechanical. He was also an accomplished, if self-taught, pianist which brought him great pleasure.

INTRODUCTION

Father had a fascination with foreign languages, though, to his eternal frustration, good Gaelic eluded him. He developed a fine basic knowledge of a number of European languages. I can still picture him now, that serious academic, lost in his studies, sitting with a cigar in his bed into the early hours of the morning, surrounded by foreign-language books and the appropriate dictionaries.

My father died at home on 24 January in 1974, aged eighty-five, after a long illness believed to be related to what is now called Post Traumatic Stress Disorder. He had made an enormous impact upon the Scottish legal profession. He was a complex, compelling and much loved man.

Nigel Dewar Gibb
Glasgow
September, 2015

Part I

Chapter 1

Winston the Warrior

Being the descendent of one of Britain's greatest generals, and having been born in the magnificent palace that bears the name of the Duke of Marlborough's most brilliant victory, it is little wonder that the light of military glory shone brightly in the imagination of the young Winston Churchill. Inspirational images of the Duke and the vast panorama of the Battle of Blenheim covered the walls of the palace and when Winston's father, the mercurial Lord Randolph Churchill, served as private secretary to his father, the then Viceroy of Ireland, the young boy was able to watch with awe and envy the martial pomp and ceremony of the parades that marched past Dublin's Vice Regal Lodge.

His early education at two schools, one in Berkshire and one in Sussex, was followed by Harrow where, within weeks of his arrival, he joined the Harrow Rifle Corps. He was just thirteen-years-old.

From Harrow Winston went to the Royal Military College, Sandhurst, after two failed attempts at the entrance exam. He applied for the cavalry rather than the infantry as this required a lower grade and following his graduation in December 1894 he became a cornet in the 4th Queen's Own Hussars. At last Winston was a soldier and the battlefield beckoned.

Frustratingly for Winston, there were no battles for him to fight. Europe, surprisingly, was at peace with itself and the British Empire temporarily subdued. So it was to Cuba that the warrior Winston departed, after seeking permission from none other than the Commander-in-Chief of the British Army, Sir Garnet Wolseley, to join the Spanish army as an observer. Here a few thousand guerrillas were defying the Spanish forces of General Campos. It was in the wilds of Cuba that Winston came under fire for the first time. He was part of a column that was trying to track down the rebels in the Cuban jungles. After a few days' march, as the column was passing through a forest, the guerrillas launched an ambush. Bullets whistled through the air, one of which struck a horse close to Winston.

The wound to the horse was the first combat casualty the twenty-year-old Winston had seen and it had a profound effect upon him. 'The bullet had struck between his ribs, the blood dripped on the ground, and there was a circle of dark red on his bright-chestnut coat about a foot wide. Evidently he was going to die, for his saddle and bridle were soon taken off him. As I watched I could not help reflecting that the bullet had certainly passed within a foot of my head. So at any rate I had been "under fire". That was something. Nevertheless, I began to take a more thoughtful view of our enterprise than I had hitherto done.'[1]

There was more fighting to come for Churchill but he found that war consisted more of interminable marches through impenetrable jungle to uncertain destinations, punctuated only by the occasional combat. Glory was as elusive as the enemy.

The deeds of men are fleeting but if consigned to print are immortalized. So it was that in Cuba Winston began his long career of self-promotion. He was commissioned to write a series of articles on Cuba for the *Daily Graphic* and these established the young Churchill as a promising war correspondent, with his own adventures foremost.

Winston returned home from his Cuban experience to find his regiment preparing for India and he had to wait until 1897 before he saw action again. It was on the infamous North-West Frontier that the Pathan tribesmen were rebelling under the Fakir of Ipi and a punitive expedition was mounted. In search of excitement, Winston once more sought the opportunity to put his actions into words, obtaining a commission from the *Daily Telegraph* at the rate of £5 a column and picking up another commission from the Allahabad *Pioneer* as he made his way to the front.

Winston was sent into the Malakand District on British India's frontier to serve in a brigade under General Jeffrey. Whilst operating in the Mahmund Valley, Jeffrey's force encountered the Pathans who proved a far different enemy to those that had skulked in the jungles of Cuba, as Churchill was to record: 'The Adjutant had been shot. Four of his soldiers were carrying him. He was a heavy man, and they all clutched him. Out from the edge of the houses rushed half a dozen Pathan swordsmen. The bearers of the poor Adjutant let him fall and fled at their approach.

'The leading tribesman rushed upon the prostrate figure and slashed at it three or four times with his sword. I forgot everything else at this moment except a desire to kill this man ... The savage saw me coming. I was not more than twenty yards away. He picked up a big stone and hurled it at me with his left hand, and then awaited me brandishing his sword. There were others waiting not far behind.

'I changed my mind about the cold steel. I pulled out my revolver, took, as I thought, careful aim, and fired. No result. I fired again. No result. I fired again. Whether I hit him or not I cannot tell. At any rate he ran back two or three yards and plumped down behind a rock.

'The fusillade was continuous. I looked around. I was all alone with the enemy. Not a friend to be seen. I ran as fast as I could. There were bullets everywhere. I got to the first knoll. Hurrah, there were the Sikhs holding the lower one! They made vehement gestures, and in a few moments I was among them.'[2]

Churchill's writing was earning him considerable amounts of additional funds and after he returned from the expedition he turned his experiences into his first book, *The Malakand Field Force*. For this he was paid the handsome sum of £600.

More opportunities for adventure presented themselves the following year when Lord Kitchener undertook an expedition into the Sudan. The 4th Hussars was not going to be involved in the campaign, but the 21st Lancers was and, with the help of his mother and his new supporter, Prime Minister Lord Salisbury, he was attached to the Lancers and head for Cairo. The success of his first book also ensured a commission from the *Morning Post*, his rates having trebled to £15 per column.

The soldier journalist reached the battle front just in time to take part in what has been described as the last classic cavalry charge delivered by the British Army. Just 300 Lancers faced some 3,000 Dervishes. The action that followed lasted only a matter of minutes.

'Two hundred and fifty yards away the dark-blue men were firing madly in a thin film of light-blue smoke. Their bullets struck the hard gravel into the air, and the troopers, to shield their faces from the stinging dust, bowed their helmets forward, like the Cuirassiers at Waterloo. The pace was fast and the distance short. Yet, before it was half covered, the whole aspect of the affair changed. A deep crease in the ground – a dry watercourse, a khor – appeared where all had seemed smooth, level plain; and from it there sprang, with the suddenness of a pantomime effect and a high-pitched yell, a dense white mass of men nearly as long as our front and about twelve deep ...

'The Dervishes fought manfully. They tried to hamstring the horses. They fired their rifles, pressing the muzzles into the very bodies of their opponents. They cut reins and stirrup-leathers. They flung their throwing-spears with great dexterity. They tried every device of cool, determined men practised in war and familiar with cavalry; and, besides, they swung sharp, heavy swords which bit deep. The hand-to-hand fighting on the further side of the khor lasted for perhaps one minute. Then the horses got into their stride again, the pace increased, and the Lancers drew out from among their antagonists. Within two minutes of the collision every living man was clear of the Dervish mass ...

'Riderless horses galloped across the plain. Men, clinging to their saddles, lurched helplessly about, covered with blood from perhaps a dozen wounds. Horses, streaming from tremendous gashes, limped and staggered with their riders. In 120 seconds, five officers, 65 men, and 119 horses out of fewer than 400 had been killed or wounded.'[3]

As soon as the Lancers had ridden through the enemy line the regiment reformed. According to Churchill he told his men that they might have to repeat the charge, to which his centre guide replied in a loud voice, 'All right sir – we're ready – as many times as you like'.

Churchill appeared unafraid even in such desperate circumstances. At this youthful time in his life, he saw the war as being 'full of fascinating thrills', and wrote 'Talk of fun! Where will you beat this'.

He asked his second sergeant if he had 'enjoyed' himself. The sergeant replied 'Well, I don't exactly say I enjoyed it, Sir; but I think I'll get more used to it next time'. At this the whole troop laughed.

These words are only a fraction of a glittering description Churchill once wrote of the charge at Omdurman. Such stories, with Winston always the central character, brought him considerable notoriety. Churchill was already beginning to realize that he might be able to make more of a mark outside the Army than in it. His father, Randolph, had been Chancellor of the Exchequer and Leader of the House of Commons, and increasingly Winston could see that politics offered far greater prospects than the military.

Before embarking on the Sudan expedition he had told Lord Salisbury that he was going to write about the campaign, 'which will from a monetary, as well as from other points of view ... be useful to me'. Winston's motives for joining the expedition were apparent even to Lord Kitchener who could see that Churchill was not going to stay in the Army and 'was only making a convenience out of it'.

The financial success of *The River War* provided Winston the opportunity to resign his commission and concentrate on writing – and politics. When he returned to the UK after his resignation on 5 May 1899, Winston, still only twenty-four-years-old, went to the headquarters of the Conservative Party and asked for a constituency at which he might stand. Robert Ashcroft, one of the Conservative Members for Oldham, invited Winston, on his own initiative, to stand with him as fellow Member in this two-Member borough, as the other Member, James Oswald, had been ill for some time. Unfortunately, Ashcroft died suddenly and Oswald resigned, prompting a by-election. In a major swing to the Liberals, both seats were lost by the Conservatives. Churchill, though, had made an impact on the political scene, and the *Morning Post* declared that 'the honours of the day undoubtedly go to Mr. Churchill ... the brilliant manner in which he has acquitted himself during the most interesting by-election to this Parliament makes his entry into the House one of the few certainties of political life'.

As it transpired, just three months after the Oldham by-election, the Boer republics rebelled against British hegemony in South Africa and war broke out on 11 October 1899. The very next day Winston obtained a commission as a war correspondent for the *Morning Post* with a salary of £250 per month, far more than he had been earning as a junior cavalry officer.

Winston sailed for the Cape on the *Dunottar Castle*, the very same boat as the man engaged to take command of the British forces in South Africa, Sir Redvers Buller, allowing the young correspondent the chance to observe the General at close quarters. He was astonished at Buller's apparent disinterest, and therefore lack of preparedness, in the conflict. Buller's lack of professionalism, one author has put it, convinced Winston that 'war could not safely be left to generals alone'.[4]

As soon *Dunottar Castle* docked at Cape Town, Winston was on his way to the front at Estcourt. When, on 14 November, an armoured train steamed out on a reconnaissance mission with a company each of the Dublin Fusiliers and the Durham Light Infantry with a 6-pounder naval gun, under the command of Captain Haldane, Churchill was on board.

Not long into its journey the train ran into a Boer patrol and came under heavy fire. The engine driver put on full steam, and the train dashed at high speed round the corner of a bend only to crash into a large stone that blocked the line, throwing three of the armoured trucks off the rails. The Boers shifted position and continued to pour fire upon the train. The small naval gun was hit by the Boers' two large field guns and bullets from a Maxim machine-gun riddled the armoured trucks. While Haldane and his men returned fire, Winston called for twenty volunteers to clear one of the trucks off the track that was half on and half off the rails.

Only nine volunteered to go out into the open with Winston, who encouraged them with the words, 'Keep cool, this will be interesting for my paper'. Under a hail of gunfire Winston and his team eventually cleared the track and the engine could head back for Estcourt. 'The engine was a sorry sight with water spurting from the tanks, the fire-box in flames, and wounded hanging on everywhere,' Churchill later recounted. 'The soldiers who were left behind then made for some houses about 800 yards distant, but one man waved his handkerchief and the Boers galloped down and called on the men to surrender.'

Churchill had managed to jump onto the engine as it pulled away, but when he saw the plight of those left behind he jumped down and ran to their assistance. Seeing the hopelessness of their situation the soldiers surrendered, leaving Winston facing the Boers alone. He tried to run but, as he himself admitted 'owing to slackness about football and other games at Harrow', he was unable to go at any pace at all.

Taken prisoner, Winston was in real trouble. By actively participating in the battle as a civilian he had broken the Articles of War and the Boers would have had every right to shoot him on the spot. The Boers, though, seemed more amused than angered when they realised whom they had captured. 'We don't catch the son of a lord every day,' Winston was told. He was also told that they would not be letting him go.

Along with sixty British officers, including Haldane who had also remained behind with his men, Churchill was taken to an improvised prisoner of war camp in the State Model Schools in Pretoria. It would not hold Winston for long.

The Model Schools were guarded by forty South African Republican Police, of whom ten, armed with rifle and revolver, were on duty at a time. The buildings were surrounded by an iron grille and a corrugated-iron fence about ten feet high. Though Winston was entirely unfamiliar with the country and spoke neither

Dutch nor Afrikaans he was determined to escape. His chance came on the evening of 12 December.

He saw that the two guards closest two him were standing with their backs turned. Winston climbed over the fence into an adjoining garden. Haldane had planned to go with Churchill but as he was about to follow one of the guards had turned round.

Winston was faced with an agonizing choice, deciding that he could not let the opportunity pass, he had to leave Haldane behind and make good his escape. Walking boldly within a few yards of the guard at the schools' gate, Winston set off on his daring escapade which would make him one of the most famous men in Britain.

Walking through Pretoria and out into the suburbs, Winston came across a railway track that headed east. He followed it for some distance until he came to a station. Here he laid in an adjacent ditch just beyond the platform until the whistle of a locomotive alerted him to the approach of a train. As he expected, the train came to a halt at the station. As it was leaving the platform Winston left the ditch and clambered onto one of the couplings and then into a coal truck.

The train travelled through the night and as daylight broke he leapt off the train as it slowed up due to an incline. Winston waited under cover all day for another night train but discovered that none passed that way during darkness. There was nothing for it, Winston would have to walk.

With the Boers at war, all bridges were guarded and Churchill had to wade through bogs and marshes. As night was falling the exhausted escaper decided he could not continue. But once again luck was Winston's friend; he knocked on the door of a house only to discover that he had stumbled upon the only English family within twenty miles.

He was hidden in one of the nearby pits of the Transvaal Collieries (helped, coincidentally by a man who hailed from Oldham) while the Boers hunted for the man who had, it was seen, broken his parole. A £25 reward was offered for 'anyone who brings in the escaped prisoner of war, Churchill, dead or alive'. The 'wanted' poster described Winston thus: 'Englishman, 25 years old, about 5 ft. 8 in. tall, indifferent build, walks with a forward stoop, pale appearance, red-brownish hair, small and hardly noticeable moustache, talks through his nose and cannot pronounce the letter "s" properly.'

The houses of known British sympathizers were searched but after a few days it was considered safe enough for him to continue his journey. He was smuggled amongst bales of wool aboard a goods train and, after two and a half days, crossed the border into Portuguese East Africa. From Lourenco Marques, the colony's capital, Winston telegraphed the *Morning Post* on 21 December: 'I am weak but I am free. I have lost many pounds but I am lighter in heart. I shall also avail myself of every opportunity from this moment to urge with earnestness an unflinching and uncompromising prosecution of the war.'

He returned by ship to Durban where he was welcomed, by most people at least, as a hero. His dramatic escape was heralded in the British press at a time when the British Army was struggling to assert itself against the highly effective Boer forces. Winston had become positively famous.

The people of Oldham now saw him as one of their own and he received a rapturous welcome, the mill-girls and machine operatives turning out en masse to greet him as he drove through the streets in a procession of ten landaus. When he told a crowded Theatre Royal about the man from Oldham who had helped him in the Transvaal mine a voice called out, 'His wife's in the gallery'. If there was any doubt who would win the next election for Oldham, it disappeared in that moment.

That autumn the Government dissolved itself, seeking a mandate from the people for its policies in the war with the Boers, which it appeared Britain was on the verge of winning. The Conservatives went to the country telling the electorate that a vote for the Opposition meant a vote for the Boers. In what therefore became known as the 'Khaki election', the twenty-six-years-old Winston Churchill was elected as the second Member for Oldham. His majority was just 230.

Chapter 2

Winston at the Helm

The autumn election of 1900 was spread over the course of a month, throughout which the Conservatives ferried their popular new Member around the constituencies that had still to cast their votes. 'Henceforward I became a "star turn" at the election,' Winston recalled. 'I was sought for from every part of the country,' being transported to London, Birmingham and Stockport to speak at packed gatherings.

Members of Parliament did not get paid in those days and as soon as the election was won by the Conservatives (with an increased majority) Churchill's thoughts turned to making money. The sales of *The River War* and the ten months' salary owed to him by the *Morning Post* meant that he was comfortable for the time being, but life as an MP was going to be costly and he decided to take advantage of his newly-won fame with a series of highly-lucrative lectures. Indeed, he did not take his seat in the Commons for the opening days of Parliament as he was on a lecture tour of the United States, and it was not until January 1901 that Winston first sat in the hall of which he would become its greatest orator.

It was not long before he showed that independence of mind which brought him notoriety and animosity in equal measure throughout his political life. He was a vocal opponent of the Government's attempts at imposing barriers to protect the trade of the Empire. So strenuously did he fight his own side, he was banished from his party, joining the Liberals, and told never to return. Churchill replied that he 'left the stupid party because he no longer wished to go on saying stupid things'.

The debate over Free Trade led to the collapse of Arthur Balfour's administration and at the subsequent election Winston, who had already crossed the floor of the House to join the Liberals, decided to tackle the hitherto safe Tory seat of Manchester North-West. This he won in what was nationally a Liberal landslide in favour of Free Trade which had been so powerfully advocated by Churchill.

Winston returned to the Commons to sit on the Front benches, becoming the Liberal Under Secretary-of-State for the Colonies. At the age of thirty-one, Churchill had become a junior minister. By the time he was thirty-four Winston had risen through the ranks to join the Cabinet as President of the Board of Trade. He was undoubtedly the Liberal Party's rising star but under a Parliamentary procedure, long since abandoned, a new Cabinet member, whose ability to represent his constituency would be diminished due to the time he would have to devote to his or her new post, had to submit himself to the verdict of his constituents in a by-election. Winston, therefore, had to fight yet another election battle. It was unusual for a new minister to be rejected by his constituents, but on this occasion it happened, and the Tory press could not conceal its delight. 'Churchill is out,' announced the *Daily Telegraph*. 'We have all been yearning for this to happen, with a yearning beyond utterance ... Winston Churchill is out, OUT, OUT.' Winston lost, it was said, because he had no principles.

This was not the view of the Liberal Party which immediately sought to bring Winston back into the Commons by inviting him to stand for Dundee. Winston won his Scottish seat with a huge majority and was back on the Front Bench. It was during this period of his life that Winston met and married Miss Clementine Hozier, daughter of the late Colonel Sir Henry Hozier and Lady Blanche Hozier.

A close associate of Churchill was Lloyd George who became Chancellor of the Exchequer. It was during Lloyd George's struggle to pass the so-called 'People's Budget' in 1909, in which new taxes upon the wealthy were introduced and social welfare programmes were created, that Churchill rose to the fore. It resulted in his appointment to Home Secretary. Churchill was now at the very heart of Government.

Though he helped to draft the first unemployment pension legislation, set up Labour Exchanges and promoted a Bill that set up the first minimum wages in Britain, his new position also brought him into conflict with the working classes. It was the miners' strike of 1910 that gave Churchill his most difficulty. In Wales there was a number of ugly incidents between the miners and police in the Rhondda Valley and Winston agreed to send in the Army in case the police became exhausted. General Sir Nevil Macready was given the authority to take control of both the military and the civil forces. Some 600 Welsh police officers, 500 Metropolitan Police officers and two squadrons of Hussars were sent into the Rhondda.

A particularly bitter riot at Tonypandy was put down without the need of the cavalry and Winston was praised for 'his foresight in sending a strong force of Metropolitan Police directly he was aware of the state of affairs in the valleys that bloodshed was avoided'. This, though, was not how it was seen by the miners, more than 500 of whom were injured with one man being killed. It was the fact that Winston was prepared to use the Army to put down the riot that particularly incensed many of the miners.

Apart from the miners' strikes, Winston also faced labour troubles in London and Manchester as well as a railwaymen's strike. There were also the Suffragettes. Winston was returning by train from a meeting in Bradford when a young male Suffragette supporter forced his way into Churchill's compartment brandishing a whip. Fortunately he was stopped before he could carry out whatever punishment he wished to inflict upon the Home Secretary.

His support for taxes upon the wealthy and opposition from the lower classes, especially the Welsh miners, meant that Churchill was no longer seen as 'the most popular man in Britain'.

Then, in 1911, Winston once again had to call out the Army. This time it was at around 10.00 hours on the morning of 3 January. The Home Secretary was in his bath when there was an urgent knocking at the door. He was informed that two or three 'anarchists', who were responsible for the recent shooting of five policemen, three of whom had died, had taken refuge in a room at 100 Sidney Street in Stepney. They had plenty of arms and ammunition and even home-made bombs.

The building was surrounded by 200 police and the group was called upon to surrender. The anarchists replied with their guns and a police inspector was wounded. The police returned fire but with no prospect of bringing the siege to a quick conclusion the Home Secretary was asked for help from the Army. Churchill did not hesitate.

This time it was the Scots Guards, the men being deployed from the Tower of London. Both sides continued to fire on the other. As the gunfight that has become referred to as the Siege of Sidney Street, popularly known as the 'Battle of Stepney', continued to rage it was seen that the building in which the gunmen were located had caught fire. The fire brigade was soon on the scene but the police were worried that the firemen might be shot if they approached the house. Winston had been anxious to be present at the siege and the decision was passed to the Home Secretary. His response was unequivocal. He could not let the firemen risk their lives. At the end of the siege the charred bodies of two of the anarchists were found inside.

Winston Churchill would be remembered, above all things, for his opposition to Germany and it was the perceived threat from the First Reich that propelled him from the Home Office to the Admiralty in October 1911. His brief was simple. He had to put the Fleet into 'a state of instant and constant readiness for war in case we are attacked by Germany'. It was this task, Winston felt, which his life as a soldier and statesman had been preparing him for.

The First Lord was a political position and whoever might be its incumbent was supposed to take only a nominal interest in the Royal Navy and its working. The First Lord was expected to be guided by the naval Sea Lords and to defer to their greater knowledge of the Senior Service. Not so Winston. In his first eighteen months in office he spent 182 days at sea, something previously unheard of. He certainly ruffled many feathers during his early months at the Admiralty, particularly when he asked lower ranks for their opinions on subjects without referring first to senior officers. This was seen as seriously undermining naval discipline. But Churchill wanted to learn as much as possible, and as quickly as possible, about his new command, its preservation as the finest in the world he saw as vital in safeguarding Britain's future. 'He felt to the quick the traditional glamour of the new office,' wrote Violet Asquith, 'the part that it played in our island history, the conviction that it was today the keystone of our safety and survival.'

His new post was one of immense responsibility. The Royal Navy consumed about a fifth of all government expenditure and was enormously important to the social and economic structure of the nation. The Admiralty was the chief industrial patron in Britain, designing and manufacturing an astonishing variety of items, from torpedoes to chamber pots. Entire towns such as Portsmouth, Chatham and Plymouth were completely devoted to, and dependent upon, the Royal Navy.

Churchill was determined that under his stewardship this great institution would flourish. He studied gunnery and watched firing practice. It was Churchill who was responsible for the development of the navy's largest gun, the famous 15-inch weapon that would out-range all others until *Bismarck* took to the seas a generation later. He visited every ship and every naval base in the United Kingdom, and those he could practically reach overseas. He travelled in warships, submarines and seaplanes or in the Admiralty yacht *Enchantress* whenever his duties did not entrap him at Westminster or Whitehall.

Winston improved conditions for the Lower Decks and increased the prospects of promotion to commissioned rank. He also fast-tracked promising young officers, notably Sir John Jellicoe and Sir David Beatty. A significant step forward was his expediting of the work on the bases at Rosyth, Cromarty and Scapa Flow. With the growing menace of Germany across the North Sea, these locations were absolutely essential.

Possibly the most important measure introduced by Churchill was that of a real Naval Staff, something that the navy, and in particular the First Sea Lord, Admiral Sir John Arbuthnot 'Jacky' (or 'Jackie') Fisher, had long resisted. This new body was able to prepare proper strategic plans and integrate them with those of the War Office.

Winston pushed forward all these measures because he was convinced, more than most, that war with Germany was inevitable. It was, in Winston's view, only a matter of time, and it was time that he desired most of all. Winston was a man in a hurry.

A chart of the North Sea, on which the daily situation of the German Fleet was marked, was pinned up on the wall behind Winton's desk in his office at the Admiralty. He used to frequently challenge his staff by asking them what action they would take 'if war with Germany happens today?' He did this to impart a sense of ever-present danger amongst his team.

Winston was always someone who had a world view of affairs and whilst he devoted his renowned energy to the Royal Navy, he also maintained a keen interest in the Army. After resigning his commission in the Regular Army he continued to write on military matters and he was aware of the military service of his brother Jack and his cousin Charles, who was the Ninth Duke of Marlborough. Both of these held commissions in the Queen's Own Oxfordshire Hussars, a Yeomanry regiment in the Army reserve that had been founded by the Fifth Duke. So, just seventeen months after leaving the Army, Winston was back in uniform as a Captain in the Oxfordshire Hussars, his commission being dated 4 January 1902.

The regiment was composed of four squadrons located at Henley, Oxford, Banbury and Woodstock. It was to this last one that Winston was first assigned, though it was the Henley squadron that Winston principally attended as it was closer by train to his London home. His duties included attending the annual camp – an event which Winston thoroughly relished. Not only did he like the military training, he also enjoyed the camaraderie of men with shared goals.

On 28 April 1905, Winston assumed command of the Henley squadron and, the following month, was promoted to the rank of major. After taking command, Winston played an active part in the regiment and in 1906 he was invited to be an observer at the annual manoeuvres of the German army in Silesia. He later recorded his impressions followed a second visit, this time to Würzburg, in 1909:

'The manoeuvres at Wurzburg [sic] showed a great change in German military tactics. A remarkable stride had been made in modernising their infantry formations and adapting them to actual war conditions. The dense masses were rarely, if ever, seen. The artillery was not ranged in long lines, but dotted about wherever conveniences of the ground suggested. The whole extent of the battlefield was far greater. The Cavalry were hardly at all in evidence, and then only on distant flanks. The infantry advanced in successive skirmish lines, and machine-guns had begun to be a feature. Although these formations were still to British eyes much too dense for modern fire, they nevertheless constituted an enormous advance ... They were, I believe, substantially the formations with which the German Army five years later entered the Great War, and which were then proved to be superior to those of their French opponents.'[1]

Churchill had seen, therefore, at first hand, the preparations for war that the Germans were making and he was determined that the force he was responsible for, the Royal Navy, would be ready to meet the challenge when it came. With this uppermost in Winston's mind, he demanded more money from the Treasury to build a fleet that could never be surpassed by the Germans. The launching of the battleship HMS *Dreadnought* in 1906 had changed the face of naval warfare in a single bound. *Dreadnought* was so superior to any previous warship, with her massive array of armament and being driven for the first time by steam turbines, that no other ship could compare with her in terms of strength and speed. It was immediately evident that whichever nation possessed the most Dreadnoughts would dominate the seas.

Germany was quick to respond. Although Germany was devoting an incredible sixty per cent of its revenue on its army, the need to compete with the new battleships of the Royal Navy could not be ignored. The result was an enormously expensive arms race between the two countries. For Germany this was an especially great investment, for the much larger class of Dreadnoughts required the enlargement of harbours, locks and the dredging of the Kiel Canal.

The Dreadnoughts themselves cost around £2,000,000 – the equivalent of almost a quarter of a billion in today's terms – but the belief that these ships held the key to Britain's security was lodged in people's minds, on both sides of the North Sea, and the race was cheered on. In Britain, when the then First Lord of the Admiralty, Mr McKenna, proposed the building of six Dreadnoughts, a popular slogan was taken up, 'we want eight, and we won't wait', that urged the Government to spend unparalleled amounts on its navy. The result was that by the time that war eventually broke out, the British fleet could boast twenty-nine of the new class of warships to just seventeen in the Kaiserliche Marine. Europe may have been sleep-walking to war in the summer of 1914 but the Royal Navy was wide awake and ready for action.

At 17.00 hours on 28 July, with the Government painfully aware that war was only days away, Winston ordered the Commander-in-Chief of the Home Fleet to have his ships take up their battle stations: 'To-morrow, Wednesday, the First Fleet is to leave Portland for Scapa Flow. Destination is to be kept secret except to flag and commanding officers. As you are required at the Admiralty, Vice-Admiral 2nd Battle Squadron is to take command. Course from Portland is to be shaped to southward, then a middle Channel course to the Straits of Dover. The Squadrons are to pass through the Straits without lights during the night and to pass outside the shoals on their way north. *Agamemnon* is to remain at Portland, where the Second Fleet will assemble.[2]

By Thursday morning the whole of the Fleet was in mid-Channel in the North Sea ready to pounce on any German warships that dared leave harbour. Though no declaration of war had yet been made, Winston also retained the naval reservists who were currently on annual training at sea. When war was finally declared on 4 August the Royal Navy was as ready as it could possibly be, and at 17.50 hours Winston sent the following message to all ships: 'The telegram will be issued at midnight authorizing you to commence hostilities against Germany, but in view of our ultimatum they may decide to open fire at any moment. You must be ready for this.'

One of the two principal duties of the Royal Navy in those early days of the war was that of safeguarding the passage of the British Expeditionary Force to France, the support of the British troops being considered vital. The other essential task required of the navy was that of defending Britain's shores from attack or possible invasion.

Nevertheless, the war at sea was always going to be subordinate to that on land. Fully appreciating this, Winston offered the newly-appointed Secretary at State for War, Lord Kitchener, the Royal Naval Division. In 1913 Winston had raised three brigades of naval infantry to form this new force. One was composed of Marines, one of men from the Royal Naval Reserve and the third from the Royal Fleet Reserve. The division would have its baptism of fire in October 1914 as the Allied armies fell back through Belgium under the weight of the German onslaught. The Belgian Army withdrew towards its National Redoubt formed around Antwerp, but so rapid had been the German advance, the Belgian Government proposed to abandon Antwerp and head for Ostend.

This move meant, in effect, that the Belgians were surrendering their country. Britain desperately wanted Belgium to stay in the fight and Winston was sent to Antwerp on 3 October to try and persuade the Belgians to hold on. With him went his brigade of Marines, with the other two brigades of the Royal Naval Division to follow the next day.

With typical enthusiasm Churchill set about convincing the Belgians to resist and, after touring Antwerp's fortifications, he persuaded them that it was possible to defy the Germans and that there was no-one better suited to lead them in their defence than the First Lord of the Admiralty.

On 5 October, Winston sent the following telegram to the Prime

Minister: 'If it is thought by HM Government that I can be of service here, I am willing to resign my office and undertake command of relieving and defensive forces assigned to Antwerp in conjunction with the Belgian Army, provided that I am given necessary military rank and authority, and full powers of a commander of a detached force in the field. I feel it my duty to offer my services, because I am sure this arrangement will afford the best prospects of a victorious result to an enterprise in which I am deeply involved. I should require complete staff proportionate to the force employed, as I have had to use all the officers now here in positions of urgency.'[3]

The importance of Antwerp has long been forgotten as the German armies swept through Belgium and into France, but at the time its retention by the Allies was seen as crucial in holding the enemy ay bay. 'Antwerp was then not only the sole stronghold of the Belgian nation; it was also the true left flank of the Allied front in the west,' noted Churchill. 'It guarded the whole line of the Channel ports. It threatened the flanks and even the rear of the German Armies in France. It was the gateway from which the Great Amphibian might emerge at any moment upon their sensitive and even vital communications. No German advance to the sea coast, upon Ostend, upon Dunkirk, upon Calais and Boulogne seemed possible while Antwerp was unconquered.'[4]

Winston threw himself into the defence of Antwerp with gusto, as Colonel John Seely, who arrived in the city the day after the First Lord of the Admiralty, recalled: 'From the moment I that arrived the whole business was in Winston's hands. He dominated the whole place; the King [of the Belgians], ministers, soldiers, sailors. So great was his influence that I am convinced that with 20,000 British troops he could have held Antwerp against any onslaught.'[5]

To have given Churchill the men and the authority to adequately defend Antwerp would have raised him immediately from his Army rank of Major to General in a single step, apart from the fact that he would be abandoning the Admiralty at the very time it needed him most of all. His request was dismissed out of hand by Prime Minister Asquith.

The British Government's reply to Winston was that he should arrange for Antwerp to be abandoned. Belgian and British forces withdrew across the Schedlt on the night of 6/7 October. Unfortunately the order to withdraw did not reach all of the 1st Naval Brigade, and only one battalion pulled out. Little short of 1,500 men were taken prisoner.

Churchill and the men of the Royal Naval Division helped to encourage the Belgians to fight on for a few more days at a time when they had considered abandoning the place before the Germans approached. The four days that the National Redoubt defied the Germans enabled the British Expeditionary Force to march up to Ypres just as the enemy was trying to sweep round the left flank of the Allied forces. At the First Battle of Ypres the Germans were stopped and the great German flanking move was prevented.

Winston's enthusiasm for the defence of Antwerp was seen as being hare-brained and its capitulation was seen as a failure which tainted Churchill's otherwise fine military reputation. Worse, though, was to come with the decision to mount the disastrous Gallipoli campaign.

When Germany declared war on Russia on 1 August 1914 both nations had amassed large concentrations of troops on their respective borders. Russia had the biggest army in the world and when she entered the war she could count an impressive total of 5,000 guns. Unfortunately, for those guns the Russian Army had only 500,000,000 shells. During the first three months of the war the Russian guns fired an average of 45,000 shells a day. The output of the Russian munitions factories did not exceed 35,000 shells *per month*. Consequently, by the beginning of December 1914, Russia possessed barely 300,000 shells, or the equivalent of little more than one week's requirement. As Winston explained: 'At the moment when the Russian armies needed the greatest support from their artillery, they found their guns frozen into silence.'[6]

Just as Russia was contending with the might of Germany, the Ottoman Empire joined the Central Powers, not to fight Britain or France, but to fight her oldest enemy, Russia. The Russians were compelled to open a second front in the Caucasus, stretching her dwindling resources still further.

The Russians, partners with Britain and France in the Triple Entente, faced utter ruin. If Russia was defeated, scores of German divisions – hundreds of thousands of troops – would be released from the fighting in the east to add their weight to the German forces on the Western Front. Defeat for the Allies in the East could well spell defeat in the West.

What Russia did possess in large numbers, however, was soldiers. Some 800,000 trained recruits were ready for despatch to the front but there were no rifles with which to arm them. If Russia, somehow, could be kept in the war until her allies could provide her with the weapons and munitions she required, her huge reserves of manpower could be guaranteed to tie down a very considerable proportion of the German Army for a very long time.

The direct threat to Russia was not the only concern of the British and French governments raised by Turkish involvement in the war. Another was the flow of shipping through the Suez Canal. It was vital that this route remained open and in Allied hands, though the territory of the Ottoman Empire reached almost to the banks of the canal.

How, therefore, could Britain and France aid Russia and defend the Canal? Every available soldier was required on the Western Front. There could be no withdrawal of troops from France or Belgium as any weakness would be immediately exploited by the enemy. With the new machines of war, aircraft, able to observe the movement of troops, any large-scale deployment was certain to be detected.

Yet there was one powerful force available to the Allies that was grossly under-employed – the combined Anglo-French navies.

The German High Seas Fleet had shown little inclination to leave the security of its harbours. Even if it should risk a fleet action, the Dreadnoughts of the Grand Fleet were more than a match for the German battleships. Britain and France could safely deploy a large number of warships to attack Turkey. This, it was expected, would relieve the pressure being exerted upon Russia and deter an attack upon Egypt and the Suez Canal. The 'ideal' method of achieving these goals, Winston declared, was by an attack on the Gallipoli Peninsula. 'This, if successful, would give us control of the Dardanelles, and we could dictate terms at Constantinople.'[7]

Nothing came of Churchill's urgings as he had warned that success could only be achieved if undertaken quickly and by the deployment of 'a very large force', and no such body of troops was available. But as the situation on the Eastern Front became ever more precarious for the Russians, something simply had to be done.

Various schemes were considered by the War Council and the forcing of the Dardanelles was advocated by Lieutenant Colonel Maurice Hankey, the Secretary to the Committee of Imperial Defence, as well as by the First Sea Lord, Admiral Fisher. The Russians themselves, through Grand Duke Nicholas, begged for 'a demonstration of some kind against the Turk'.[8]

Kitchener, consequently, asked Churchill what could be done, suggesting that a naval 'demonstration at the Dardanelles' might be sufficient to hold back Turkish troops to defend Constantinople. Churchill was no longer interested in attacking Turkey, which, without large numbers of troops, he considered impractical. He had his own plan for assisting the Russians – a direct attack on Germany across the North Sea. In this plan, Schleswig-Holstein would be invaded, the Kiel Canal seized and troops landed on the Pomeranian coast with orders to march the 100 miles to Berlin. This scheme was favoured by Fisher, who declared on 22 December that, 'The Baltic is the only theatre on which naval action can appreciably shorten the war'.

The Secretary to the Committee of Imperial Defence, Maurice Hankey, produced a memorandum on 28 December setting out his views on how to break the deadlock in the West and help Russia in the East. He was entirely in favour of attacking Turkey directly, with the expected support of Bulgaria, and he believed that 'there ought to be no insuperable obstacle to the occupation of Constantinople, the Dardanelles, and Bosphorus'.

Churchill did not believe that anything could be done by ships alone and he pressed Kitchener to find troops for a combined naval and military assault. The latter replied that every man was needed on the Western Front and none could be spared for operations in the East. The whole burden was pushed onto Churchill's shoulders.

Churchill summoned his Admiralty War Group to consider Kitchener's proposal. It was not well received. However, Churchill had used some of his funding from his Naval Estimates to keep a number of old battleships in fighting condition and these 'expendable' ships might be deployed without the need to draw modern ships from Home waters. Some plan, the group decided, might be worked out but before any moves were considered. Winston sought the views of the man on the spot, the commander of the British squadron in the Mediterranean, Vice-Admiral Sackville Carden. 'Do you consider the forcing of the Dardanelles by ships alone a practicable operation? It is assumed older Battleships fitted with mine-bumpers would be used preceded by Colliers or other merchant craft as bumpers and sweepers.'

When Carden and others considered this plan they concluded that if a squadron of eight battleships tried to rush through the Dardanelles, the powerful Turkish coastal batteries were likely to sink six and severely damage the other two. Carden did not believe that the Strait could be forced in such a manner, but, 'They might be forced by extended operations,' he explained, 'with large numbers of ships'.

Carden had formed his views from an enterprise he had conducted on 3 November, shortly after Turkey's entry into the war. Carden, under instruction from the Admiralty, had steamed up to the Dardanelles and bombarded the Turkish forts at the entrance to the Strait. After a twenty minute bombardment and two lucky hits, the outer forts of Kum Kale and Sedd el Bahr were put out of action. The Turks had not responded. This gave Carden a false impression of both the strength of the forts and of the Turks' willingness to resist. This encouraged him to believe that if attacked in force the forts and their defenders would soon be overcome.

Admiral Henry Oliver, Winston's Chief of Staff, and Sir Henry Jackson, Chief of the Admiralty War Staff, were also in favour of an attack upon the Dardanelles. Both men believed that Carden's concept of a step-by-step reduction of the Turkish forts could succeed.

Such extended operations, however, were not really going to benefit Russia; she needed help quickly. The idea of opening a second front – something more than just a naval demonstration – was however beginning to appear increasingly attractive to the British planners. It was becoming disturbingly obvious that, as the trench systems became deeper and wider, there was little prospect of any decisive action on the Western Front for the foreseeable future. The harsh reality was that the war which everyone believed would be over by Christmas was going to be a very long struggle indeed. As always, such thoughts were put into powerful rhetoric by Winston: 'My impression is that the position of both armies is not likely to undergo any decisive change – although no doubt several hundred thousand men will be spent to satisfy the military mind on the point ... Are there not alternatives than sending our armies to chew barbed wire in Flanders?'

Everyone knew exactly what Churchill meant. There was clearly an alternative but it was not the direct amphibious assault across the North Sea that Churchill (and for that matter Lord Fisher) wanted. Lloyd George spelt out quite clearly what the only realistic alternative was: 'The Dardanelles appeared to be the most suitable objective, as an attack here could be made in co-operation with the Fleet. If successful, it would re-establish communication with Russia; settle the Near East question; draw in Greece and, perhaps, Bulgaria and Roumania; and release wheat and shipping now locked up in the Black Sea.'

This all made complete sense. As one historian has written, 'The idea had a strategic clarity and logic that was almost unique among the campaigns of the First World War. Its potential for achieving decisive strategic results in an era of strategic stalemate seemed to be enormous.'[9]

Kitchener was pleased that his plan was now appreciated: 'The German lines in France may be looked upon as a fortress which cannot be completely invested with the result [that] the lines may be held by the investing force whilst operations proceed elsewhere.' That elsewhere was Gallipoli.

It was not just a case of knocking Turkey out of the war. If she was defeated Turkey might be persuaded to join the Allied cause. This would ensure that none of her territory was seized by Russia for the two countries would then be Allies.

With no alternative plan on the table, attention turned to the practicalities of forcing the Dardanelles and attacking Constantinople. Winston still wanted any naval attack to be supported by up to 60,000 troops, but he had to plan without them.

It was at this point, as the Admiralty staff worked on the details of the operation, that Fisher first began to voice his concerns. Then, on 21 January, he wrote: 'I abominate the Dardanelles operation, unless a great change is made and it is settled to be a military operation.' As the days passed, Fisher's opposition became resolute and he decided that he could no longer remain at the Admiralty if the operation went ahead. He threatened to resign.

Apart from the impracticality of trying to force the Dardanelles, Fisher was concerned that it was not only obsolete battleships but the very latest warships that would take part in the operation, thus reducing the fighting capacity of the Home Fleet. Winston sought to allay Fisher's fears, as did Kitchener, and Fisher was persuaded to continue in office.

Carden's premature, and fairly pointless attack in November had in fact alerted the Turks to the likelihood of an Allied operation against Constantinople. It was clear that any such expedition by Britain and France could only be delivered through the Dardanelles and into the Bosphorus. Forewarned, the Turks would be ready and waiting.

At 09.51 hours on 19 February 1915, from a range of 9,500 yards the old battleship HMS *Cornwallis* opened fire on the outermost Turkish fort on the Anatolian shore of the entrance to the Dardanelles Strait. This marked the start of one of the most ignominious episodes in British naval history. Little was achieved that day with the forts showing no signs of being subdued. Likewise on 25 February when the bombardment of the forts was resumed, the Turks still appeared capable of resisting every effort made against them. Further operations in early March also failed. It all proved too much for Admiral Carden, who relinquished his command.

Kitchener had also finally accepted that troops would have to be deployed and he began to gather together what forces he could muster. Meanwhile another major attempt to force the straits by the British and French fleets took place on 18 March. By the end of the day, three battleships had been sunk and another badly damaged and still the Turks remained in control of the straits.

It was on 25 April that British, Australian, New Zealand and French troops landed on the Gallipoli Peninsula. They failed to achieve any of their objectives.

Fisher became more strident in his opposition to the whole campaign against Turkey and as each day brought only bad news from the East he threatened to resign yet again. On 15 May he told Winston that he had made up his mind to take no further part in the 'foolishness' unfolding in the Dardanelles.

The following morning Fisher carried out his threat and resigned for the last time. To compound the problems facing the Government, a report in *The Times* the previous day on the desperate shortage of shells which had affected the outcome of the Battle of Aubers Ridge on 9 May, caused outrage. Asquith saw only one way out of the mounting political crisis – to form a war-time coalition with the Conservatives.

Churchill knew that his political career hung in the balance. His walk across the floor of the Commons to sit on the Liberal benches in 1904 had never been forgotten by his former colleagues and would not be forgiven. The breach with Fisher was seized upon by Bonar Law, the Conservative leader, who was 'specially emphatic as to the impossibility of allowing Mr Churchill to remain at the Admiralty'.[10] There would be no place for Winston in a government which included the Conservatives.

Winston, still believing there would be a role for him in the coalition, told Asquith that he hoped to be offered a position, but not *any* position; Winston would accept only a 'military department'. If this was not possible he wanted 'employment in the field'.

Whilst having to leave office was a long fall from grace, Churchill was actually quite keen to take a direct part in the fighting. One of Lord Fisher's complaints about Winston was that 'At every turn he will be thinking of the military and not the naval side ... His heart is ashore, not afloat! *The joy of his life is to be 50 yards from a German trench!*' He had also been deadly serious when he offered to resign his ministerial post for an Army command, admitting that having 'tasted blood' he was 'like a tiger' seeking more action. A political career, he had said in Antwerp, 'was nothing to him in comparison with military glory'.

It was at Antwerp that an Italian journalist painted the following picture of Churchill who appeared utterly unafraid under fire: 'I was in the battle line near Lierre, and in the midst of a group of officers stood a man. He was still young, and was enveloped in a cloak, and on his head wore a yachtsman's cap. He was tranquilly smoking a large cigar and looking at the progress of the battle under a rain of shrapnel, which I can only call fearful. It was Mr Churchill, who had come to view the situation himself. It must be confessed that it is not easy to find in the whole of Europe a Minister who would be capable of smoking peacefully under that shellfire. He smiled, and looked quite satisfied.'

There was no military department for the independently-minded Churchill in the Coalition. He was offered the Duchy of Lancaster. This role is effectively one of a minister without portfolio and the holder of this post has a seat in cabinet, but with no real authority. Winston left the Admiralty on 25 May 1915.

His involvement at the heart of affairs continued, however, as he was given a seat on the Dardanelles Committee, which was to all intents and purposes the War Council. In this capacity he penned a memorandum to ministers on the futility of the policy being adopted on the Western Front. 'We should be ill-advised to squander our new armies in frantic and sterile efforts to pierce the

German lines. To do so is to play the German game. As long as the process of attrition works evenly on both sides we are on the road to victory. But a few weeks of an attempted offensive may inflict irreparable injury upon our newly gathered military power.'

Though Churchill sought to influence ministers, he knew that the direction of the war effort was in the hands of Kitchener and his own successor at the Admiralty, Arthur Balfour. He later described the situation he was now in: 'In this position I knew everything and could do nothing. The change from the intense executive duties of each day's work to the narrowly measured duties of a counsellor, left me gasping. Like a sea-beast fished up from the depths, or a diver too suddenly hoisted, my veins threatened to burst from the fall in pressure. I had great anxiety but no means of relieving it; I had vehement convictions and small power to give effect to them … I had long hours of utterly unwanted leisure in which to contemplate the frightful unfolding of the war. At a moment when every fibre of my being was inflamed to action, I was forced to remain a spectator of the tragedy, cruelly placed in a front seat.'[11]

His thoughts turned increasingly to leaving the Government altogether and taking up an active post with the Army. He sought action and no better place offered him more fulfilling excitement than fighting the enemy in the front line. Others also saw that Winston might want to return to soldiering, and he was offered command of a squadron of the Oxfordshire Hussars by Lieutenant General Sir William Campbell in charge of Southern Command.

It was on 6 November that the Dardanelles Committee sat for the last time. Winston knew, for the immediate future at least, that his voice was no longer going to be heard. Five days later Asquith announced the formation of a new Cabinet War Committee which would from then on dictate war policy. That new body would not include Winston Churchill.

On 12 November 1915, Winston tendered his resignation from the Duchy of Lancaster. For the first time in ten years he was out of office.

Three days later Winston delivered his resignation speech to the Commons, which was well received, especially by *The Times*:

'The House of Commons is traditionally prepared to be generous to a personal explanation, but Mr. Churchill succeeded yesterday in evoking something more than the sympathy which always awaits a retiring Minister. The Prime Minister, who paid him a graceful and almost unqualified tribute, said no more than the truth when he declared that Mr. Churchill "had dealt with a very delicate situation, not only with ability and eloquence, but also with loyalty and discretion." Punctuated by cheers from all parts of the House, and accorded an ovation at the close, the speech was an undoubted Parliamentary triumph.'

Winston decided immediately to join his regiment in France. He knew that he would be welcomed by the Oxfordshire Hussars and that a position would be made for him. When Max Aitken (Lord Beaverbrook) visited the Churchill household he found the 'soldier-statesman was buckling on his sword'. Winston was off to war.

Chapter 3

The Western Front 1915

The war that Winston was about to join was, in some regards, not dissimilar to that he had experienced at Antwerp, with poorly-prepared trenches and intense artillery bombardments delivered by unseen hands dealing death from afar. There was, though, one vital difference – hope. At Antwerp the Belgians expected to be defeated and their willingness to resist when they knew they were going to be beaten was correspondingly diminished. The men of the British Expeditionary Force knew that they would not be beaten.

The great German offensive of 1914 had been halted and the Germans forced to dig in to defend the territory they had won. By 1915 it was the Allies who were on the attack, repeatedly battering against the enemy lines in a bid to achieve the breakthrough that would end the stalemate of trench warfare and drive the invaders back over the Rhine.

The initial aim of the Chief of the French General Staff, General Joffre, was to recapture the important French industrial centres, particularly the coal and iron ore mines, occupied by the Germans. If the war was to be won France would need all its industrial strength, so, in December, Joffre launched an attack upon the enemy salient which reached its furthest point westwards at the town of Noyon. In what was called the First Battle of Champagne, the French Fourth Army attacked the German positions from 20 December 1914 until the middle of March 1915. Little was achieved and the French lost more than 93,000 men, twice as many as the Germans.

As the Battle of Champagne wound down, the British Expeditionary Force undertook its own offensive with the aim of capturing the high ground of the Aubers Ridge and, in so doing, threaten the Germans in occupation of the city of Lille. Although the British broke through the German front and captured the village of Neuve Chapelle, the German Sixth Army carried out counter-attacks and the British offensive was halted. What became known as the Battle of Neuve Chapelle was a far smaller engagement than that in Champagne, and casualties were correspondingly lighter, but total losses were comparatively even, with both the British and the Germans each losing around 10,000 men. The significance of the Battle of Neuve Chapelle was that it indicated that it was possible to break through well-prepared defensive systems – the first time this had been achieved since the advent of trench warfare in the autumn of 1914.

The BEF, along with the Belgian Army and the French Eighth Army, formed the northern part of the trench system that ran from the Channel to the Alps. After the Battle of Neuve Chapelle the British adopted a defensive stance around the Belgian city of Ypres in Flanders which they had held since October 1914. After having been blocked in their initial attempts to reach Paris in August 1914, the Germans had tried to sweep round the Allies' western flank. Not only would this move cut off the BEF from the Channel ports, it also offered the prospect of being able to press upon the rear of the main French forces that faced east. As soon as German intentions had been revealed British divisions raced to prevent the German 4th Army from reaching the Belgian coast.

Their objective was to reach the city of Ypres. This was a vital road and rail communications centre and if the Germans could capture the city, the route to the coast would be firmly in German hands. The leading elements of both the BEF and the German 4th Army reached Ypres within days of each other. The Germans launched an attack on the hastily-prepared British positions on 19 October 1914 but, in what was defined as the First Battle of Ypres, the Germans were held.

On 27 October the Belgian King, Albert I, ordered the sluice

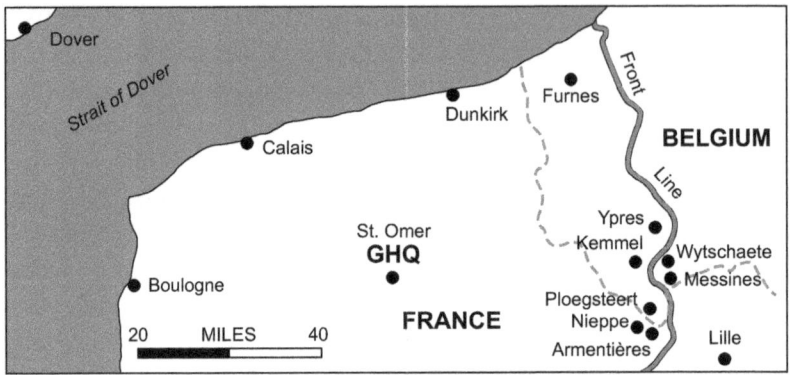

Above: The Western Front in relation to Ploegsteert.

gates to be opened and the flat land to the west of Ypres down to the sea was inundated. Ypres, and its immediate environs, from that moment onwards, became the most westerly point occupied by the opposing forces, the positions held by the BEF forming a salient that protruded into the German occupied areas. This salient had to be held at all costs.

The Germans launched another attack upon Ypres on 22 April 1915, which lasted for more than a month. Once again the BEF hung on to most of the ground it occupied but the German 4th Army, under the command of *Generalfeldmarschall* Albrecht, Duke of Württemberg, gained some territory, compressing the salient even tighter and pushing the front line closer to Ypres' centre. The Second Battle of Ypres, as it became known, also saw the Germans use gas on a large scale for the first time in warfare, adding to the daily perils of the troops in the trenches.

The British were not slow to follow suit. Once again the French sought to attack in the Champagne and Artois regions and Sir John French who commanded the BEF agreed on a joint assault. On 25 September 1915 the British launched their biggest offensive of the year at the Battle of Loos, the attack being accompanied by the discharge of chlorine gas.

On that first day the British almost achieved the big breakthrough that both sides had aimed for since 1914. A shortage

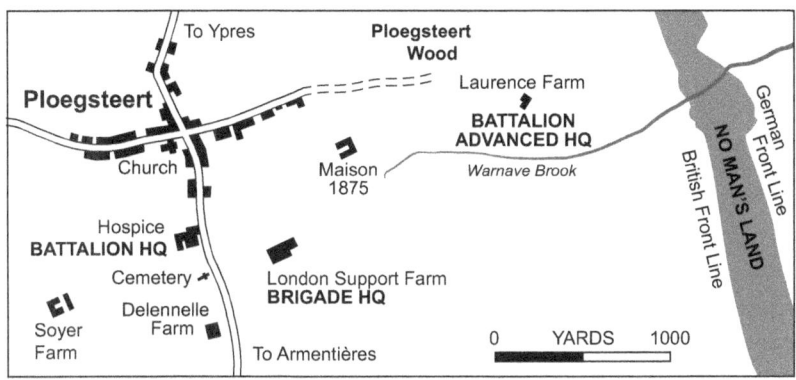

Above: The immediate area of the front around Ploegsteert.

of shells for the artillery, and French's failure to allow his reserves to be deployed quickly enough to exploit the early successes, enabled the Germans to recover and over the following days they re-took much of the ground they had lost. The corresponding French offensive, known as the Third Battle of Artois, also failed.

The battle was the first major engagement undertaken by the recently-recruited 'New Army' battalions, the all-volunteer force that had been raised by Lord Kitchener. The 'Your King and Country Need You' call-to-arms first appeared on 11 August 1914. It explained the new terms of service and called for the first 100,000 men to enlist. This figure was achieved within two weeks. Army Order No.324, dated 21 August 1914, then specified that six new divisions would be created from units formed of these volunteers, collectively called Kitchener's Army or K1. One of these was the 9th (Scottish) Division.

Regarded by many as one of the best fighting formations of the First World War, the 9th (Scottish) Division, which Winston would eventually join, was given the task of capturing the main German strongpoint in the Loos sector, the infamous Hohenzollern Redoubt. The Scots stormed the redoubt but were driven out by a German counter-attack. Another attempt was made upon the redoubt on 13 October, but this failed, resulting in 3,643 casualties, mostly in the first few minutes of the assault.

The Battle of Loos was the last major offensive of 1915, and Sir John French sought only to consolidate the positions the BEF held throughout the winter. The 9th Division was moved northwards to Ploegsteert which is some nine miles south of Ypres and at the very southern extremity of the salient. To those who served there during the war it became known as 'Plugstreet'.

Much of Flanders is flat with a very high water table. This meant that after digging just a few feet the men encountered water. Persistent shelling by both sides churned up the ground, bringing the water to the surface and creating a sea of mud.

Just what it was like for the men of the 9th Division was described by Second Lieutenant Edward Underhill writing from Ploegsteert in November 1915: 'The conditions here are appalling. I never knew what mud was till I got here ... We have had about three days' continuous rain, and the result is the trenches are flooded and the country round is a sea of ankle-deep, and in some places today I have been over my knees in it. I took 150 men to do drainage work under the R.E.s on the communication trenches on the left where we were before we came out. It was an endless, hopeless task. The walls had caved in in places, and as soon as the muck was cleared out it caved in again, and it all had to be done again. The fire trenches were 2 or 3 feet deep in water, and they were talking of abandoning them.'[1]

Being south of the Ypres Salient, which was the main focus of the German effort, meant that Ploegsteert was a comparatively quiet sector of the front line. Whilst there were no major offensives undertaken by either side in the Ploegsteert sector, there was, nevertheless, shelling from both sides which inevitably meant casualties, but these were light compared to those suffered by the troops in and around the suburbs of Ypres.

Winston was fortunate that circumstances took him to this somewhat safer part of the battlefront. But no such considerations were in Winston's mind when he wrote in his resignation letter: 'I am an officer, and I place myself unreservedly at the disposal of the military authorities, observing that my regiment is in France.'

Chapter 4

Winston With The Grenadiers

Major Winston Churchill of the Oxfordshire Hussars crossed to France on 18 November 1915 to join his regiment. His departure, wrote the historian Frank Brennand, 'was a painful one':

> His faithful secretary was openly crying, and Lady Randolph Churchill was appalled at the thought of Winston leaving the Admiralty to wallow in Flanders mud. Clementine Churchill, surely one of Winston's greatest pieces of luck in a lucky career, stood by calmly, as she had to do so often, both between and during the wars.[1]

The news of Winston's journey had preceded him and he was met at Boulogne by a car sent by the Commander-in-Chief of the British Expeditionary Force, Sir John French, who invited Churchill to join him at his headquarters at St Omer. Winston was pleasantly surprised and was, of course, happy to oblige, but he felt he should inform his regiment and asked the driver to stop off at Bléquin where the regiment was based. He spent a few hours there before continuing on to General Headquarters.

Winston was warmly received by Sir John French. The two men had known each other since the Boer War in which French commanded a cavalry division. Sir John had served as Chief of the Imperial General Staff between 1912 and March 1914 and had worked closely with Churchill as First Lord of the Admiralty. During that time they had become close friends.

They talked at length about the war, including the fact that the

Government was putting pressure on the sixty-four-years-old Field Marshal to relinquish his command of the BEF. The two men must have felt they had much in common.

Sir John sought to find a role for the former Cabinet minister that would seem appropriate to his status. He suggested to Winston that he should become one of the Commander-in-Chief's aides-de-camp at GHQ, or that he might take command of a brigade. This was hardly a difficult choice. Winston, forever the soldier, who had long dreamed of leading men into battle, was thrilled at the prospect of becoming a brigadier-general. Only months before he had offered to resign his ministerial post to take command of the defence of Antwerp as a general officer only to be told that promotion from major straight to general simply was not possible. Now, it seemed, he was to become a Brigadier-General. Such sudden promotion, Churchill felt, was not as inappropriate as it might appear, as he later wrote, 'having been trained professionally for about five years as a soldier, and having prior to the Great War seen as much actual fighting as almost any of the Colonels or Generals in the British Army'.[2] That night, after a hot bath and a lavish meal with champagne, he wrote to his wife Clementine and told her that he was 'entirely happy'.

There was not an immediate opening for Winston, but war always presents opportunities and French promised to arrange a brigade for him as soon as possible. Winston could have remained within the comfort and luxury of the fine château where GHQ was housed, but this was not his way. The war was near at hand and Churchill wanted to be part of it. He also felt that he needed some experience in the front line before taking command of a brigade of three or four battalions. This, of course, made complete sense and French was glad to facilitate this. Winston asked if he could gain that experience with the Guards and, on 19 November, Major General Lord Cavan, the commander of the Guards Division, was asked to visit St Omer, where Churchill's request was put to him. It was decided that Winston would have his training with the Grenadiers.

Anxious to be in action as soon as possible, that same day

Churchill travelled the twelve miles to La Gorgue to the headquarters of the Guards Division to meet the senior officers of the division. He returned to St Omer for the night and prepared to join the Grenadiers the following day. He wrote again to Clementine that night and could not help but refer to the Duke of Marlborough in his letter. Winston now really believed that he had made the right decision to leave Parliament and he was genuinely excited with his future prospects. He told Clementine that he did not know which battalion of the Grenadiers he would be joining but that he would be participating fully with the battalion's routines and taking his turn with the men in the trenches. Winston's attitude to war and his unpretentious courage is revealed in his observation that to his 'surprise' he learnt that the Guards, when not actually engaged in a major attack, had had only about fifteen men killed or wounded every day. Such numbers might trouble some men, but Winston cited this figure to illustrate to his wife that being at the front was, in his words, 'harmless'. When he was not performing his tour in the trenches Winston would be returning to GHQ where he would be able to have the hot baths so dear to him.

'I am very happy here,' he assured Clementine. 'How I ever could have wasted so many months in impotent misery, which might have been spent in war, I cannot tell.'

After spending the morning at St Omer, Winston travelled to La Gorgue for lunch and was informed that he would be attached to the 2nd Battalion, Grenadier Guards which was due to go into the front line that very afternoon near Neuve Chapelle. Cavan took Churchill to the battalion's headquarters and introduced him to Lieutenant Colonel George Jeffreys. Winston recalled that his reception was as frosty as the weather:

> 'It was a dull November afternoon, and an icy drizzle fell over the darkening plain. As we approached the line, the red flashes of the guns stabbed the sombre landscape on either side of the road, to the sound of an intermittent cannonade. We paced onwards for about an hour without a word being spoken on either side.

Then the Colonel [spoke]: 'I think I ought to tell you that we were not at all consulted in the matter of your coming to join us.'

I replied respectfully that I had no idea myself which Battalion I was to be sent to, but that I dared say it would be all right. Anyhow we must make the best of it.

Then was another prolonged silence.

Then the Adjutant [said]: 'I am afraid we have had to cut down your kit rather, Major. There are no communication trenches here. We are doing all our reliefs over the top. The men have little more than what they stand up in. We have found a servant for you, who is carrying a spare pair of socks and your shaving gear. We have had to leave the rest behind.'

I said that was quite all right and that I was sure I would be very comfortable.

We continued to progress in the same sombre silence.[3]

The spirit of unity and camaraderie that Winston had enjoyed in earlier times with the Oxfordshire Hussars and the warmth with which he had been greeted at GHQ, having, as he told his wife, been received back as 'the prodigal son', must have already seemed a very distant memory.

The 2nd Battalion, Grenadier Guards' War Diary recorded Churchill's arrival in straightforward terms: 'The brigade took over line of Trenches opposite PIETRE. All in a very bad state, communications trenches flooded and front line breastworks crumbling and were not bullet-proof. Major Rt Hon Winston Churchill, who has just resigned from Government, arrived to be attached to the Battalion for instruction, and accompanied the Battalion to the Trenches.'[4]

Apart from the socks and shaving kit carried by his soldier-servant, all that Winston went into the trenches with was his khaki Oxfordshire Hussars uniform, his peaked cap and his Colt .45 which he had purchased before travelling to France.[5]

The battalion reached the front as dust began to darken further the grey Artois skies. Its headquarters were set up in what Winston described as 'a pulverized ruin' called Ebenezer Farm. Its battered and badly damaged walls, padded with sandbags, provided some protection for the officers.

The meal that evening was a sombre affair, finished off with tea sweetened with condensed milk which did not appeal to Churchill at all. The battalion had suffered appalling losses since its arrival in France with the BEF and Jeffreys was one of the few officers who had survived since the beginning. He had seen too much suffering and he had little interest in small talk with a politician who, it was considered by some, had sent many men to their deaths in the futile campaign against the Turks.

After dinner Churchill had to decide where he was to sleep. He was offered a place in the signal office in the farm but he found that the office was only about eight feet square and was already in use by four signallers. The only alternative was outside in a dugout some 200 yards from the farm – this being offered to him by the battalion's senior major.

This turned out to be 'a sort of pit four feet deep', containing about a foot of water.

'I thanked the Second-in-Command for the trouble he had taken in finding me this resting place,' noted Churchill, 'and said that on the whole I thought I should do better at the signal office … The bullets, skimming over the front line, whistled drearily as we walked back to Ebenezer Farm. Such was my welcome in the Grenadier Guards.'

Winston was not impressed either with the condition that the trenches had been left in by the outgoing battalion. Nevertheless, he was happy to be away from the world of politics. 'Filth and rubbish everywhere,' he wrote, 'graves built into the defences & scattered about promiscuously, feet and clothing breaking through the soil, water & muck on all sides; & about this scene in the dazzling moonlight troops of enormous bats creep & glide, to the unceasing accompaniment of rifle & machine guns & the venomous whining & whirring of the bullets which pass overhead. Amid these surrounding, aided by wet & cold and every minor discomfort, I have found happiness & content such as I have not known for many months.'

Winston, though, was not content to stay at battalion headquarters and he asked if he could be where the action was in the firing trenches. A thirst for action was not the only driver that prompted Winston to make this request, a thirst of a different kind also played its part, as Bill Deedes, the former editor of the *Daily Telegraph*, related: 'He [Churchill] was with Grenadier Guards, who were dry at battalion headquarters. They very much liked tea and condensed milk, which had no great appeal to Winston, but alcohol was permitted in the front line, in the trenches. So he suggested to the colonel that he really ought to see more of the war and get into the front line. This was highly commended by the colonel, who thought it was a very good thing to do.'

Churchill later conceded this to be the case: 'I have always believed in the moderate and regular use of alcohol, especially under conditions of winter war. I gladly moved my handful of belongings ... to a Company in the line.'

In fact when the Grenadiers' second-in-command went home on leave Colonel Jeffreys invited Churchill to take over the absent officer's duties. Winston regarded this as one of the greatest honours he had ever received, but he turned the offer down, perhaps still preferring more time in the trenches than condensed milk and tea at headquarters.

Edward Grigg, who had also served on a newspaper, in his case *The Times*, and whom Churchill knew, was in charge of the battalion's No.1 Company, and he was delighted to offer Winston a place in his dugout. It was there that Winston spent his next night, 21 November 1915, once more informing Clementine that it was no more dangerous than at battalion headquarters. This was because that, although there was nothing between No.1 Company and the enemy, he was below ground in a dugout and therefore not exposed to gunfire, whereas at Ebenezer Farm any movement outside the farm buildings had to be above ground where stray bullets skimmed through the air.

The front held by the battalion ran for 700 yards from Moated

Grange Trench to Sign Post Lane. The trenches were in poor condition. They were originally part of an older trench line built by the Germans and then re-built by the new occupants, but with little care. The Grenadiers therefore devoted much time to cleaning up and strengthening the defences, and Churchill joined in the reconstruction work.

This tour of duty in the front line lasted forty-eight hours, during which time the battalion had two men killed and two wounded from the intermittent shelling and the constant vigilance of the enemy snipers.

After its two days in the front line on the evening of 22 November the battalion moved to reserve billets some three miles away at Bout Deville. The billets, which the 2nd Grenadiers' War Dairy described as 'poor', were within earshot of the gunfire at the front and were still well within range of the enemy's artillery.

Winston wrote to his wife informing her that he was slowly making friends with the men. Even Colonel Jeffreys' attitude to the former First Lord was mellowing as he saw how Churchill was happy to share the discomforts of the front line alongside the rest of the battalion.

Equally, Churchill was impressed by the organisation and discipline of the Grenadiers. Although most of the original Regular Army officers had been lost to the battalion over the previous year the traditions and standards of the Guards had been maintained. He acknowledged that it had been a wise decision to join the Grenadiers for his induction into service on the Western Front.

Happy though he was as a soldier once again, Churchill had no intention of relinquishing all of his home comforts and he asked his wife to send out a 'small' box of food each week to supplement his rations. That small box, he pointed out, was to include sardines, chocolate, potted meats and 'other things which may strike your fancy'.

Winston was once again in the trenches with the Grenadiers on the night of 25 November 1915 and the following day he had a very fortunate escape. He was in the dugout with Edward Grigg when he received a message from Lieutenant General Richard Haking who was the commanding officer of XI Corps. If Churchill was to command a brigade, then Haking might well be his Corps Commander.

Winston had been summoned to Haking's headquarters at Merville for 16.00 hours, a car being sent for him. This would mean Churchill had to leave the dugout and walk to the Rouge Croix crossroads where the car would be waiting in broad daylight. The tracks leading from the front were periodically shelled and targeted by small arms fire. But, as Churchill remarked, he had no choice but to comply and for all he knew it might be positive news about his future appointment.

So, after cleaning himself up as best he could, Churchill tramped the three miles across the rain-drenched and windy open ground. Soon after he had started on his trek, accompanied by his servant carrying his coat, the German artillery open fire, shelling the roads and trenches in retaliation, Winston assumed, for a bombardment that had just been delivered by the British artillery.

Winston eventually arrived at the crossroads, covered in sweat and mud, only to find no car or driver. Presently a Staff Officer turned up to say that the car had been forced off the road by the heavy shelling. That was understandable, but then the Staff Officer, a Colonel, told Winston that Haking only wanted a general chat with him and that any day would do. Churchill was understandably displeased. He took his leave of the Staff Officer and retraced his steps through the muck, shelling and bullets to his dugout.

Night was creeping in as he made his way back to the front. He could see, and hear, that the trenches were coming under heavy fire. The shrieking of the projectiles and the brilliant red bursts of the explosions became more intense as he approached the Grenadiers' positions. But, by the time he reached No.1 Company the bombardment had ceased and all was quiet again. Winston duly related this incident in some detail to Clementine – not because his life had been risked unnecessarily, but because it probably saved his life. Around a quarter of an hour after Winston had left his dugout, a shell landed just a few feet from where he had been sitting. The dugout was completely destroyed and an orderly who was sat inside was killed. Another orderly and an officer were badly shaken. All their equipment and effects were buried in the mud and debris.

Winston and his servant had escaped death by mere chance and it prompted him to describe this event at length to Clementine to show her that there was no point in her worrying he might be too reckless and expose himself. 'It is all chance,' he wrote. This can hardly has eased her concerns.

'In war,' Churchill later mused, 'chance casts aside all veils and disguises and presents herself nakedly from moment to moment as the direct arbiter over all persons and events. Starting out in the morning, you leave your matches behind you. Before you have gone a hundred yards, you return to get them and thus miss the shell which arrived for your express benefit from ten miles away, and are no doubt shocked to find how nearly you missed the appointed rendezvous. You stay behind an extra half-minute to pay some civility to a foreign officer who has unexpectedly presented himself; another man takes your place in walking up the communications trench. Crash! He is no more. You may walk to the right or the left of a particular tree, and it makes the difference whether you rise to command an Army Corps or are sent home crippled or paralysed for life.' Churchill had challenged chance before and would so again.

Winston was at the front to understand modern warfare, or at least the warfare that the Western Front had become. He learnt how to push saps forward and to fortify trenches, as well as saw the effects of the first truly industrialised war. He also saw, as he had done in his youth, that he was unafraid of bullets and shells. When on the morning of 26 November the trenches were bombarded, he wrote that it did not cause him any sense of anxiety or apprehension, 'nor does the approach of a shell quicken my pulse, or try my nerves or make me bob about as do so many'. This was a feature of Winston's character which he found puzzling. He seemed not to fear danger as others did and he was at a loss to explain this.

Even those not in Churchill's battalion came to learn or hear of his exploits. Corporal Walter Gilliland was serving in the Royal Irish Fusiliers: 'Near here Mr. Winston Churchill is stationed and a cooler and braver officer never wore the King's uniform. He moves about among the men in the most exposed positions just as though he was wandering the lobbies of the House of Commons. During the Ulster business before the war there was no man more detested in Belfast [he had addressed a gathering of Unionists, telling them to prepare for Home Rule], but after what we have seen of him here we are willing to let bygones be bygones and that is a big concession for Ulstermen to make.

'The other night his regiment came in for a rough time, and a party of the men were buried under the wreck of a section of trench blown up by the enemy. This explosion was followed by a terrific bombardment from the enemy's guns, and from hundreds of machine guns posted everywhere. Amid it all, Mr Churchill was moving about serenely, doing his best to extricate the unfortunate men. Bullets spluttered around him knocking over his men left and right, but he seemed to bear a charmed life, and never betrayed the least sign of nervousness. His coolness is the subject of much discussion among us, and everybody admires him.'[6]

It was also when he was with the Guards that Winston showed his softer side. On the night of 25/26 November 1915, whilst he was on duty, he came upon a sentry who was asleep at his post. This was a very serious offence as it endangered the whole company. The penalty for this was at least two years imprisonment and could even result in the death sentence. The sentry was obviously terrified at being caught, but Winston did not report him. 'He was only a lad,' said Winston.

Winston was learning much about life in the trenches. Above all he saw that there was a numb indifference to casualties. Soldiers were killed, it was what happened in war. The men simply got on with their duties or fatigues.

Churchill's time in the front line gave him the opportunity to think about how the war in the trenches could be won. It had become painfully obvious that attacks in the open across No Man's

Land against machine-guns in well-fortified defensive positions was suicidal. During his time at the Admiralty, Winston had set in motion moves to develop what would eventually become the tank. The building of such armoured fighting machines was a complex and expensive task and whilst tanks would prove to be fearsome weapons of war, their introduction would still not stop men being shot. Winston, therefore, considered some form of personal armour. 'For the specific object of protecting men from machine gun bullets during the short walk across from trench to trench, shields are indispensable,' he wrote as part of a memorandum he had typed up for him at GHQ, a report which he titled *Variants of the Offensive*. These bullet-proof shields could be carried by individual soldiers or pushed along by several men. They would be 'lined along the parapet [of the trench] and picked up by the men on the signal to advance'. These collective shields, four feet high and fifteen feet across, would be capable of protecting up to fifteen men, and would be fitted with wheels or, ideally, with caterpillar tracks.

Winston proposed that they would be 'disposed secretly along the whole attacking front two or three hundred yards apart': 'Ten or fifteen minutes before the assault these engines should move forward over the best line of advance open, passing through or across our trenches at prepared points. They are capable of traversing any ordinary obstacle, ditch, breastwork or trench. They carry two or three maxims [machine-guns] each and can be fitted with flame apparatus. Nothing but a direct hit from a field gun will stop them.'

Under the protection of the shields the men could cut any wire that had not been destroyed by shelling. Winston also proposed using a form of oxyacetylene cutting equipment which could be carried by the soldiers to cut quickly through heavy barbed-wire entanglements.

On 27 November 1915, the battalion left the front and marched back to the reserve billets, the men singing *It's a Long Way to Tipperary* as they reached the village of Riez Bailleul. The following day Lord Cavan asked Winston to join him for lunch at La Gorgue.

During the meal the Major General told the Major that he it was not necessary for him to return to the trenches. He had experienced life, and death, in the front line and now understood the circumstances and conditions the men fought under well enough. He could now remain at headquarters until a brigade became available to him. Churchill, predictably, was not interested in hanging around at headquarters. He told Lord Cavan that 'he wouldn't miss a day of it', and that he was keen to get back to his place in the line. He duly re-joined No.1 Company.

During his next period in reserve Winston accepted Sir John French's offer to stay at GHQ. When he arrived at St Omer he found that Sir John had been recalled to London and the talk at headquarters was of the Field Marshal's imminent removal from command of the BEF. Sir John returned to France in the knowledge that he had only three weeks in post. Sir John consequently urged Churchill to take a brigade immediately before the Field Marshal was dismissed and Winston lost his sponsor.

Winston agreed and he wrote to his wife on 4 December 1915, to tell her that within a week or two he would become a Brigadier-General. The eminently sensible Clementine cautioned against such assertive statements in a letter two days later, advising him to go step by step in the accepted manner. 'Get a battalion now,' she wrote, 'and a brigade later'.

Winston's imagination had been fired, though, and he was becoming increasingly excited with what he saw as a promising military career, as it was mooted that before long he would be commanding a division. Then, on 10 December he was told that he would be given the 56th Brigade of the 19th (Western) Division. This was composed of four Lancashire-raised Service battalions.

Before he could take up his new command he was due another spell in the trenches with the Guards. In this forty-eight hour period a remarkable incident occurred which he told his wife about. A party of ten Grenadiers under Second Lieutenant The Honourable William Alastair Darner Parnell raided across No Man's Land and occupied part of the opposing German trench. This, they found, was largely deserted and waterlogged, but they came upon a three-man German picket. They 'beat the brains' out of two of the Germans with clubs and triumphantly dragged the third one back to the British lines as a prisoner. What the Grenadiers did not mention was that young Lieutenant Parnell accidentally fired his pistol, killing one of his own men. The rest of the Grenadiers pretended that their comrade was killed by the Germans and Parnell was awarded the Military Cross.[7]

Winston, who had been happy to be away from Westminster, found himself drawn back into the world of politics when he received a letter from Lord Curzon, the Lord Privy Seal, telling him that there were serious divisions amongst the Cabinet and that the Allies were to accept defeat at Gallipoli and pull out all the troops, which disappointed Winston. It was politics nearer home, however, that would disappoint him far more deeply.

Word had reached the House of Commons that Churchill, a mere major, was going to be given command of a brigade by Sir John French. Winston's many enemies in the Conservative Party 'whose vindictive spleen remained unslaked' were determined to oppose this.

On 16 December 1915, Sir Charles Hunter, also a Major in the Army, asked the Under-Secretary of State for War, Mr Harold John Tennant, whether or not it was true that Winston had been offered a brigade, and for how many weeks he had served at the front as an infantry officer. The Under-Secretary replied: 'I have no knowledge myself, and have not been able to obtain any, of a promise of command of an infantry brigade having been made to my right honourable and gallant Friend referred to in the question. On the second point I have consulted books of reference and other authentic sources of information, and the result of my investigations is that my right honourable and gallant Friend has never commanded a battalion of infantry. No report has been made to the War Office of the movements of Major the Right Honourable Winston L.S. Churchill since he proceeded to France on the 19th November. If he has been serving as an infantry officer between that date and today, the answer to the last part of the question would be about four weeks.'

Charles Hunter persisted in demanding to know if Winston was going to skip the normal rules of promotion and be offered command of a brigade. In a joke about the advanced age of the generals in the British Army, Sir C. Scott Robertson interjected by saying that Mr Churchill couldn't possibly be offered a brigade as he was under sixty! Mr E. Cecil was not to be deflected from pointing out that, 'if this appointment were made it would be thought by very many persons both inside and outside this House a grave scandal'.[8]

In fact it was not only Winston's enemies that were opposed to his rapid advancement, his friends also saw no good coming from him being promoted over the heads of officers with far greater claims to general rank than a Major in the Oxfordshire Hussars.

When Churchill returned to GHQ on 14 December 1915, Sir John French was no longer there. He had been summoned back to the UK, his days as the commander of the BEF rapidly drawing to an end. Whilst Churchill was at St Omer he received a telephone call from London. It was Sir John French. He had something unpleasant to say.

That morning he had received a letter from Prime Minister Asquith vetoing Churchill's promotion.

Though not always a firm supporter of Winston, Lord Beaverbrook was indignant at this seemingly vindictive intervention by Asquith. 'A Premier may have to throw a colleague overboard to save the ship,' he wrote, 'but surely he should not jerk from under him the hen-coop on which the victim is trying to sustain himself on the stormy ocean'.

French was due back at GHQ to formally hand over to his successor, General Douglas Haig, and Winston wanted to question Sir John on the reasons behind the refusal of the Government to allow him to take a brigade, so he remained at St Omer. Sir John arrived back in the evening of 17 December.

Having been promised a brigade, Winston was very dejected at being offered only a battalion. He even contemplated simply giving up his Army career to return to Westminster. The determining factor for Winston would be how the new Commander-in-Chief viewed him. If Haig was prepared to give Winston a chance to prove himself capable of high command then all might be well after all and no-one could say that he had not earned his spurs on the battlefield.

On Sir John's last day as commander of the BEF, 18 December, he spoke to Haig on a 'delicate personal matter'. Haig later recalled that meeting at St Omer:

> He did not look very well and seemed short of breath at times. He expressed a wish to help me and the Army in France to the best of his power at home. Then he said that 'There was a delicate personal matter' which he wished to speak about. This was that he wanted to give Winston Churchill an Infantry Brigade. This had been vetoed but he was anxious that Winston should have a battalion. I replied that I had no objection because Winston had done some good work in the trenches and we were short of Battalion COs. I then said goodbye.[9]

Having bade his predecessor farewell, Haig dealt with the situation promptly, no doubt because, as Haig himself noted, 'Winston Churchill then appeared'. This time it is Churchill who recounted what followed next:

> I was called in and had an interview with Haig. He treated me with the utmost kindness of manner & consideration, assured me that nothing wd give him greater pleasure than to give me a brigade, that his only wish was that able men shd come to the front, & that I might count on his sympathy in every way. He had heard from Cavan of the 'excellent work' that I had done in the trenches … I was greatly reassured by his manner wh. was affectionate almost. He took me by the arm and made the greatest fuss. I used to know him pretty well in the old days when he was a Major & I was a young MP, but I am bound to say the warmth of his greeting surprised me.[10]

So Winston, his ruffled feathers having been agreeably smoothed, acquiesced. He would take command of a battalion.

That battalion, Churchill learnt later in the day, was intended to be the 9th Battalion, King's Royal Rifle Corps. However, it was then discovered that this battalion was about to return to the UK; Winston's posting was cancelled.

As no position was vacant Winston had to wait for his new command so he decided to return to Britain, which of course meant a return to the hotbed of political intrigues at Westminster. Winston was soon absorbed in the machinations and manoeuvring and he realised how much he missed politics and being at the heart of the country's decision-making. It appeared that the Government was about to tear itself apart, which would present Winston with an opportunity to re-establish himself in front line politics. It was the front line in France, however, that he had to contend with first, and on 27 December 1915 he returned to St Omer.

On 29 December Winston and Captain Edward Spiers, a former acquaintance, whom he had first met before the war, went to a section of Vimy Ridge held by the French to see how they did things. They were both shocked at the number and size of the rats they saw running in and around the trenches. Winston observed that they served a useful purpose in that they ate the dead bodies, of which there were always many.

Spiers had spent time with the French and so was a good guide. He took him to a spot at Notre Dame de Lorette where there was a ridge facing the French behind which was a declivity. According to Spiers the French had repeatedly attacked the German positions there but no one had ever returned alive. This was because about fifteen yards below the ridge trenches had been dug into the rear slope. When any French troops mounted the ridge they stood out clearly against the sky and were easily 'popped' off by the Germans.

It was on New Year's Day 1915 that Winston was finally informed that it was a battalion in the 9th (Scottish) Division that he would command. He immediately wrote to his wife, telling Clementine that he was not allowed to say which battalion it was or where it was to train. All he could say was that it was a few miles to the left of where he was before with the Grenadiers. That battalion was the 6th (Service) Battalion, Royal Scots Fusiliers.

Part II

With Winston Churchill at the Front

Chapter 5

With Winston at the Front

The 6th (Service) Battalion of the Royal Scots Fusiliers was part of the 9th (Scottish) Division, commanded by Major General William Furse, the first of Kitchener's 'New Army' divisions to cross to France. At the time that Winston took command of the battalion it consisted of thirty officers and around 700 men. Churchill presented himself to Furse on New Year's Day and dined with him at his headquarters at Merris. This gave Winston a chance to learn something about his battalion from someone who had seen it in action.

It had been formed at Ayr in August 1914 in response to Kitchener's appeal and came under the orders of the 27th Brigade. After training the battalion was sent to France on 11 May 1915, in time to take part in the Battle of Loos that September. The battalion had lost heavily in that battle, suffering more than fifty per cent casualties. The gaps had been filled with young and inexperienced officers and Winston asked if he could have with him Captain Edward Spiers of the 11th Hussars who had been serving as a liaison officer with the French 10th Army, and Captain Archibald Sinclair. Spiers was regarded as being too young to hold a position in such a weakened battalion, but he was allowed to have Sinclair as his second-in-command.

The battalion had been in the front line of the Ypres Salient for two months and had just pulled out to recover in reserve billets at Moolenacker near the town of Meteren, about five miles short of the Belgian frontier and ten miles back from the front line. The battalion was not due back at the front until 20 January. This gave

Churchill almost three weeks to get to know his battalion, and, perhaps more importantly, for the men to get to know their new lieutenant colonel. He knew that he had a difficult job on his hands as the battalion had lost most of its senior officers but he told Clementine that he was confident he could bring the battalion up to scratch: 'This battalion is the weakest in the brigade and makes the least good appearance. The young officers have not the command to make their companies drill and march really well. They can do a plain job all right; but the polish is at present lacking.'

As one officer pointed out, though, the battalion that Winston had conducted his training in was the Grenadier Guards – any comparison between the two was inevitably going to be unfair. This was particularly the case when it is borne in mind that the Grenadiers only spent forty-eight hours in the trenches at any one time, whereas the Royal Scots Fusiliers generally endured six days in and six days out of the line.

After the losses at Loos the battalion had little rest, being thrown into the Ypres Salient spending a harsh winter in the Flanders mud. After trudging four miles through mud up to their thighs they had just a few days rest before Winston arrived with his boundless energy. Little wonder then that the men could not match up to the standards of the Guards.

Winston saw all this as a great challenge. His attention was first directed towards ensuring that his men's equipment was adequate and well looked after. Gas helmets, rifles in good order, trench discipline and routine,' was how he described his initial focus. 'I shall give them some very precise drill and marching,' he told his wife. As Captain Dewar Gibb recalled, Colonel Churchill's instructions were not quite as 'precise' as he might have hoped, as will shortly be revealed.

The chapters that follow in Part II are based upon
'WITH WINSTON CHURCHILL AT THE FRONT'
which was written by Captain X, the late Professor
Dewar Gibb, and published by
Gowans and Gray Ltd. in 1924.
Professor Gibb's words remain unaltered and
uncorrected.

The lighter weight, slightly indented text has been added
to support and complete the account.

Chapter 6

The Thunderbolt

One morning in December 1915 I fell in with the Transport Officer in the unsavoury courtyard of the farm which housed the Battalion H.Q. of the 6th Royal Scots Fusiliers, and in exchanging rumours he told me as a fact that almost immediately Winston Churchill was coming to take over the Battalion. Not to be outdone I said I knew, and had further heard that Lord Curzon had, the day before, been made Transport Officer of the adjoining battalion and was already in a position to teach him, Scott, his job.

I was about to communicate further news of a similar nature when I began to suspect from Scott's unquenchable solemnity that he might after all be making an essay in the truth, and having put him on his honour I gathered from him that it was so and that beyond all doubt this was a rumour that was going to come true. You know, perhaps, the haunting effect of those book titles whose meaning is not self-evident, such as "Cometh up as a flower" and "What will he do with it?" and how you apply them in all sorts of absurd situations and wonder if this at last is what the author means. Just so there was running perpetually in my head, "The wonderful thing that has happened to our boys," only with the epithet quite changed. It was all I could do – keep on muttering this – stunned.

He was expected to arrive that day and to take over from the C.O. after lunch. I felt it incumbent on me to impart the news to the other company officers, so I hastened off to the company parade-ground, where my wretched platoon was performing without enthusiasm what was known as trench-clearing drill.

At first I had no chance, as the C.O. was there, urging us to greater exertions because the Brigadier was expected, and the little fellow would have been enraged if he had detected any symptoms of a conversational nature. I therefore had to resign myself to the inculcation of a spirit of aggression in the troops. Presently, however, the Colonel came up to me with a darkened brow. He was obviously not himself, and I thought that his worried expression portended something unusual. And at last, after a certain amount of leading, he told me that Winston Churchill was to relieve him of his command that very day. I assumed a look at once of sympathy and resignation, and said I had heard it was so. I could not, however, say that I was glad.

> It was not until Monday, 3 January 1916, that Lieutenant Colonel Winston Churchill set off from St Omer to join his battalion at Moolenacker Farm. He had sent a message ahead that he wanted to meet all the officers for lunch, following which he would inspect the whole battalion. His somewhat unorthodox arrival was recorded by one officer, F.G. Scott:
>
> 'Just before noon an imposing cavalcade arrived. Churchill on a black charger, Archie Sinclair on a black charger, two grooms on black chargers followed by a limber filled with Churchill's luggage – much more than the 35 pounds allowed weight. In the rear half we saw a curious contraption: a long bath and boiler for heating the bath water.'[1]
>
> At first sight this may have appeared to reflect the decadence of this aristocrat that had been dropped into their midst from the cossetted comfort of Blenheim Palace but, as Gibb later fondly recalled, Winston shared his bath with his officers and it was a great luxury they enjoyed amidst the privations of life in the shell holes and trenches.

The officers duly assembled for lunch which was a truly memorable, or possibly, forgettable experience, as Lieutenant Edmund Hakewill Smith, the battalion's only surviving regular officer, recalled. 'It was quite the most uncomfortable lunch I have ever been at,' he later told the historian Martin Gilbert. 'Churchill didn't say a word: he went right round the table staring each officer out of countenance. We had disliked the idea of Churchill being in command; now, having seen him, we disliked the idea even more. At the end of the lunch, he made a short speech: "Gentlemen, I am now your Commanding Officer. Those who support me I shall look after. Those who go against me I will break. Good afternoon gentlemen." Everyone was agreed that we were in for a pretty rotten time.'[2]

The men, however, would soon change their opinion of Lieutenant Colonel Churchill.

Chapter 7

The Arrival

When the news spread, a mutinous spirit grew. Everybody liked the old C.O. and nobody could see why any prominent outsider should come in and usurp his place so easily. Why could not Churchill have gone to the Argylls[1] if he must have a Scottish regiment! We should all have been greatly interested to see him in a kilt and, besides, the Argylls were accustomed to celebrities in their ranks since Ian Hay had celebrated their deeds in his remunerative volume.

Or again, we should all have been glad to see him once for all oust and utterly displace the Brigade Commander, who had jarred upon us since the day he stopped the Battalion's leave for a fortnight on finding in our front line a well-rusted bayonet, the property of some migratory and irresponsible sapper. We should even have been glad to see him replace the Divisional General who, although popular, was always unduly anxious to involve us in unpleasant and dangerous brawls with the Germans opposite.

Indeed, any position at all in the Expeditionary Force seemed not too exalted for Winston if only he had left us our own C.O. and refrained from disturbing the peace of the pastures of Moolenacker. However, the uselessness of this line of thought soon became obvious to everybody, and we felt instead that we might more profitably seek to interest or amuse ourselves in the possession of an ex-cabinet minister as our Colonel.

Winston arrived that very day at noon at Battalion H.Q. and it was not long before certain red-hatted gentlemen from

Divisional Headquarters at Merris also dropped in on us, which was *not*, as they would fain have made us think, a daily occurrence, and really must have had some connection with Winston's advent. Nobody who knows the many uncomplimentary things which were said by the regular officers serving in the B.E.F. regarding Winston Churchill as a soldier would ever have believed that they could have been so extremely friendly, not to say forward, as some of them were while he was in command of his battalion.

In the afternoon, our billet was visited, and along with the other Company officers, I was presented. My Company-Commander manifestly "had the wind up," as we had a beastly tumbledown old farm, which it was impossible to make really comfortable for the men, and, of course, as there is no such thing as giving a reason in the Army, the blame was liable at any moment to fall on Gibb's head. The Staff Captain of the Brigade, who really deserved it, was

(*a*) a Staff officer

(*b*) a Peer's son, and

(*c*) a Gordon Highlander,

and hence inviolable and immune from criticism. However, Churchill said little or nothing, and after peering into the barn which housed the men, he faded softly from our ken for the time being, and we were left in our usual condition of troubled peace. The receipt of Orders that evening, headed by the Colonel's name, *plus* strings of decorative letters, filled us with a childish interest.

Chapter 8

The Battalion

This book is excusable, if at all, only as an account of Winston Churchill as a battalion commander in the Great War, yet it will probably be not amiss if I devote a few lines of it to describing in outline the battalion which he was called upon to command. It is impossible to say whether or not it was by his own choice that he came to a Scottish regiment, but his oft-expressed views regarding Scotland and the Scots (which a Scottish historian could not without blushes record) make it very probable that he had a large say in the decision to appoint him to the command of a battalion having a depot at Ayr rather than Aldershot.

The battalion was the 6th (Service) Battalion of the Royal Scots Fusiliers. The regiment itself was born in 1678, at which date the ancestors of the world-famous Highland regiments were prominent chiefly in certain hanging dramas, not altogether unconnected with the stealing of cattle. It is therefore of considerable antiquity, and its fighting record may be said, without immodesty, to be as noteworthy as its age. Let the superstitious attach such significance as they will to its early connection in less happy circumstances with a name which gave a title to James Graham of Claverhouse, under whom it fought at the battle of Drumclog.[1]

The battalion, which was of the "First Hundred Thousand," had won laurels and golden opinions at the Battle of Loos. As a result, however, it had returned to billets with a very inconsiderable proportion of its men and only two officers. It had then been built up by reinforcements, and although still somewhat ragged – and not less so by reason of a recent and thoroughly unpleasant sojourn in the wood misnamed "Sanctuary," near Ypres – it was in a fair way to become again as fine a unit as when it left England in the spring of 1915.

The men were very largely Lowland Scots, with a sprinkling of Englishmen. The Scots Fusiliers are the Ayrshire and Galloway regiment, and comprise many miners from the Ayrshire coalfields. As a first line service battalion it contained a fair proportion of regular N.C.O.s. The officers were extremely young, perhaps exceptionally so for those early days. We boasted only one regular officer and he had only left Sandhurst after August 1914. He was very much chagrined at finding himself in a Kitchener battalion, but he came to learn that the expression of these sentiments was unpopular, and perhaps will be the greater soldier one day from having grasped the fact that people may be soldiers though they have never seen Sandhurst. He was a pleasant, chubby, shortnecked youth and, being bombing-officer, was christened the "Bomb-boy" by Winston. He even – *horresco referens* – used to "lecture" on bombing, and exuded bombs and fuses at every pocket in the most brilliant and terrifying fashion.

The Adjutant was but little older. He was a nice, laughing, young man, of a very engaging address and endowed with an unusual power of expressing himself in emphatic profanity, distinguished by the undulating intonation of a dweller in the Eastern Cheviots. He was oppressed, however, by the late hours which the advent of our energetic C.O. forced him to keep, and later resigned in favour of one of the company commanders, a sombre and conscientious advocate, briefless, I think, from the Parliament House, in Edinburgh.

Then there was Kemp the signalling officer, whose signalling days with us, however, did not last long, as part of a whizz-bang hit him, and made it necessary for him to be taken to England.

The acting second-in-command was Ritchie, an older man, of about 26. A most efficient officer, and now a regular, he was relegated to the obscurity of a company by the advent of Winston's *fidus Achates*, whom he brought to us from the 2nd Life Guards and constituted second-in-command. This was Archibald Sinclair, a Scottish Laird, of Thurso, and he remained with the battalion throughout Winston's stay.

It was a great pity that that remarkable man, Joe Dunbar, our M.O., left us within a week or so of the change of government, as he was beloved by us all, especially well for his hearty contempt of vermorel-sprayers, his thorough and real efficiency as a doctor, and his earnest and loving participation in the rites of Bacchus wheresoever and whensoever these were celebrated throughout the Battalion, and indeed throughout the Brigade areas.

These men constituted the C.O.'s entourage. The companies contained many good fellows and many good officers. Among them was Ramsey of D Company, a most gallant and efficient officer, who possessed in the highest degree that quality, more desirable than any other in the late war, an ever present appreciation of such humour as lay in the most humourless situations. Foulkes of A Company, most deplorable of horsemen but most lovable of men: and Harvey of C Company, handsome and impressive. B Company was under Gibb, who later became Adjutant.

> Apart from the memoir he subsequently wrote, Dewar Gibb maintained a diary, albeit infrequently, during this time. It is evident that it took many weeks before he warmed to Winston, and his words at the time present a slightly different picture to that subsequently painted by Gibb in his book.
>
> His first entry is when Winston arrived on 4 January: 'WSC arrives in a motor car with piles of luggage and a Guards Officer. He shook hands all round and orders Archie Sinclair to be second in command; I feel excessive annoyance … 3 officers supplanted.'[2]

Chapter 9

Settling Down

Winston, in the most businesslike way, at once set about knowing his officers. He summoned them all to the orderly-room at 2.30 p.m. on the day of his arrival. I think that Battalion H.Q. were situated in a more than usually dirty farm. Certainly the farm people were more than usually dirty and unprepossessing. Yet certain of them found favour in the sight of the Regimental Sergeant-Major and of the signallers – *anglicé* telephone-operators – who lived in the kitchen, which was the ante-room to the orderly-room. And whether by means of the sign-language, or by dint of that reiteration which works such wonders, the dirty ladies of the house had come to understand that the new Colonel was somebody.

Winston therefore made fitting entry on this his formal accession to power, for not only was there much clicking and saluting on the part of

(a) the officers,
(b) the Sergeant-Major, and
(c) the prisoners,

but the ladies rose up to the accompaniment of loud whispers of "*Monsieur le minister!*" "*Monsieur le Colonel!*" "*Ah, c'est lui?*" "*C'est votre minister?*" and in this way imparted to the proceedings at once an irregular air of friendliness, and an international colour, which produced a most happy effect and one worthy of the occasion.

First of all the Company Commanders were called into the orderly-room and were introduced formally by the retiring

Colonel. Then the rest of the officers came in and were presented. After each officer had come up and saluted and shaken hands Winston relapsed into his chair and scrutinised him, silently and intently, from head to foot. It was not easy to know how to parry this unconventional attack on one's composure. It was necessary to stand at attention, of course, so that no relief could be sought in the diversion of a mere social and friendly conservation. I found myself forced to stare hard back at him and trust to time to bring this, like all other trials, to an end. So I stared, but I admit the experience was distasteful to me. And what particularly annoys me about it in retrospect is that when some months later in a new battalion I took over a company and tried this device when my platoon sergeants were named to me, I think it upset me more than it did them and I never knew their names to the end.

That was orderly-room No.1, which terminated after we had all been "vetted" in this novel fashion, but orderly-room No.2, held the next day, was all bustle and business. There had been consultations and alarums, and, on the part of the Adjutant especially, a burning of midnight oil. Indeed, the increasing pallor of that functionary was now giving rise to comment and it was rumoured that he was having a "hell of a time."

At any rate next day's orderly-room was a very impressive spectacle. We no longer had an ancient and far from sober-looking military policeman as escort to the prisoners, but a smart, tall soldier with a great deal of equipment on, and with bayonet fixed. The Regimental Sergeant-Major (always in my opinion the most ludicrous-pathetic figure in any battalion) had polished his buttons to such an extent that they shone through the dim and unwholesome atmosphere of our miniature Old Bailey like some pure, clear, emanation of the fine flame of discipline burning within his bosom. His attitude, too, towards his inferiors was more distinctly harsh, masterful, and unmannerly, while the prisoners obviously stood in some doubt as to whether he was not empowered there and then to order a holocaust of them without bringing them before the C.O. at all.

There were other signs of the times to be noticed, such as the absence of cats from the orderly-room: the cessation of what I always understood were "winnowing" operations in the granary immediately overhead: the exclusion of the orderly-room sergeant and his satellite, till then prime actors in the daily kaleidoscope of orderly-room: and even a slight sympathetic smartening up of the clothing worn by the officers.

"War is declared, gentlemen," observed Winston to an audience now thoroughly aroused to attention, "on the lice." With these words did the great scion of the house of Marlborough first address his Scottish Captains assembled in council. And with these words was inaugurated such a discourse on *pulex Europaeus*, its origin, growth, and nature, its habitat and its importance as a factor in wars ancient and modern, as left one agape with wonder at the erudition and force of its author. I became forthwith a prey to the most lively apprehensions lest I should fall a victim to its foul attentions, in which event I saw but little likelihood of ever being clean again.

When Winston's masterly biography of the louse was completed, and in order that we might not abandon all hope, he called upon the Doctor, hitherto a silent but not unmoved listener, to suggest remedies and make proposals, and thereafter he created a committee of company commanders to concert measures for the utter extermination of all the lice in the battalion. I may here say that it was done, and done well, after three or four days spent in toil as unsavoury as any I have ever devoted myself to. I remember the Corps Commander passing the billet when we were busy with our hot irons, extruding the lice from trousers and shirts. One of the men saw him and looked at his friend saying,

"There's that wee General – is it no?"

"Aye, that's him. The last time I saw him was at the Orchard: – the wee —— spoke to me."

"Did he, Jock? He didna ken ye the day!"

"Whit could the man hae said? Gied me an order to turn a —— —— machine-gun on this —— shirt o'mine?"

We were certainly a liceless battalion. At a late period of the war the HQ staff invented a beautiful little word to signify this process: a word happily blended of a purely Latin prefix and a purely Anglo-Saxon noun – the word "delouse."

Once a party of men sailed from France to England, and on arrival the utmost horror and indignation were created by the discovery that they were "*un*deloused." At the time we speak of, however, this word had not come into being, and we had to refer to it in our pride by way of periphrasis, but we were to an unparalleled degree an utterly "deloused" battalion.

From day to day the C.O. introduced particular little innovations which he liked and by the end of ten days he had produced a manifest smartening up on every side. Ritchie indeed sarcastically observed that he had only come "to teach us to click our heels and polish our guns and to turn us into a first-class eye-wash battalion," but that was too sweeping a statement, and it was only just to admit that he improved us greatly. Meantime he improved *on* us. All the company commanders were invited to dine in the H.Q. mess and there learnt a little of the charm and courtesy of the man as distinct from the Colonel. No doubt he sought to win us, but for that he is only to be admired, and his capacity for coaxing and charming the best even out of the most boorish is a gift which I never ceased to wonder at. He materially altered the feelings of the officers towards him by this kindliness and by the first insight we thus gained into the wonderful genius of the man. And so he began a conquest which when he left us was complete – a complete conquest achieved in two or three short months and over men of a race not easily moved or won over.

The men meanwhile seemed to be delighted with their new Colonel. Obviously each man thought that he himself was the person whom Winston's coming was especially designed to honour. Many of them did not know even his name correctly: he was Lord Churchill, Viscount Churchill, Sir Winston Churchill, even the Duke of Churchill, but whatever his name was, his being there was a feather in their caps. For a week their letters told of nothing else and after the wave of correspondence had rolled towards Scotland for a week, it rolled back again to France till the latest day of his stay, in the form of applications for leave, for discharge, for pay, for pensions, for lost birth-certificates, return of erring husbands, everything and anything which the writers conceived his influence would be useful in effecting. The Adjutant grew more rapidly bald in the conduct of his administrative duties at this period, as the Colonel insisted on the most scrupulous justice being done to every inquiry, however trifling.

Chapter 10

Settling Down (Continued)

Our nights were spent in wondering what he'd do next, our days in doing it. There were still a few special ideas which he wished to introduce into his battalion.

One, much resented, was the practice of acknowledging all orders by the use of the single word "Sir." We were forbidden to say "Yes, sir" or "No, sir." When you try to say "Sir," each time you are told to do or not to do something, you feel at first that you are merely straining language and putting a rein upon your enthusiasm. To introduce into this silly little monosyllable all the enthusiasm you felt about carrying out the orders of a new and rather fearsome C.O. appeared at first an almost impossible task, but in the end we improved. Beautiful and inspiring was the spectacle presented by Harvey lisping out eloquent "Sirs" in response to the C.O.'s curtain-lectures in orderly-room, but no one of all the rest ever did it quite so convincingly or well. I suspect the nasty trick grew up in the neighbourhood of Chelsea.

> However, the 'fearsome' new commander was turning out to be far more considerate of his men than had been at first anticipated. It was found that if a man was put in front of Winston for some misdemeanour he would ask them if they had fought at Loos. If the answer was in the affirmative the Colonel would dismiss the charge. Inevitably, word soon got around and before long everyone in the battalion claimed to have fought at Loos. Churchill's leniency was not

appreciated by some of the officers and NCOs as Gibb explained later in his memoir.

As promised Winston was going to mount a determined assault upon lice and whilst the battalion in its reserve quarters a delousing committee was formed. Second Lieutenant Jock McDavid (who Gibb referred to as MacDavid) and the French liaison officer attached to the 9th Division, Lieutenant Emile Herzog, were sent to the nearest town, Bailleul, to find baths for the men. Winston had suggested that large brewery vats might be suitable and, luckily, the two officers found a deserted brewery.

From the outset Winston was keen to see that his men were treated well, and indeed promised them an improvement in their circumstances. True to his word a large supply of new uniforms soon arrived as well as the recently-issued steel helmets, the battalion being amongst the first to receive them. The men also noticed an improvement in their rations. Having a famous politician as the commanding officer clearly had its advantages.

Life in reserve was relaxed and Winston did not impose any undue measures. Each morning was devoted to exercise and drill but after lunch the men were free to rest and relax.

One morning, Winston and Sinclair joined in with bomb-throwing practice, which Winston described to Clementine as a job to be approached gingerly: 'You pull out the safety pin, and then as long as you hold the bomb in your hand nothing happens. But the moment you throw it – or release your hand – the fuze begins to burn and then 5 seconds afterwards there is [a] real good bang and splinters fly all over the place. As soon as you have thrown it, you bob down behind the parapet, until the explosion has occurred. Sometimes the men are stupid – drop the bomb in the trench or close to it – then the bombing officer [the previously-mentioned 'Bomb-boy'] – a young Sandhurst kid – deftly picks it up and throws it away with perhaps 2 seconds to spare.' Winston added, no doubt to ease his wife's anxieties, that 'It is perfectly safe as long as you do it right.'

Football was, of course, a usual afternoon activity for the men which Winston promoted. A field was rolled out and goalposts erected. Football jerseys and balls were acquired and the 6th Royal Scots Fusiliers played against neighbouring battalions. Winston rarely missed a game and was hugely proud of his team which won, it is claimed, all its matches.

An officer with the Royal Scots Regiment (not to be confused with the Royal Scots Fusiliers) wrote of one divisional running race that was organised at this time: 'There was a very strong field with teams from nearly every unit in the division. But the audience completely mobbed us; for the rumour had gone round, carefully fostered by his own battalion, that Winston Churchill, who had just joined the division, was a starter. Disappointment ran high when it turned out to be a common C.O. who had been mistaken for the famous man.'[1]

Winston believed wholeheartedly in sport for the men and on 16 January, for example, he organised, or at least arranged for, a combined sports day and concert. The sports were such things as mule races, pillow fights and obstacle races, whilst the concert in the evening took place in a large barn. The men sang with gusto, but, as Gibb noted earlier, with the usual intentional misquote of the words.

'The men enjoyed themselves immensely,' Winston told his wife in a letter describing the day's activities, 'Poor fellows – nothing like this has ever been done for them before. They do not get much to brighten their lives – short though they may be ...'

The concert was recalled by Corporal John McGuire: 'I have never forgotten a concert in a barn where Churchill suddenly climbed on top of an old wagon. He could not sing for nuts, but in his deep nasal voice he belted out the out the old stable song: 'My old tarpaulin jacket.'

The next day was spent rehearsing for a route march in which all four battalions of the 27th Brigade were to take part. This was Winston's chance to show the brigadier how much his battalion had improved in the fortnight he had been in command.

Whilst the men were drilling Winston attended a lecture on the Battle of Loos given by Colonel Arthur Holland.[2] It was a tale, Winston observed, 'of hopeless failure, of sublime heroism utterly wasted and of splendid Scottish soldiers shorn away in vain ... Afterwards they asked what was the lesson of the lecture. I restrained an impulse to reply "Don't do it again". But they will – I have no doubt.'

Everyone was now ready for the route march, as Gibb recalls in continuing his memoir:

Winston was very sound in his ideas about singing on the line of march. All that need be said regarding this question has long ago been said, and there is no room for doubt that the singing soldier halves his fatigue. Some soldiers, however, sing more readily than others, and ours were not of the most tuneful. This was partly due to the fact that the knowledge of words was at a premium. One verse, or, at most, two, was all they could manage, and the more they were urged to sing, the less they would sing. However, there were rehearsals and recitals in the barns of nights, and perhaps some of the companies found their trudging through that unspeakable Flemish mud a little alleviated by it all. My company was endowed with a thorough knowledge of only one song, which, while it is not an uncommon song, I feel sure you will not find it in the delightful little brochure on "Tommy's Tunes," which will go to show successive generations of jeunes filles what, among other things, Daddy did in the Great War. That work is of a wholesomeness beyond reproach. My soldier's poor repertory was not. It was of an unsurpassed profanity. The only fragment that still lingers in my memory of this song which I said they did know runs as follows:

> "I'll paint, and you'll paint,
> We'll both paint together – oh
> Won't we have a hell of a time,
>   painting one another, oh!"

It will easily be understood that by ringing the changes on the word "paint," the rest of the verse may remain pretty much the same and yet afford a bewildering variety of mental pictures. That indeed was the simple, artless plan, and the results were astonishing. I think the company felt that to sing other songs in their entirety was to put a slight upon this magic inexhaustible fountain of impurity. Only very seldom at any rate did the strains ascend of such classics as: –

> "Marching, marching, marching,
> Always jolly well marching!"

Our company's singing was adversely commented upon by Winston during the first route-march. We were second company, and in passing through the village of Merris the men were busy inventing adventures and ever fresh adventures in song for their hero and heroine. Afar off I saw the Colonel coming down the column and my heart leaped, for here was our company singing lustily and I felt sure of praise. Winston's large black horse loomed in sight, and then the amazing thing happened. The first platoon – mine – was seized, for the first and last time in its existence, with a devastating attack of modesty and dried up like a mountain rill in summer. The contagion spread and in a moment the company was marching mute – mute of modesty:

Why are your men not singing Captain Gibb?" shouted the Colonel to our Company Commander.

"They *were*, sir, but they think – they thought – they're afraid that –" but Winston had passed on down the column shouting "Sing, sing" as he went.

Gibb turned to me, but did not pass on the rebuke, having a sense of justice.

"Curse these fellows," he said; "like a lot of ——- schoolgirls. They don't care a hang for us, but because the man is a cabinet minister, they must needs study his ——— feelings, ——— and ——— them!" Gibb always looked extremely staid and respectable, but his language was dreadful.

> In his diary, Gibb recalled the route march on 7 January: 'WSC "capered about on his horse and generally behaved in an absurd fashion." … "Is this man going to be quite impossible, I wonder?" Fraser and I, however, enjoyed his peach brandy, whisky and cigars enormously - much needed to counter the horrors of trench warfare. WSC talked about the fleet, high command, law. I let him know that I was a lawyer.'[3]
>
> Whilst the officers of the battalion were already becoming enamoured with their new commander, the Other Ranks initial meeting with Colonel Churchill filled them more with puzzlement than wonderment. This event had taken place the very first afternoon after the 'uncomfortable' lunch the officers had endured.
>
> The men were paraded for Winston's inspection, and the enthusiastic new commander was keen to show how he could handle a battalion. The men had their rifles at the slope when Winston arrived. The Assistant Adjutant, Captain Gibb, reported that all the men were present and correct. Taking his position at their head Winston shouted out 'Royal Scots Fusiliers! Fix Bayonets!' Of course the men could not possibly fix bayonets with the rifles sloped on their shoulders. A few men took their rifles down and started to fix their bayonets, whilst most of the battalion simply stood mystified and immobile, unsure how they were to carry out their Colonel's instructions.

Gibb then advised Winston to call out 'Order Arms' and then fix bayonets. This was an instruction the men could follow.

Winston then carried out his inspection of the ranks, following which he gave the order 'Sections Right!' This was a cavalry order and would have been quite familiar to the troopers of the Oxfordshire Hussars, but to the men of the Scots Fusiliers it meant nothing and again they stood confused waiting for an instruction they could obey.

This parade, and the subsequent bayonet practice, was one that Gibb later recalled with some embarrassment:

On the second day of Winston's tenure of office he gave orders that all the companies should parade in a certain slushy meadow, when he intended personally to inspect the work of each company and meet the officers and men in their official capacity. I had command of our company that day and we were bidden to come forth first and display our prowess. I was given a free hand, so I chose company-drill, which I knew, and which I thought Winston as a cavalryman was as little likely to know as anything. And the company-drill went off to my own entire satisfaction. Then we paused, while the Colonel went along each platoon and spoke to the men. They loved that. They always do love a chance of spreading themselves to one of the "high heid yins" as they call them.

"What is your age?" asked the Colonel of His Royal Beeriness No.6 in the rear rank.

"41, sir," was the reply.

"41? An excellent age: it's my own."

He was very nice to them all, and as I have said they responded well, but I didn't like some of the buttons I saw and I had no eye for the humour of the situation; I felt there was more to come.

We were now at one of those frequently recurring epochs of the War when the General Staff discovers that all the innovations suggested by the War Office were only so many useless encrustations on military science and technique, and the bayonet had just been re-discovered, and its cult hysterically proclaimed in myriads of silly little coloured booklets, issued for official use only (and by no means to be taken into the front-line trenches). Winston had not been out long enough to know that no attention should be paid to these publications, which would all be condemned in the ensuing month, and he had been affected by this meretricious enthusiasm for the bayonet.

"Mr. X. [i.e. Gibb], will you put your company through a few bayonet exercises?"

I parried that and summoned the Company-Sergeant-Major. He played up like a man and had begun to bellow orders at the men before the C.O. saw what had happened.

"No, no, I want you to do it," he said then to me. So I took up the tale. As I have never been interested in bayonet fighting and held decidedly unorthodox views on it, I can honestly say I felt most uncomfortable. I summoned up to my aid all the mystic phrases which I had heard in the past and which I imagined might convey something to my willing company, but all the time I felt sure that I should have been better understood by a company of British soldiers in front of Sevastopol in 1854 than here in Flanders in 1915.

"I want you to take a rifle and bayonet yourself and demonstrate, Mr. X., demonstrate."

Officious hands thrust the necessary implements into mine, and I began to indulge in a wild series of warlike gestures. I felt that it all bore no possible resemblance to bayonet exercises as "laid down," but I had to do something, and so I went on lunging and parrying and thrusting, all the while wondering if Winston would have me reduced to the ranks afterwards for such an exhibition of buffoonery. And matters were *not* helped out by the fact that the other companies and their officers were standing around, and at ease, to witness this amusing spectacle, and that I had already heard one hastily stifled cackle from Ramsey, whom I knew to be even more ignorant of the whole subject than I was.

Above: Lieutenant-Colonel Winston Churchill and Captain Dewar Gibb pictured during the former's time as Commanding Officer of the 6th (Service) Battalion, Royal Scots Fusiliers in 1916. (Nigel Dewar Gibb)

Below: Captain Dewar Gibb, middle row on the right, pictured with other officers of the 6th (Service) Battalion, Royal Scots Fusiliers in 1916. Captain Bryce Ramsey in on his right. (Nigel Dewar Gibb)

Left: Lieutenant-Colonel Winston Churchill pictured in uniform, sporting his characteristic blue French Army helmet, during the winter of 1915-1916.

Below: Winston Churchill pictured watching German Army exercises in October 1913 – the original caption states that the Kaiser was also present. In less than three years, Churchill would find himself in the trenches of the Western Front facing the men of this very army. (US Library of Congress)

Above: Major Winston Churchill, once again wearing his French helmet, stands with General Émile Fayolle and other officers, including Captain Edward Spears (third from left), at the headquarters of XXXIII Corps, French Army, at Camblain L'Abbé in the Pas-de-Calais while visiting the French front line on 15 December 1915. Churchill's visit came during the training he was undertaking with the Grenadier Guards. (Historic Military Press)

Below: Led by Dewar Gibb, the men of the 6th (Service) Battalion, Royal Scots Fusiliers march down to Port Glasgow during their departure from the city en route to the Western Front. (Nigel Dewar Gibb)

Left: Two officers of the 6th (Service) Battalion, Royal Scots Fusiliers. Captain Dewar Gibb is on the left, whilst standing to his left is Captain Bryce Ramsey. (Nigel Dewar Gibb)

Below: Churchill and the men of his battalion arrived at Ploegsteert on 26 January 1916. They would find a scene not dissimilar to this view of one of the village's snow-covered shell-blasted streets which was taken in the winter of 1916/17. (Courtesy of the Australian War Memorial; P01835.066)

Right: British troops in a front line trench at a corner of Ploegsteert Wood a few months after Churchill had left to return to the UK and politics. (US Library of Congress)

Below: The environment in which Churchill served in early 1916. This view shows British soldiers in a trench protected by barbed wire near a corner of Ploegsteert Wood. There were no major set-piece battles in this area. In fact, after the fighting in late 1914 and early 1915, it became a quiet sector where units were often sent here to recuperate and retrain before returning to take part in more active operations. (Courtesy of the Australian War Memorial; H09032)

Above: A view of the area around Hyde Park Corner, near Ploegsteert Wood, showing a German 5.9-inch shell burst. Note the small white splashes where the fragments are hitting the water. The road shown leads to Messines, and the duckboard track continued to the reserve support and front lines near Prowse Point and St. Yvon (St. Yves). (Courtesy of the Australian War Memorial; E01516)

Left: Dewar Gibb at his home at Shandon on the Gareloch, Dunbartonshire, during the 1930s. (Nigel Dewar Gibb)

Above: Winston Churchill pictured during his time as Prime Minister in the Second World War. This photograph was taken using only the light of fires burning as the result of an air raid on London in early 1944 – the original caption is dated 9 March 1944 – when Churchill decided to venture out to see the work of the emergency services first-hand. He was accompanied by his daughter, Mary Spencer-Churchill, who can be seen to his right in her ATS uniform. (Historic Military Press)

Below: During the Second World War, whilst Professor of Law at Glasgow University, Dewar Gibb offered to give lessons on law to Polish officers stationed nearby. In this group photograph of the 'class' he can be seen siting sixth from the left. On his right is Colonel Kornel Krzeczunowicz; to his left Professor Christian Fordyce. (Nigel Dewar Gibb)

Above: Dewar Gibb aboard his yacht on the Gareloch off Shandon. (Nigel Dewar Gibb)

Left: Dewar Gibb pictured in the 1940s. (Nigel Dewar Gibb)

I don't think Winston can have taken his little yellow and pink and blue booklets much to heart, for at last the horrid farce came to an end, and no great harm done. I was not privileged to see the other companies drill, but I am told that Ramsey took a bold line and quenched criticism by giving his men company drill at the double, and making them present arms on the march, to the discomfiture of MacDavid, the Adjutant, whose facial control was not sufficiently developed to cope with a strain so sudden and so unexpected.

> Again, in his diary Gibb made a brief reference to such experiences, this time referring to events of the 6th: 'Did 1 hour drill with my Company before WSC who doesn't know much about it all; he was cavalry ... He saw all the officers in the afternoon: he gave absurd points for attention, singing on the march, and allocated bodyguards for all officers in trenches.'[4]

I cannot say that after this I read with much enthusiasm in orders that on the following day the battalion would parade at 9.30 a.m., and that Company Commanders would be mounted. At all times a C.O.'s parade is an utter abomination, and not one of us could contemplate with calm the prospect of seeing added to the horror of it the spectacle of the four Company Commanders on their "horses." It may be imagined that this would only affect the four wretches principally concerned, but it is not so, for an uncontrolled and fiery infantry charger in a small field together with a great many men armed with rifles forms a source of danger, alarm and panic. Fortunately our company beast, which I always thought resembled a large trench rat (and which was called "Eagle") was pretty steady, so I made up my mind to bolt from the *mêlée* which I felt sure was inevitable.

The company paraded betimes and I distinctly saw a large number of clean buttons among them and in one part I saw four men together with their equipment put on in the same way.

Cheered to see my troops playing up like this, I leapt into the saddle and putting myself at the head of the company I marched them off, to the accompaniment of our usual solitary asthmatic piper, whose bearing never failed to leave me with the impression that he was making a greater effort to keep in step with the pony than to register a reasonable percentage of correct notes in his one air, "Campbells of Redcastle."

The scene of operations was a field about 2½ acres in extent with trees scattered about in it at intervals the least convenient. Underfoot it was wet, it was nowhere level, and in short it was at all points in perfect contrast to what a parade ground ought to be. There were two companies there when I arrived, and the Regimental Sergeant-Major was just outdoing himself. "Getting hell" from him there were: –

The Markers.
The Company Sergeant-Majors.
The Band.
All other ranks.
The objects of his *sotto voce* remarks were: –
The C.O.
The Adjutant.
The other officers,
The ——- mud.
The ——- rain.

The horses were in a remarkable state of calm, which I feared must presage a storm. Nothing and nobody else was in a state of calm. One didn't expect it of the functionary alluded to above, but others, ordinarily more or less stolid, were fussing about, fastening straps here, covering dirty buttons with other straps there, pushing and pulling, dressing up, dressing back and behaving generally in a panic-stricken and utterly unsoldierlike fashion.

D Company, however, was not fussing nor fretting – nobody was dressing it up or back – it was not being bellowed at by the R.S.M. or the Adjutant. D Company was not there at all: it was in a state of absence.

Then Sinclair, the Second-in-Command, arrived. The high spirit of his horse communicated itself to the horses of the company commanders, unspeakably increasing the misery of those officers. After he had called the Battalion to attention he was followed quickly by the C.O., who was at once saluted with the remarkable announcement, "D Company absent, Sir," which might have daunted a lesser man on first assuming command of a battalion.

We stood and waited, and after mistaking the transport, a milk-cart, and a gang of red-throated staff for the company, it at last marched on with the piper gaily playing "The Barren Rocks" and Ramsey looking well-fed and happy. Nothing was said then, but Ramsey was later called on for explanations. These were two-fold. To the C.O. he said his watch was wrong. To us he said he did it to pull Winston's leg. Neither explanation was true, in all probability. He escaped with a caution.

Then we presented arms. We presented arms quite a number of times, Winston returning the compliment by touching his hat to us. The ponies, too, did not let the feat of arms pass unnoticed. Foulkes's took him for a short stroll to a muck-pond. Mine fortunately did no more than lose its dressing. Harvey's and Ramsey's turned about and glowered at their companies.

Having done with handling arms, we were put in motion. Now Winston was a cavalryman and his commands might legitimately have been expected to lack all the precision of phrase that is expected of an infantry Colonel. They lacked that, it's true, but that was the least of it.

We set off in column of fours and an early fence made it necessary to wheel, which emergency was met by the command: "Head of the column three-quarters left wheel."

Unhappily the head of the column was at the disposal of poor Foulkes, already too much occupied in curbing the forwardness of his horse to be able to spare a moment for translating such a command into the language of "Infantry Training." Imploringly he turned round, and his horrid beast, encouraged by this, made a straight line for the Colonel in midfield. Meantime the company was up against the fence and with the resource of men determined, as British soldiers are said always to do, to think for themselves, it started to "mark time in front."

At last Foulkes was borne back to them, and having gleaned the Colonel's wishes during his short escapade, he wheeled them to the left and relieved a tense situation. It is rumoured that during this impasse the Colonel turned to Sinclair and whispered "Shouldn't they gallop, Archie?" This is probably untrue, as it came from MacDavid, still smarting under a rebuke by the C.O. for the unauthorized addition to his uniform of a yellow bandana handkerchief, three quarters of which flaunted bravely from his left sleeve.

The horses only became unmanageable when we began to march in column of companies, constantly turning about and wheeling and forming. Sometimes I was beside my company, sometimes in front, sometimes behind. Never, save by accident, was I where I should have been, and the other equestrian performers on the field were in no better case. The companies lurched forward, the subalterns swore, the horses rammed the companies from behind and before, the commands ground out unceasingly, as one or other fence of the wretched enclosure was encountered and the upshot of the whole matter was a *mêlée* of blasphemous humanity and outraged horseflesh.

It was all rather astonishing to us, for we had come to have a real regard for Winston's sense of propriety and decorum and orderliness in matters of duty. And to the end we never saw eye to eye in the matter of ceremonial parades. I think the root of the evil was the horses. It was one of the lesser triumphs in organization of the General Staff to allow infantry officers, and infantry temporary officers at that, to go to foreign theatres of war, where horse-riding was practically essential, without making the least provision for training them to sit on a horse.

In France it was often essential to use horses, as in riding long distances to visit new trenches before taking over, and the plight of a poor devil suddenly presented with a frisky pony and ordered to ride long miles over vile cobbled streets and past line upon line of badly driven mechanical transport was one of the direst ever devised and brought about by the stupidity of mankind. Winston did not realize, I think, that ninety per cent of his officers could not ride and that in any event officers on battalion parade are more efficient when unmounted. True, the spectacle *should* have been more imposing with what looked like horsemen in the field, but the reality was sadly different.

We did have one inspection at Moolenacker, when Sir Charles Fergusson, the Corps Commander, visited us. On that occasion we had no horses and the whole thing would have passed off well had not the Pipe-Major, when called upon to play the music during the General Salute, chose to introduce a most unseemly variant on the usual air and struck up with "The Drunken Piper."

> Whilst the training, parades and route marches continued, the moment when the men of the 6th RSF would be required to head to the front line and into the trenches was fast approaching. Consequently, on 20 January, Winston rode up to examine the section of the front that his men were to take over.
>
> To his surprise he found that it was much better than any other part of the trenches he had previously seen. The trenches had duck boards for the men to walk along, and drainage ditches had been dug. This meant that the soldiers could live and fight in dry conditions. The parapets were strong and bullet-proof and the dugouts provided good shelter.
>
> The place itself was called Ploegsteert which is a little more than a mile inside the Belgian border with France and just over nine miles to the south of Ypres. It was described by Winston as 'a long row of well-built brick houses, some of them four storeys high, looking blankly towards the enemy across flat, soppy fields'. He saw that the village itself had so far not been badly damaged,

except for its church. Some of the houses had holes in them but they were perfectly habitable and weatherproof.

In typical military fashion many houses had been taken over as canteens and cafés and the remainder as billets and headquarters. The battalion was billeted in and around three farms: Soyer Farm, Delennelle Farm and what was known as Maison 1875. Winston's headquarters was to be in what had formerly been the workshop of the Sisters of Mercy and was generally known as the Hospice, which was situated on the Ploegsteert to Armentières road. When the battalion was not actually on duty in the trenches it was there where Churchill would stay, but his advanced headquarters was to be at Laurence Farm on the road leading out of the village to the east where the trenches faced the enemy across No Man's Land.

On the 24th the battalion received its orders to commence its move towards the front. It was to reach the support area behind the front line in and around Ploegsteert itself on the 25th and then take over in the trenches on the 26th.

'We went into Plugstreet ... with our tails well up and pipes playing,' wrote one officer, 'for we were fit and hard, and ready to cope with the Boche on level terms once more, thanks to that Heaven-sent rest; and God help the Boche when taken on under such conditions by a Scottish division.'[5]

As Gibb mentioned, before leaving Moolenacker the commander of II Corps, General Sir Charles Fergusson, inspected the brigade and, to Churchill's delight, he declared himself 'astonished' at the improvement he saw. There seems little doubt that this was because the men genuinely tried their best for someone they considered was concerned for their welfare. Churchill had made his mark in little more than three weeks.

Winston wanted to make the last night before moving off to the front a memorable one. There was a very real chance that not all of his officers would survive the following weeks and so he laid on a special dinner at the Station Hotel in the town of Hazebrouck. He also invited Major General Furse and Colonel Holland. This proved to be, in Winston's words, an elaborate feast, with oysters and 'lots' of champagne. It was the first time that all his officers had been gathered together round a table for dinner. The men were much moved. They had never been treated like this since joining the army.

Gibb, too, remembered that last night before leaving for the front:

At last the time drew nigh for our return to the trenches, a prospect at no time exhilarating, but now one calculated to give rise to the greatest uneasiness. I myself recollected some remarks of Winston's when he said: –

"We will go easy at first: a little digging and feeling our way, and then perhaps later on we may attempt a deed."

It was just such "deeds" that were becoming unpleasantly popular at this epoch. Trench-raiding was becoming all the cry and of course the printing-presses of the General Staff – manned by bronzed category C warriors, somewhere near Rouen and Étaples – were working night and day to cover with bad English in worse type reams of paper, which, whatever purpose it might serve, would certainly never serve its ostensible initial purpose of being read. To raid trenches was unpleasant enough: to read about the various flat-hatted regiments who had done it was out of the question.

Pray do not think, dear tender heart that pulsates and throbs at the reading of the warlike, stirring, beautifully written tales of Philip Gibbs, Beach Thomas and the rest, that I intend to disparage the martial spirit of the gallant men who won the war. Far from it. But know that the ordinary mental state of men slogging to and from trenches was miles and miles from the heroic.

Years ago the writers of school stories wrote about boys called Eric who were pure, truthful, keen, energetic and industrious. Now they write about the average schoolboy who, it must be admitted, does not ordinarily possess these virtues in any remarkable degree. They are mostly all capable of fine things in emergency, but as a rule they avoid work, they know the uses of the ready lie, they swear, they over-eat themselves – in a word they do not live upon a plane of epic achievement. So precisely is it with our soldiers: they might have said with truth in the words of Holy Writ that for them all things were *lawful* (*e.g.* trench-raids) but not all things expedient. Capable even of chastity of language they doubtless were, but in the main the words of Uncle Toby remained true in 1914, and true it was that "our troops swore dreadfully in Flanders."

To return, our attitude to trenches was hostile and more than ever hostile in view of the possibility of a serious and definite rupture with whatever enemy chanced to be opposite to us. However, for the moment – the moment before going in – we were placated with *panis et circenses*, like Roman proletariat of old time. Winston gave a dinner-party in Hazebrouck, in the Station Hotel, to his officers and to one or two others, among them the Brigade Major and the Officer Commanding the Divisional Train, a personage with whom it was highly advisable, if we would have our comforts, to stand well.

The dinner was a *succés fou*. As a prelude, the officers had the advantage of an afternoon in Hazebrouck where drink and sweets and *Vies Parisiennes* and most remarkable postcards could be and were bought in large quantities, and even more venturesome enterprises embarked upon. There was a certain Rue St. Hilaire – but there, I believe, the later fighting put a term to the activities of a great part of Hazebrouck: if the Rue St. Hilaire still stands, it can only be as a most amazing instance of divine clemency.

I wish I could write of the dinner-party as it merits to be written of. But only salient features remain in my memory, no bad test of its success. I distinctly remember that the Pipe-Major made a devilish row marching round the table in the most persistent fashion. The C.O. however recognized, as many

Englishmen do not, that the pipes are instruments capable of playing definite airs, and on learning that one of the airs played was "Bonnie Dundee" he instructed the Pipe-Major to play it again.

I also recollect an eloquent speech by the C.O., in which he gracefully alluded to his three ties with Scotland; his wife, his constituency, and his regiment. This was of course greeted with salvoes of cheering. The Brigade Major, too, made a speech. He was Norman Teacher, a Scots Fusiliers regular officer and one of the most gallant of men, killed while in command of the 1st Battalion at Passchendaele later in the war.[6]

After this a period of unmitigated and apparently causeless good-will set in, during which I observed with much pleasure an officer perform a feat which I thought had been a figment of the imagination of many generations of too temperate novelists. Gradually, gently, gracefully, he relapsed under the table. Winston observed him in the performance of this classic act with an expression of entire *bonhomie* and amusement, and my heart warmed towards him for it.

About 11 p.m. we plunged into the cool of a starlit, lovely night and were confronted with our horses, more than impatient for the green fields of Outtersteene. Not otherwise than when the high-spirited entrants for the Derby or the St. Leger fret and paw at the starting-post did these noble ponies chafe when confronted with the insurmountable barrier of the gate across the railway at Hazebrouck station, to the extreme alarm and consternation of their none too capable riders; even so also when the ridiculous train had gone on its smoky path and the gate was slowly lifted, did they crowd through the opening and shoot down the road towards their billets in a wild and headlong career.

After a mile of this course I found it possible to induce a spirit of moderation in my beast, and I sought to restrain also my companion the Bomb-boy. He, however, like Gallio, cared for none of these things, and he was soon beyond my ken, jolting and bumping and tearing down the road like an ill-tied sack of potatoes on his fat little beast. On nearing home, after many a mile, I was met by wild men, who came from their billets and shouted incoherent expressions of good-will at me. There were others who missed their way and paid midnight visits to Meteren, Rouge Croix, Strazeele and other peaceful towns and only arrived home at an hour when their ardour had sensibly abated. I believe the Doctor and the Transport Officer did not even try and only came home with the milk. It was a most successful evening.

> Before leaving for the front Winston penned a letter to his four-year-old son, Randolph: 'I am living here in a little farm ... The Germans are a long way off and cannot shoot at us here. It is too far. So we are quite safe as long as we stay here. But we can hear the cannons booming in the distance and at night when it is all dark we can see their flashes twinkling in the sky. Soon we are going to close up to the Germans and then we shall shoot back and try to kill them. This is because they have done wrong and caused all this war and sorrow.'
>
> On 22 January, Churchill penned a letter to his first cousin, Charles Spencer-Churchill, the 9th Duke of Marlborough, whom he referred to as 'Sunny': 'I have been commanding this battalion for the last 3 weeks, & now in a few days I shall take them into the line. I have paid a couple of visits to the trenches & they are the best & most comfortable I have seen, in what is now a large & varied section[?] of the front. They are dry, well supplied with dugouts, good communications, good wire, & minor conveniences. Our battalion H.Q. will be in a farm about 500 yards from the front line. Few of the buildings in this area are much knocked about but this farm has been hit a good many times & is a target. This is the blemish on an otherwise harmonious scheme.
>
> 'When we go into 'rest' we only retire about 1500 yards, and so we shall dwell for the next few months

continually within range of the enemy's artillery, field as well as heavy. Things are however fairly quiet at present on this sector; tho' no doubt we shall stir them up a bit. We shall not be far away from that wood in which you used to take an interest in the early days of the war. The battalion is one of the 9th (Scottish) division which fought heroically at Loos, storming the German trenches with a loss of 6000 men out of about 9000 engaged. It is in consequence shattered & only 2 officers who were present in the battle are still on duty. I have no regular officers (except Archie Sinclair) who I brought with me & made 2nd in command) & hardly an officer over 25 years. The average must be about 23½. ... Re. these circ's. you will realise that my task is not an easy one, & that a very great deal of labour & responsibility will fall on me when we are actually in contact with the enemy.

'The battalion has improved since I came & the utmost loyalty & wish to do right characterizes everybody, & I am hopeful that we shall get in all right. But think what the professional soldiers will have said 2 years ago of a battalion so composed & efficient.'[7]

With preparations complete, the time to move forward to the front finally arrived. It was at 08.00 hours on 24 January 1916 when the 6th Battalion, Royal Scots Fusiliers marched out of Moolenacker led by Colonel Churchill. The battalion reached the support line two and a half hours later, being temporarily billeted in the village of La Crèche.

The battalion which the Royal Scots Fusiliers were to relieve, the 8th Battalion, Border Regiment, numbered approximately 900 men, whereas the severely reduced 6th RSF could only count around 700 in its ranks. With 1,000 yards of trench (Nos. 103 to 112) to hold the battalion would be thinly spread. Though Winston was acutely aware that the battalion had not been able to make its numbers up after the Battle of Loos and was still under-strength, he was confident that this would not affect its ability to defend its section of the line: 'Although we have only 700 men instead of 900 wh [*sic*] our predecessors had,' he continued in his letter, '1,050 wh we ought to have, we have more machine guns – so important. Rest assured there will be no part of the line from the Alps to the sea better guarded.'[8]

The positions the battalion were to hold actually consisted of two parallel lines which ran along flat ground from the estaminet at Le Gheer to the Warnave river. The two lines were linked by communication trenches.

Winston moved into the Hospice for just one night before the battalion took over the trenches. In a letter home, he described his temporary new quarters to Clementine:

'I am extremely well-lodged here – with a fine bedroom looking out across the fields to the German lines 3,000 yards away. Two nuns remain here [actually mother and daughter] and keep up the little chapel which is part of the building. They received me most graciously when I marched in this morning, saying that we had saved this little piece of Belgium from the Germans, who were actually there for a week before being driven out … On the right and left the guns are booming; and behind us a British field piece barks like a spaniel at frequent intervals. But the women and children still inhabit the little town and laugh at the shells which occasionally buff into the old church.

'It is very quiet on the front today, and really from your point of view this is an ideal part of the line. It is very unlikely to be the scene of a big attack by either side. It has no great concentration of German artillery opposite it. The trenches are good, well wired, with a broad interval between the lines. The houses have been little damaged. Some of the men of the battalion we are relieving call it "The Convalescent Home". I think instead of being anxious you ought to set your mind gratefully at peace. The Btn we are relieving has lost 70 men only in 4 months; whereas in one day where I was before, the Grenadiers lost 20 – doing nothing.' No doubt this did not set Clementine's mind at rest and she probably considered seventy men lost as seventy too many.

Before the final move into the trenches, Winston delivered a speech to his officers. Though they had spent far longer at the front than their CO, his experience with the Grenadiers had taught him much about the practicalities of trench life. More interestingly, his advice mirrored his views on life and the war in general, though his interpretation of the word 'moderate' with regards to alcohol might be more of a reflection of his times and his social class: 'Don't be careless about yourselves – on the other hand not too careful. Keep a special pair of boots to sleep in and only get them muddy in a real emergency. Use alcohol in moderation but don't have a great parade of bottles in your dugouts. Live well but do not flaunt it. Laugh a little, and teach your men to laugh – get good humour under fire – war is a game that is played with a smile. If you can't smile, grin. If you can't grin, keep out of the way till you can.'

As we have seen, Churchill, it seemed, loved the drama and excitement of warfare and he was utterly unafraid of danger. Winston would follow his own advice over the course of the next few weeks. He did indeed play the game of war with a smile on his face.

Chapter 11

In the Line

Winston spared no pains to enter the front line in command of a *corps d'élite*. Like most battalions on foreign service, ours corresponded in actual strength and numbers at few points with the recognized establishment. This was apparently due in some measure to the reluctance on the part of the authorities to make promotions within the battalion to fill vacancies.

Whatever was the cause, the C.O. didn't like it and embarked on a vigorous campaign designed to put matters right. Not only did he open a long distance bombardment by means of the usual paper ammunition, in triplicate, but he paid personal and, I believe, highly disconcerting and unpopular visits to the Headquarters of the Brigade and Division. I believe that in many cases a stout resistance was offered, but in the end Winston did achieve results which would not have been possible to other commanding officers. It was an excellent thing for the redthroats to be thus shaken out of their usual lethargy by having to answer straight questions verbatim instead of evading the issue or returning blunt refusals by post for no known reason, but the essay did not tend to render more popular their courageous assailant. It need not be added that this fact in no way disconcerted him.

On a cold raw day in January the Colonel and the Company Commanders with a few other important officers of the battalion moved out of the billeting area in a motor omnibus, bound for the neighbourhood of Armentières and Plugstreet. It shall be here interpolated that if in 1919 omnibuses were scarce in London and elsewhere on account of so many having been taken away for military needs in France, that scarcity is not materially due to the number taken away for the transport of Scottish soldiers. Now and again, on occasions of joy-riding or of quasi-joy-riding, a few individual tam o'shanters crowned the top of a bus, but when it was a matter of relieving tired soldiers of a long march, then the omnibuses were reserved to the exclusive use of the Sassenachs. I don't know why. Scotsmen can "old soldier" it with the best and it is surprising that they did not just help themselves, but certainly it seemed to be a point of creed with the Q side of the Staff that only the English infantrymen (and of course the few Irish who fought the war) should travel otherwise than on their flat feet.

At any rate this time we had a bus, and the bus went on and on through a lot of horrid dingy towns till we came to Pont de Nieppe, or Nieppe, I forget which, when we had to come down and walk. At this time the Armentières region was comparatively intact, but was far from entrancing. We walked for some miles over exceedingly dirty roads – not dirty with the honest knee-deep clay of Ypres, but with the soot-laden mire of a manufacturing district. There were batteries unpleasantly close which continued to go off and frighten us and make us wish to go back again. Winston by this time had donned the French helmet[1] which we were all to become so familiar with and was in great fettle.

"Here we are," he said, turning to me, "here we are, torn away from the Senate and the Forum to fight in the battlefields of France."

"Yes" I replied. I often said merely "yes" on these occasions, as I felt that the time was quite inappropriate for me to enlarge on his observations, and still more so for me to contribute any thoughts of my own. Some men in unpleasant surroundings like to dwell on them and pity themselves: other men never condescend to notice them. Winston belonged to the latter class – he did not care a rush for them, or if he mentioned them he did so only to make light of them.

We came at last to the village of "Plugstreet" which it would be mere pedantry for the Anglo-Saxon ever again to call "Ploegsteert." It had an unpleasant reputation at this period and was not considered by any means a cushy spot. There was a beastly place called the "Bird-cage" in the Hun front line.[2] It was said the enemy kept there a large gun which could be raised and lowered pressing a button and which *was* raised and lowered at uncertain intervals and blew the trench opposite to atoms. I now believe this to have been a lie, invented by Old Bill[3] and his kind for the consumption of new drafts, but at that time I believed it, and, believing it, shuddered at it.

On our arrival, however, Plugstreet was calm and peaceful and the village itself was singularly intact: all the *estaminets* were doing business and there were remarkably few mouse-holes. The church tower, a very high one, still held its head aloft for the gratification of the superstitious. We picked our way up towards the trenches along the course of the brook known as the Warnave, and came to a large farm known as "Maison 1875" about half a mile in a direct line from the front. This was practically whole and used as a rest billet. To the end of our time there it was never seriously shelled, and I cannot imagine why, as the enemy must have known quite well it was always full of soldiers.

The line we were to take over was being held by the 8th Border Regiment, and we were shown all the beauty spots by them in the most approved fashion. Winston was in his element. Very few of the people seemed to recognize him, but on the way down from the trenches my guide said to me: –

"Excuse me, Sir, but your commanding officer is very like Mr. Winston Churchill."

I agreed and said that the resemblance had often been remarked. It was the blue tin-hat which prevented people from recognizing him with certainty.

On our way back we went into a farm-house and made the usual distribution of *largesse* in return for some dirty water doing duty as coffee and for some stale bread, and after that we ambled back to Armentières and went home in our omnibus.

On the following day we lined up on the road at Moolenacker in column of fours and set off for the trenches. It was a warm day, and there was the usual cursing and grousing, but eventually we reached a small village near Steenwerck and put up there for the night. We arose at what Ramsey always referred to as "the crack of dawn" and pushed on to Plugstreet via Le Romarin.

Our arrival provoked no emotion in the breasts of the inhabitants, but, had they only known, it meant that most of them would say farewell to their homes within a very few days, as a result of the retaliation by the enemy for the bellicose attitude of our Division as a whole. We did not, however, think of telling them about "Windy Bill": we were too sadly accustomed to him.

We did not relieve that day, but got down in our billets. The Battalion Headquarters were at the Convent [the Hospice], where the nuns were still abiding, and what with a piano and the nuns' cooking, I believe there was little for them to complain of. We went to Delennelle Farm, which was large and comfortable and had good barns. It was adorned by Alice, the daughter of the house, and disfigured by an enormous Saxon hound left by the Huns, which bit or tried to bite everybody and which we eventually shot. The officers lived in a row of small houses opposite. Other companies were at Soyer Farm and Maison 1875.

The first night was passing away very well when about 4 a.m. I was aroused by an orderly with a message. Ramsey was sleeping in the same room and I went and found a match and read the message, we damned our C.O. as heartily as he was ever damned before. That energetic and unresting spirit had observed that the wind was in the right quarter for German gas and had sent round pieces of paper to each of the Company Commanders to signify this and to tell us to be specially alert and warn our sentries and so on.

"Good God," said Ramsey, "the man's daft."

"Daft or not daft, I'm hanged if I'm going out at this time of night on any such quest," I replied and told the orderly to go away. It was all very wrong, I dare say, but such energy was too novel to be appreciated fully at first blush and – there was no gas after all.

The next afternoon we had an orderly-room at the Convent and we were informed by the C.O. that as the following day was the Kaiser's birthday we might expect a doing when we went into the trenches. With this chastening thought we retired to rest.

> The relief of the 8th Borders took place during the early hours of 27 January and was, for Winston, a satisfactorily smooth operation, with the entire battalion safely ensconced in the trenches before daybreak at 05.50 hours, as he told Clementine:
>
> 'The relief was accomplished this morning before daylight with the utmost precision in under 2 hours. I don't think the Grenadiers ever did better. We now hold about 1,000 yards of trenches and I am responsible for this whatever happens. We have so far had no losses – though there has been shelling and sniping and our parapet has at one place been blown in. All is proceeding regularly and the day has been quiet and normal in spite of being the Emperor's birthday.
>
> 'I spent three hours in the trenches this morning deciding in all the improvements I am going to make in them, and looking into the arrangements of the company commanders. It is now dark and we are able to light our fire without being betrayed by the smoke, so that we shall have a hot dinner as usual.'
>
> From his Advanced Headquarters in the buildings of Laurence Farm, Winston had telephone lines running to each of his companies and to brigade headquarters, so that he could be contacted by, and could contact, every important person very quickly. He was particularly pleased that he could ring up brigade and request an artillery

bombardment from the divisional artillery, should the enemy prove troublesome, in thirty seconds. Time would show that this system was very efficient but only when the telephones actually worked!

That day the shelling of the occupied lines was quite light, though at around 14.30 hours the enemy's 4.2-inch howitzers delivered a salvo, though no casualties were reported.

Winston had told his officers to make themselves as comfortable as possible without flaunting their wealth and Churchill had every intention of doing exactly the same. He asked Clementine to send him large slabs of corned beef, stilton cheese, cream, hams, sardines, dried fruits, and a big steak pie. He also wanted her to ship out to him every ten days three bottles of brandy and, of course, his cigars.

His requests were entirely unrealistic. Not only was there a war on and, as he should have been well aware from his time at the Admiralty, the German U-boats were endeavouring to strangle Britain's maritime imports. Though rationing was two years away, food was already becoming harder to obtain. The main limiting factor, however, was that the prescribed weight allowance for parcels to the troops in France and Belgium was just seven pounds.

Nor was life at the front quite as congenial as the picture Winston had portrayed, as his wife no doubt gleaned from a letter her husband wrote on 28 January, disguised as a humorous incident: 'While I was passing the convent [not to be confused with the Hospice in Ploegsteert], a good sized shell burst in its ruins … A fountain of brickbats went up into the air; and I watched them carefully from 50 yards away, to dodge if any fell near me. Suddenly I saw, almost instantaneously with the explosion, 5 or 6 black objects hurtling towards me – You know how quick thought is.

'I had time to think they were splinters, to argue that they could not belong to the same explosion, and to reach out for another solution, before I saw that they were frightened birds!'

He later asked Clementine if she 'liked' him writing about such occurrences, which he called the 'ordinary incidents of life' in the trenches. He acknowledged that being at the front was dangerous but, in his words, 'not vy dangerous'.

Writing up the entry in the battalion's War Diary for the 28th, Sinclair noted that the weather was fine before adding: 'Aircraft very active. Artillery exceedingly quiet. Enemy snipers active all day. 1 casualty.'[4]

Gibb also related those first hours back in the trenches:

We relieved at 2 a.m. next morning – I think it was 2 a.m. It was shockingly early and Winston was given credit for it all and heartily cursed. Yes, we had a nice moonlight flitting into our new quarters and felt – as soldiers love to feel – that we were really ill-used. Our company was on the left and adjoined the 11th Royal Scots. It was about 80 yards from the Huns and the brutes began to shell us just after breakfast. The O.P. was just behind our support line in a ruined estaminet, Le Gheer, and both the O.P. and our front line had a nice time. The small gunner officer, who had breakfasted with us and whose complexion reminded one of the interior of pink cream chocolates, dived below to the cellar of his beastly estaminet and we thought he was dead. At least there was no retaliation from our guns. After knocking our parapet about and exposing our vitals somewhat the guns stopped.

I was sitting thinking of the fun we'd have in repairing the *lacunae* that evening with the machine guns rattling on us when Winston appeared with his escort. Already a few of the men were throwing little bits of earth across the gaps from either side in a half-hearted effort to patch them up. But Winston stopped all that.

"Let them remain as they are till dark," he said. "Don't let the enemy see we are hit or that it is anything material."

I *think* that is what he said. I didn't understand: my methods of making war and making trenches were child-like in their directness, but of course I left the horrid gaping chasms, as I was told. However, I had a man wounded through one of them and then I threw discipline to the winds and patched them up.

It may be well to say here that although we oft-times differed from the Colonel and on many points, we did him not infrequently, and especially at first, grave injustice. Certainly at times his ideas were too *recherchées*, too subtle, to stand the practical test of everyday trench fighting, but whatever he said, whatever order he gave, however startling the innovations he made, it was always worth while to ponder them before too hastily condemning them.

He walked as frequently as not off beaten paths, but his course was more frequently than not a right one, as well as a fresh one. One idea of his, however, which perished through the strictest non-observance by all concerned was that while in the trenches each officer should have a "body-guard," to consist of his bâtman, or orderly, or both, in order that his precious life should never for a moment remain needlessly unguarded. As in many cases a bâtman was shared by two or three officers, as bâtman were also mess waiters, and as even bâtmen require sleep at times, it was obvious from the outset that this idea would never be carried out, and it never was. But it was only a small minority of his innovations that were quite unworkable, and, when once they proved unworkable, he never insisted on the continuation of fruitless attempts to carry them out.

From the very day of our arrival in the line, it was apparent to all that Winston's motto was going to be "Work," in the sense of trench-building and trench-repairing and improvement. And first of all he singled out Ramsey to be a sort of works inspector. This was a singular choice, since Ramsey, though exceedingly able, was regarded by us all as the finest specimen we had of the "old soldier," a term which is not synonymous with "enthusiast for hard work." However, the change was hailed with delight by Gibb, in whose company Ramsey was serving, and who had found his new Second-in-Command too independent in his methods and in his attitude of mind towards constituted authority. Ramsey himself was extremely pleased, as he had discovered a lair in Lancashire Support Farm where he had, in any event, predicted for himself many long nights of uninterrupted repose, but where he now considered himself, in his new capacity, as absolutely immune from interruption.

"You fellows don't understand Winston," he said to me, on the night of his "appointment." "You don't know how to manage him. You all say, 'Yes, Sir' and 'No, Sir' and do what he tells you to do, and then you get cursed at the orderly-room. If you simply treat him with contempt and come on to parade late and don't care a dam, he gives you a cushy job. Look at me. Now I'm going to have a nice, soft, comfortable life in a nice – a really nice dugout (do you know it? with a bed, man, a bed) and there Ramsey is going to sleep from dewy eve until the crack of dawn while all you other poor blighters are standing-to, and firing off your guns and wetting your feet out in front. This is decidedly a *bon* job, and maybe I'll get a Military Cross. It's the sort of thing they're given for.

This oration annoyed me, but annoyance was of short duration. That very night, and not so very long after the "master of works" had shed his boots and laid himself down on his expanded wire bed, a call came from the C.O. to attend him in the front line, and when Ramsey got up to the line he was given as many orders and as much work as would have satisfied a man who really liked work. I believe he did not return to his expanded wire bed that night, and during his tenure of office he was by no means so often in repose as even an officer with his company. It was a great grievance and so changed was his attitude towards his new post that he was able to describe it tersely to me a few days later as being "bloody awful."

For Winston certainly got some work out of his battalion. Early and late he was in the line. On an average he went round three times a day, which was no mean task in itself, as he had plenty of other work to do. At least one of these visits was after dark, usually about 1 a.m.

In wet weather he would appear in a complete outfit of waterproof stuff, including trousers, or overalls, and with his French light-blue helmet he presented a remarkable and unusual figure. He was always in the closest touch with every piece of work that was going on, and, while at times his demands were a little extravagant, his kindliness and the humour that never failed to flash out made everybody only too keen to get on with the work, whether the ideal he pointed out to them was an unattainable one or not. To see Winston giving a dissertation on the laying of sandbags, with practical illustrations, was to come inevitably to the conclusion that his life-study had been purely of poliorketics and the corresponding counter-measures. You felt sure from his grasp of practice that he must have served apprentice to a bricklayer and a master-mason, while his theoretical knowledge rendered you certain that Wren would have been proud to sit at his feet, or even such a master of the subject as Uncle Toby Shandy.

And yet sometimes Winston was wrong about those sand-bags and 2nd Lieut. Stickinthemud was right. In fact while professing a great admiration for the Colonel's zeal and enthusiasm as regards building of parapets and traverses and parados, I must confess that he did not seem to be able to get into touch with the actual practical handling of these accursed sand-sacks. It was a case of the "last infirmity of noble minds."

Of course we were somewhat prejudiced against him as a Master-Builder, because of a very unfortunate method he adopted of egging on his troops to greater efforts. That method lay in inviting us to compare the work we did with the work done by the Gordon Highlanders, who occupied these trenches alternately with ourselves. Now everybody knows that it was customary in France for battalion "A" on taking over trenches from battalion "B," to proceed to condemn battalion "B" for having done no work on these trenches, or alternatively for having done their work in so incompetent and unsoldierlike a fashion, that the trenches were in a worse state than ever and would have been much better had battalion "B" left them alone and confined themselves to washing their dirty faces and picking up the spare pieces of bully beef they were apparently too dainty to eat. When that was the etiquette it obviously was doubly irritating to be told by your own C.O. that battalion "B" really did better work than you did. I don't know whether Winston realized this, but it was a very sore point with us all for a long time. Had it been any other regiment it would have been less tiresome, but we had already heard so much of Gordon achievements[5] both from their own lips and in the daily papers that to have them again hurled at our heads by our own C.O. as a pure type of soldierly energy was a little too much. Many of us confessed our inability to see any trace of the Gordonian occupation save a litter of Woodbine packets (empty), but that was perhaps spiteful.

> Perhaps it was because of the workload imposed by Churchill, or the general difficulties that accompanied a posting in the forward trenches, that there were just three brief entries in Gibb's personal diary in the last days of January.
> On the 21st, for example, he wrote: 'Went with WSC to the trenches in Nieppe, Armentieres and Ploegsteert. Our bit is 80 yards from the Huns! A bit too close as we're used to 400 yards.' This was followed by, on the 27th: 'WSC came up and was very nice.' Two days later, the 29th, Gibb recorded that 'I'm fed up with the Rt Hon Colonel at the moment!'[6]
> The day before Gibb had penned his last remark above, the 28th, was fine and again the artillery fire was 'exceedingly' light, according to the battalion War Diary. Enemy snipers, on the other hand, were busy and the men had to take great care moving around. Luckily, only one man was hit.

In order to help the 6th RSF adjust to life back on the front line, their first spell back in the trenches was to last just two days. All subsequent tours were to be the usual six days. So, on the 29th, the battalion was relieved in turn by the 8th Battalion, Gordon Highlanders and, once again, the operation was conducted without a hitch and completed by 06.25 hours.

'The relief went off like machinery,' Winston proudly announced. 'No casualties; and all over in 4 minutes under the 2 hours I estimated for. Our companies marched into billets in admirable order going through the village in brisk parade step – unheard of outside the Guards. There is no doubt that officers and men try vy hard to do everything I tell them. I am extremely pleased with the officers who are working splendidly'.

Winston had every intention of making life as pleasant as possible in the support lines as he had proposed in the trenches. Always of great concern to Churchill was a bath and at the Hospice he found, to his delight, a 'splendid' bath and a 'tolerably' hot water supply. 'I am now going to sample it,' he told his wife that day, describing it as 'that first of comforts'.

In the Hospice Winston had a comfortable well-furnished room on the ground floor with a large bay-window that looked straight out on the front line, though it was barely out of rifle range of the German trenches. It was in this room that Churchill continued to add to his *Variants of the Offensive*[7] whenever time permitted.

That first morning back in Ploegsteert Winston rose at 04.00 hours, had breakfast with some of his staff at about 07.00 hours and then attended Mass in the Hospice's little chapel. According to Winston the old vicar was very gracious: 'His church is shattered, and the house in wh he lives is freely shelled: but he sticks to his post and "flies his flag".'

Being in reserve did not mean that the men were

completely safe as Plugstreet was well within the range of the German artillery. There was a Royal Artillery battery behind the Hospice which the Germans repeatedly targeted, largely avoiding hitting any of the buildings in Ploegsteert. Winston was pleased with the Germans for this: 'It is satisfactory that they ignore the houses, and have ignored them so long: for the artilleryman – particularly the Bosch artilleryman – is a creature of habit and sticks to the target he sets his fancy on. The guns are so accurate that even a hundred miles away one is safe or almost so.'

Those words were perhaps just too tempting for the Fates to ignore and just after Winston had finished his delightful hot bath, the Germans made another attempt to silence the British battery. Winston was feeling 'deliciously' clean and contented when there was a loud explosion and a great cloud of soot was shaken from the chimney of the Hospice and billowed over the well-washed lieutenant colonel. Winston cursed the German gunners who had misjudged the distance, the shell exploding prematurely, shattering the windows of the Hospice and thoroughly covering Winston in sticky, black grime. In fact five High Explosive shells fell around the Hospice but without inflicting any further damage. At the same time, a fresh wind was blowing from the southeast – providing ideal conditions for the enemy to launch a gas attack and everyone was on the alert.[8]

Even though the battalion had only spent two days in the trenches, there was much to be done to clean and repair equipment. There was also time for Winston to reflect on his new role, of which he gave his mother a glimpse: 'Commanding a battalion is like being the captain of a ship. It is a vy searching test and a severe burden. Especially so when all the officers are young and only soldiers of a few months' standing: and when a hundred yards away lies the line of the German army with all its devilments and dodges.'

Having committed himself to the life of a soldier, Winston desperately wanted to prove himself. He was not interested in what he termed 'mediocracy' and he would not return to civilian life until he had made a name for himself. At this time Winston was too heavily involved in managing a battalion of infantry to be concerned about his former life as a politician and there was no reference to the management of the war during his early days at Plugstreet.

When he was at GHQ with the generals and staff, however, such wider topics were the subjects of discussion and letters from home still referred to parliamentary matters. Winston would soon be drawn back into the intrigues of Westminster but in the trenches he was thoroughly occupied with commanding his men in battle. He put his thoughts into words in a letter to Clementine:

'I like this sort of work vy much. It occupies me and I hope to be able to do it well. I don't think there is much difference in safety between the trenches and our "rest billets". Both HQrs, advanced and support, registered and shelled. But it takes an awful lot of shells to do much harm; apart from bad luck. On the whole I prefer the trenches where there is always something going on, and where one really is fighting in this great war for the triumph of right and reason. No doubt about it – one is doing the real thing.'

Winston's enthusiasm in his new role was not always appreciated by his men, as Lieutenant McDavid related. On 1 February the battalion returned to the front, taking over from the 8th Gordons, this time for one of the standard spells of six days. On the first night Winston wanted to inspect the battalion's forward posts in No Man's Land along with a patrol led by McDavid.

'The Colonel's first visitation of our posts in No Man's Land,' McDavid recalled, 'nearly brought the whole British

Army into action. Clad in his long trench waterproof, shining knee-high trench boots and blue steel helmet, with his revolver and powerful flash-lamp attached to his web-belt, he preceded me on the journey through the wire. All went well until we were within a few yards of the first post. The enemy machine-gun fire swept the sphere of operations.

'We all made a dive for the shelter of the shell crater, which was now somewhat overcrowded, and consequently we had to keep in a crouching position. Suddenly a blinding glare of light appeared from the depths of the hole and with it the CO's muffled request to "Put out that bloody light!" It was only a matter of seconds before he realised his crouching posture was responsible for pressure on the contact switch of his own flash-lamp, and corrective action quickly followed.'[9]

Winston enjoyed the thrills of such expeditions into No Man's Land which he frequently undertook, but for those that had to accompany him it could be a nerve-wracking experience. Lieutenant Hakewill Smith recalled undergoing patrols similar to that described by McDavid: 'He [Winston] would often go into no-man's-land. It was a nerve-racking experience to go with him. He would call out in his loud, gruff voice – far too loud it seemed to us – "You go that way, I will go this … Come here, I have found a gap in the German wire. Come over here at once!"

'He was like a baby elephant out in no-man's-land at night. He never fell when a shell went off; he never ducked when a bullet went past with its loud crack. He used to say, after watching me duck: "It's no damn use ducking; the bullet has gone a long way past you by now."'[10]

According to the historian Martin Gilbert, Winston did not put himself in danger merely for the fun of it. He wanted to show his men that he would share their risks alongside them. He was not only a politician but also an aristocrat from one of the country's leading families and such persons were not to be seen crawling around in No Man's Land. That Churchill was prepared to do this, and clearly enjoy it, was a revelation to the common men of which the battalion was composed.

Winston actually made no less than thirty-six forays into No Man's Land. An article in the Royal Scots Fusiliers' regimental magazine written by Corporal John McGuire describes one of these expeditions. McGuire was in charge of bombers and scouts and was awarded the Military Medal for a single-handed attack on a German machine-gun post. One evening Winston asked McGuire if he felt like 'going out tonight?' Of course the NCO could not refuse:

'I strapped on a revolver and two mills bombs, and at midnight Winnie turned up with his adjutant. He wore his trench helmet, trench coat and Sam Browne belt with revolver. We topped the parapet and slipped through a gap in the barbed wire known only to scouts.

'Ten yards farther on I lay down on the second line of trench concertina wire enabling the other two to cross. From there we crawled on our stomachs across muddy ground punched with shell holes. Near the German lines we settled in a hole and listened to the Germans talking. After two hours we crawled home.

'This was the pattern for all our trips. While we were out our own side never fired but the Germans, worried by the silence, sent up verey lights and followed up with heavy machine-gun strafing. I often thought we'd "had it" but Churchill showed no fear. He would smile and say, "They know I'm here, McGuire, they know I'm here."

'The men were delighted with him. He was a new type of commander who took an interest in everything. He would inspect the feet of the men on sentry duty. If their feet were wet he ordered dry socks for them. "What were your father's politics?" he asked me once. "Liberal," I replied. "A wise choice," he commented ... I will always remember him for his warm humanity.'

Churchill certainly exuded an air of fearless, and relaxed, confidence which was reinforced when he started painting. In the midst of the German shells which often fell in the areas immediately behind the front line around Laurence Farm, Winston would set up his easel in the courtyard, put on the latest popular gramophone records and start to paint. One officer, Lieutenant Edmund Hakewill Smith, recalled one of Churchill's artistic outbursts:

'Winston started painting the second or third time he went up to the farm, Each time we were in the line he spent some time on his paintings. Gradually, too, the courtyard became more pitted with shellholes. As his painting came nearer to completion, he became morose, angry, and exceedingly difficult to talk to. After five or six days in this mood, he suddenly appeared cheerful and delighted, like a small boy at school. I asked him what had happened, and he said 'I have been worried because I couldn't get the shell-hole right in the painting. However I did it, it looked like a mountain, but yesterday I discovered that if I put a little bit of white in it, it looked like a hole after all.'[11]

It was not only art that drew Winston's attention, but also music – though the latter was not always for the most obvious reason. On one occasion he summoned the band of the 9th Division to Ploegsteert, as bandsman Lance Corporal Robert Fulton recalled:

'A figure appeared. It was Winston Churchill. He was carrying his own Chair – it was a .303 Ammunition Box. He says this will do Lads. We fixed up and started our programme. He sat in the middle.

'A young lad from the RAMC sang that beautiful old Ballad "Sunshine of your Smile". Then shelling started, some well off the mark and some mighty near accompanied by a few overhead shrapnels. Well, with plenty of ducking and a broad smile on Winston's face we got through it. At the end he thanked us all.

'He said "Lads I am sorry bringing you into such a precarious position but I am going to let you into a little secret. Last week the Germans had a band at the back of their lines playing to them and our artillery got on them and all you saw was instruments & drums going into the air and I really wanted to see if their artillery were as good marksmen as ours".'[12]

The unusual appearance of the French blue steel helmet that Winston wore (as he felt that the Fusiliers' Glengarry bonnet did not suit him) caused some alarm when he made his sudden appearances, as C.E. Lyne, who was serving in the same sector at the time, remarked: 'About this period of static warfare rumours and gossip about spies became widespread, strange lights were reported flashing from church towers, German soldiers dressed as Belgian civilians were occasionally arrested. It was even reliably reported that train loads of Russian soldiers were seen crossing England but were not arriving at any known destination.

'One day Fawcett came into Battery Headquarters in a state of some excitement and said: "I believe we have got a spy in our sector because I have just seen a bloke dressed in a Frenchman's steel helmet and queer garments and speaking in a guttural voice, who said 'This is a good place for an OP'. 'Actually,' said Fawcett, 'I thought it was a bloody awful place, so I'm quite sure he is a spy, so let's go and arrest him."

'W. and I, who were the only ones in headquarters at the time, persuaded Fawcett not to, on the grounds that if he really was a spy he would hardly be likely to draw attention to himself by wearing queer garments, so we never did arrest him, which is just as well because we discovered that a Colonel Churchill, who was commanding a formation of "Jocks", I believe the Sixth Battalion of Royal Scots Fusiliers, had been given a sector of the Plugstreet trenches.

'We were none of us politically minded and the name Churchill meant nothing to us and in due course we became accustomed to the sight of Churchill in his queer attire on his way to and from the trenches from time to time. But we never got accustomed to his insatiable desire to 'stir up the Hun', which he used to do by calling up our gunners, usually between midnight and three a.m. to fire twenty rounds of high explosive at the German lines. It stirred them up all right but the shells they fired in return were not against the Jock trenches but against our guns and the inhabitants of Plugstreet and in the end, our peaceful life was completely disrupted and the French authorities had to clear the remaining civilians out of Plugstreet altogether. I managed to get hold of a picture of Churchill wearing the strange garments in which he had so startled Fawcett at the time when he came into our quiet area in Plugstreet. From this moment Plugstreet began to die.'[13]

Winston was convinced that the Germans were concentrating their fire on Ploegsteert because they knew that the famous ex-Lord of the Admiralty was posted there, but C.E. Lyne's explanation seems far more likely.

On 3 February, Winston's battered headquarters suffered another heavy blow and on this occasion he and his immediate staff were inside. The dramatic incident was described by Winston in a letter to Clementine: 'We had just finished an excellent lunch and were all seated round the table at coffee and port wine, when a shell burst at no great distance making the window jump. Archie [Sinclair] said that at the next one we would go into our dugout in the barn just opposite and we were discussing this when there was a tremendous crash, dust and splinters came flying through the room, plates were smashed, chairs broken. Everyone was covered with dust ... A shell had struck the roof and burst in the next room.'

Winston, as was so often the case, played down the incident. Lieutenant McDavid, who was also in the room at the time, was hit on the finger and had to be evacuated back to the UK. In a letter written to Churchill's biographer Martin Gilbert many years later, McDavid recalled just how close his CO had been to also being wounded: 'Winston was toying about with his lamp. He was sitting playing with this thing when the shell came along. A piece of shrapnel almost split the battery holder in two – it lodged in the metal of the battery holder. It was less than two inches from his right wrist. If it had been any nearer it certainly would have taken off his wrist.'[14] How the course of history might have changed but for that precious two inches![15]

For Gibb, or Captain X, the departure of the wounded Lieutenant McDavid was a defining moment in terms of his service under Churchill. Unaware of this, on 1 February, Gibb had written in his diary that 'WSC throwing his weight around and laying down the law about all sorts of things'.

On 4 February Gibb was allowed on leave, and was still in the UK on the 13th, which was his twenty-eighth birthday. He returned back to the Western Front, and the trenches, on 16 February.

It was on 25 February that Winston asked Gibb to be his adjutant. Only three days earlier he had written that 'From this hour I am done with him', yet this closer relationships with Winston quickly had its effect, for on 8 April he wrote he that he, 'ADG', was considering 'writing a book about his time with WSC!'

Winston evidently appreciated Gibb's abilities for his entry of 30 April was, 'WSC going to run ADG for a Staff job. Says, "I have a non-mistake brain, a prime requirement." He's a damn good sportsman, that's what he is.'

Having taken over from McDavid as Adjutant, Gibb also related the incident when McDavid (whom he calls MacDavid) was wounded:

Very early in our occupancy of the Plugstreet trenches, a whizzbang came through the roof of the farm in which the Battalion Headquarters mess was and very nearly – by a foot or two – blotted out the Colonel and his retinue.

MacDavid the Adjutant was wounded in the thumb by a piece of a soup plate, and we soldiers in the line agreed that it served him right for sybaritic indulgence in such luxuries as china. But the outcome of the occurrence was an outburst of the most feverish eagerness on the part of Battalion Headquarters to sandbag themselves and render such accidents less probable for the future. The wretched Ramsey was summoned and was forced to devise shelters and scarps and counterscarps and dugouts and half-moons and ravelins – to indent for this and that – to organize huge working-parties, and to have the work completely executed in some ludicrously inadequate time.

That little farm presented such a scene for the next few days as must have been witnessed at the erection of the Pyramids. It swarmed with activity – men coming and going and carrying (and cursing) and climbing and hammering and shovelling, while Ramsey looked on and commanded and implored and directed and misdirected and a thousand times a day, and wished himself back in B Company. And as soon as ever he relaxed, came Winston, quite cool and fresh, and indicated his further desires.

At last the work was completed, and a great wave of satisfaction swept over the front line that now at length Battalion Headquarters were safe and that not only Winston, but also the youth MacDavid and the mascot-like Bomb-boy could repose almost as safely as in the dear home-land. Yes, it was an unpopular venture in entrenchment, but after all an inconsiderable item in the long tragic catalogue of the injustices endured by the P.B.I.[16]

We did a lot of good work on the trenches in any case and it is only fair to say that Winston sternly resisted all temptations to perpetuate the memory of the workers by conferring on our new works territorial names in any way connected with their originator. So we were denied our "Dundee Promenade," and our "Admiralty Avenue." But if any of you soldier-readers knew the "Fusilier Slits," know that they were built by us.

> Without doubt, Winston took a great interest in the trenches themselves and their construction, not being willing to accept that the ones his battalion inhabited were as good as they might be. As a consequence he had a conversation with the officer in command of the Royal Engineer section attached to the 9th Division, Major Gordon Risley Hearn. Major Hearn then visited the Ploegsteert sector with Winston, and, through him, Churchill learnt how and where the trenches should be drained, at which points they should be particularly reinforced and where dugouts should be located. When Hearn returned to divisional HQ he left behind a Lieutenant of Engineers – Lieutenant Francis Donald Napier-Clavering, 64th Field Company RE – and a party of his men to put in hand the work that the Major had advised.
>
> As might be expected, Winston was thoroughly intrigued with the work of the Engineers and he was often bombarding the Lieutenant with questions. In particular, Winston wanted to know how thick the parapets of the trenches needed to be to stop a rifle bullet. Napier-Clavering said that the parapets should be at least three feet thick. Of course, Winston wanted to know if the RSF's parapets measured up. He told Napier-Clavering they would go up to the trenches that night and measure the thickness of the parapets. 'Bring a stick with you three feet long,' demanded Winston.

That night they walked up to the front and climbed up onto the top of the parapet with Napier-Clavering's stick, measuring the earthwork along the entire battalion position. The twenty-two-year-old Lieutenant had never seen anything quite like it in his short military career:

'Up went a Verey Light. Churchill was on his knees measuring the depth of the earth with the stick. The Hun machine guns opened up, belly high. Why the hell weren't we killed I just don't understand. I didn't want to die; I wanted to kill some of the Hun first. "For God's sake keep still, Sir," I hissed. But he didn't take the slightest notice. He was a man who had no physical fear of dying.'

On his very first visit to the front Winston had noticed a small abandoned convent (referred to earlier) very close, just 100 yards, to the trenches that had been reduced to rubble. The cellars were deep and secure from the gunfire but, like so much of Flanders that was below ground level, were flooded. Now that he was at the front for a few days Churchill had the opportunity to drain the cellars and thus provide him and his staff with a far safer headquarters than the conspicuous Laurence Farm and one that was measurably closer, around 700 yards closer than the farm, to his men in the forward trenches.

The cellars were slowly cleared and became what Winston called his 'Battle Headquarters'. Just 400 yards from the German trenches, Winston also christened the new HQ 'The Conning Tower'. Laurence Farm, however, continued to be Winston's main headquarters, where his staff were already well-installed. Instead, he had sandbags piled up inside all the walls and the floor above. His intention was to make it shell-proof from all but the heaviest projectiles.

As well as having noted his CO's enthusiasm for his surroundings in the front line, Gibb also recorded his observations on how Churchill interacted with those around him:

It was always a matter of especial interest to watch our Colonel in his relationships with his superior officers, those men who while a thousand times smaller in all essentials were yet by the accident of the time in a position to issue orders to him. Such of us as expected to see sparks flying were disappointed. The Colonel's bearing was studiously respectful, but no General whom I ever saw with him was ever rash enough to be very critical or very severe.

During his command of the Battalion, we had to deal with two Brigade Commanders. The former of these two shall remain nameless. The Battalion disliked him and into the Colonel's feelings I was not permitted to see. What was to Winston an occasional cause for stumbling, namely, the setting of too hard a task, was General X's constant failing. I do not think that I ever encountered the gentleman, in the trenches or out of the trenches, without conceiving a sincere desire to punch him upon the head. My one consolation was that everybody else was given equal or better reasons for conceiving a similar desire, and I more than suspected that such an excess of zeal and unreason was not autogenous or self-begotten, but that a considerable amount must have been due to copious injections from a superior source.

I remember a visit of his on one occasion to Battalion Headquarters at Lawrence Farm just after that stronghold had been considerably knocked about by shelling and various protective works destroyed. He sent for the Colonel, who arrived promptly and greeted him in debonair fashion. The General at once opened out about the defective condition of those same protective works.

"Look here, Churchill," he fussed, "this won't do, you know. There's no protection at all here for men. You ought to get something done – build something to make it safe. Men cannot go on living here: look at that sentry there – it's dangerous, you know, it's positively dangerous."

The Colonel was pardonably nettled.

"Yes sir," he replied, "but, you know, this is a very dangerous war."

And with that let us leave General X. I once thought I'd look him out after the war, and declare another war on him on my own account, but upon my word it's not worth while. I suppose every New Army officer made several such resolutions and probably kept none of them. His successor was General Trotter, who was from the outset *persona grata* in the Headquarters mess. The Colonel always held him up to us as the pattern of a soldier, which I believe he was, and during his short stay our relations with the Brigade were of the most friendly and pleasant nature.

Within a few days of our arrival at Plugstreet the face of nature, including nature as adorned by the habitations of man, altered considerably, and for the worse. Down went all the church towers opposite our line – the Hun was shelled incessantly and of course he did not fail to retaliate both on our line and on our back areas.

Soon a doleful and ever-increasing line of refugees began to file out of Plugstreet with their gear on little carts or on their backs, carried as best it might be. We were besieged by applicants for a loan of our transport waggons and the C.O. never refused to help them when it was at all possible to spare the waggons. The nuns were among the first to go, and indeed the convent [Hospice] became so unhealthy that it was left completely unoccupied, a large farm nearer to the trenches becoming henceforth the Headquarters of the Battalion out of the line in this sector. The houses once vacated, it became our main recreation to watch the Hun shelling Plugstreet and to see the bricks and clouds of red dust flying sky-high by the hour.

In the comparatively early days when Churchill was with us it so happened that going over the top was not in the fashion, and so it unfortunately is not my part to chronicle any wild deeds of valour on the part of our redoubtable Colonel with his Scottish dogs of war slipped from the leash. In a quiet time, however, he did contrive to enliven our trench-fighting to a considerable extent, and on more than one occasion seriously to scare the Huns opposite to us.

IN THE LINE

Going round the line on a beautiful morning about one or two o'clock the Colonel would see perhaps a man or men brought in badly wounded on patrol. This sight brought with it apparently a desire to get some of his own back. I remember well one evening in particular, when we had two men seriously wounded and one killed.

Winston's coming into the dug-out in the front-line where my company commander was sitting, just returned from leave, and recounting his experiences, exciting and highly discreditable, to an enraptured audience. The blue helmet appeared round the door and we heard a voice say: "Come on, war is declared," and we were bidden all to turn out and superintend the rapid-fire of our half-waking platoons.

We found that Winston had arranged for almost all the guns of the Division to support our little alarum, and as soon as the rifle-fire began there was a perfect blaze of artillery behind us and the Hun very soon became alarmed and fired off rockets "of every colour m the summer solstice" as Ramsey put it. Unfortunately he did not confine himself to firing off rockets, but fired off a multitude of whizzbangs[17] and other unpleasant projectiles as well. Just as the enemy field guns began, the Colonel came along to our trench and suggested a view over the parapet. As we stood up on the fire-step we felt the wind and swish of several whizzbangs flying past our heads, which, as it always did, horrified me. Then I heard Winston say in a dreamy, far-away voice: "Do you like War?"

The only thing to do was to pretend not to hear him. At that moment I profoundly hated war. But at that and every moment I believe Winston Churchill revelled in it. There was no such thing as fear in him.

These little intervals did good in very dull times, but they were not invariably popular. Especially were they unpopular with Gibb, the Adjutant. The position for him was an invidious one. He remained of course at Battalion Headquarters and it was his pleasant task to keep touch with the Colonel and the artillery. It was all very well when we were getting support purely from our own covering battery, though even then the battery officers didn't like being asked to fire off their cannon in the middle of the night, merely to get the wind up. But the C.O. was a great friend of General Tudor, who commanded the Divisional artillery, and he did not hesitate therefore to call for more efficient support than could be rendered by a mere 18-pounder battery.

The wretched Gibb used to sit with the telephone to his ear receiving alternately messages from the C.O. in the line and heated inquiries from the people at the battery and Divisional Artillery Headquarters. A typical scene ran as follows: –

C.O. (*loquitur.*) Hello: Gibb? Just ask the battery commander to give us ten more rounds.

Gibb. Sir. (*Sotto voce*.) Hell.

Hello, Beer battery, Hello.

Beer Battery. Hoosthat?

Gibb. Get me your officer. (When officer came.) I say, Scots Fusiliers here, *would* you mind giving us ten more rounds?

B.B. No damn fear.

Gibb. Oh, look here, my Colonel really *must* press for it, we're killing a deuce of a lot of Huns up here. Do, like a good fellow.

B.B. You've had about fifty rounds already, my dear man.

Gibb. Yes, I know, but really this is the lot. Thanks awfully.

A pause; the ten rounds are delivered. Then a buzz.

C.O. Hello: Gibb?

Gibb. Yes, Sir.

C.O. Look here, just give General Tudor my compliments and ask him to give us some retaliation, say twenty rounds from – (I forget – some thundering great batteries). He won't mind.

Gibb. (Won't he?) Sergeant Signaller, what's the call for Divarta?

S.S. Couldn't say, Sir, we never call them.

Gibb. Oh, we'll call the ——— brigade. Hello, Brigade. Give me the C.R.A. Yes, damn it, the C.R.A. Hello, Divarta; oh, that the officer on duty? I say, this is Scots Fusiliers. My Colonel wants you to give him twenty rounds from your (large bore cannon). Can you do it? Yes, Colonel Churchill.

Art. Officer. Quite out of the question. Good gracious, why do you want it? Is the Hun attacking?

Gibb. (sweating) No, no, we're just keeping up an offensive spirit. (Jesting desperately) See Divisional Orders *passim*.

Art. Officer. My dear fellow, what the devil are you talking about? For God's sake go to sleep.

Gibb. No, but really my Colonel is most anxious about this. I'm sure General Tudor will agree.

And after a while and after much further argument they would give in and the night would be rendered hideous by repeated series of shocking explosions, during which the entire Division awoke from its slumbers and asked itself if this was the Great Push or only another of Winston's tunes on a borrowed fiddle.

Half an hour later the C.O. would return with his following all in great fettle about the row they had created, and puzzled by the merely half-hearted acquiescence of the Adjutant in these rejoicings. However, there would be a few drinks and then the lucky ones turned in, thinking it was rather a good joke to possess a C.O. who could keep the whole Division off its sleep, the G.O.C. included, for half an hour and no apparent reason.

> Whilst on his first six-day tour of duty in the trenches, on 6 February, Winston received a summons from GHQ at St Omer ordering him to make his way immediately to London Support Farm and take over command of the brigade. This, Churchill believed was his much-desired promotion. He had continued to believe that Haig would offer him the chance of commanding a brigade as soon as Asquith's ban was lifted. Poor Winston had misread the situation completely. Haig had been warned to beware of Churchill as a possible Government spy, let alone a popular journalist who was always ready to put pen to paper.

Bonar Law, the Leader of the Conservative Party, was 'very strongly pressed to help Churchill to an appointment of this kind,' wrote Lord Beaverbrook. 'He responded with an unswerving antagonism to Churchill. He thought to give Churchill an influence on the conduct of affairs in France would be a disaster. [Equally] Lloyd George would not give any countenance to projects for Churchill's preferment.'[18]

Winston hurried to Brigade Headquarters as ordered only to find that he had been instructed to take over the brigade because its commander, Brigadier-General Henry Ernest Walshe, was absent. Walshe was due back the following day. When he reached London Support Farm he received another summons, this time telling him to join General Furse at Divisional Headquarters in Nieppe.

So off went Winston again. When he arrived for lunch he found that Furse also had another guest, Lord Curzon, the Lord Privy Seal. Suddenly, and quite unexpectedly, politics was on the menu once again. Winston, though, was still enchanted with his new job and he urged Curzon to go with him to see the trenches at first hand. Curzon agreed.

Later Winston told his wife about Earl Curzon's visit to the front line: 'It was very quiet and we successfully avoided the shells and the machine gun bullets, both of which came discreetly and tactfully in the places where we had left or in those we had not reached.'

On 7 February, the battalion was relieved by the 8th Gordons. The spell in the line had been, according to the War Diary, a 'very quiet period'. Though the RSF had 'lost no men killed', three men had been wounded.[19] The relief on the 7th would not appear to have been made without incident, for 19-year-old Private William Rossell is listed as having been killed in action on that date.[20]

For the time being, Churchill would continue to devote most of his energy to soldiering, but he had been involved in politics for more than fifteen years and, in the back of his mind, his political ambitions remained as alive as ever. The crisis over the failure of the Gallipoli Campaign had, by early 1916, been overtaken by the issue of conscription, and it was a subject close to Winston's heart.

The Military Service Bill was announced at the beginning of January and received Royal Assent on the 27th of the month.[21] In 1914 Winston had advocated some form of compulsory military service, realising that Britain's voluntary armed forces were small in comparison to those of the major Continental countries where military service was obligatory. At that early stage of the war conscription would have been utterly unacceptable to the vast majority of the population. There also appeared to be no such need as the rush of volunteers outstripped the British Army's capacity to absorb the vast numbers that lined the streets outside recruiting offices throughout the country.

The war, which so many believed would be over by Christmas, proved not only to be a far more protracted affair than had been wildly predicted, but far more deadly. Casualties were on a far greater scale than anyone had ever imagined. There had never been anything like it. Instead of counting casualties by the thousands or at worst tens of thousands as in earlier conflicts, the battles of the Great War resulted in the loss of hundreds of thousands of men. Volunteer recruitment could not maintain the flow of replacements needed. Conscription was simply inevitable.

The first step in that direction came with the Military Service Bill which fell short of wholesale conscription but specified that men from eighteen to forty-one years old were liable to be called up for service in the army unless they were married, widowed with children, serving in the Royal Navy, a minister of religion, or working in one of a number of reserved occupations.

Along with the Defence of the Realm Act, which had been introduced in 1914, this new Act was possibly the most important piece of legislation in placing Britain onto a 'total war' footing. The Bill that went on to become the Act was introduced to the House of Commons on 5 January by the Prime Minister, H.H. Asquith. Despite the fact that conscription – compulsory active service – had deeply divided not only Parliament but the entire nation, the Act came into force on 2 March 1916. Such was the depth of feeling, in April 1916, for example, that over 200,000 people had demonstrated against the Act in Trafalgar Square. Other commentators defined the legislation: 'The action which we are taking now should have been taken early in 1915, and that the months now ahead of us should have been devoted to the creation of 30 new divisions, so that we might have possessed this coming summer a large strategic reserve fit to throw into the scales of war at the decisive point and at the decisive hour. This was not possible without a stronger dose of compulsion, a greater restriction of the lists of reserved trades, and a preliminary determination that trade should take second place to victory.'[22]

Sir John Simon, the Home Secretary, resigned on 1 January in protest at the bill. Winston hoped that a split in the government would give him the chance to re-establish himself in Cabinet. Whilst he was in the front line and so close to the enemy positions, his mind was fully occupied with his military duties, but when in reserve he had time to read the newspapers and ponder on his future: 'Peace out here,' he told Clementine, 'and crisis at home are disturbing combinations for my mind'. Winston longed for action, be it either on the front benches or in the front trenches.

After the visit of the Lord Privy Seal Churchill went back to the 27th Brigade Headquarters where he learned that Walshe had been delayed and that he was to remain in command of the five battalions and around 4,000 men for a second day. Because his position was only temporary Winston did not trouble himself to learn the machinery of command at brigade level.

Winston's few days at Brigade Headquarters revealed to him how poor the organisation of the BEF was at times. Writing that there was a lack of drive throughout much of the administration of the Army, he added 'Take the telephone system for instance. It is grotesque. You cannot get through. When you do you cannot hear, there is always a dog fight going on over the wires. They have stuck in the main to the same little field instruments that an army on the move uses instead of making a perfect system wh cd so easily be done. And how vitally important it might be in a battle! If we had been content at the Admiralty to paddle along at that feeble pace, we shd never have mastered the German submarine. Then of course there ought to be 10 times (at least) as many light railways on the front. This war is one of mechanics and brains and mere sacrifice of brave and devoted infantry is no substitute and never will be. By God I wd make them skip if I had the power – even for a month.'

The return to the reserve billets on 7 February allowed Lieutenant McDavid, who had been hit in the finger during the bombardment of Laurence Farm, to return to the UK. McDavid had been completely won over by Winston, as he later wrote:

'[Churchill] joined a conglomerated mess of young civilians and old reservists both of whom had experienced hell since they arrived in France in the spring of 1915. Morale was low, understandably so. After a very brief period he accelerated the morale of the officers and men to an unbelievable degree. It was sheer personality. We laughed at lots of things he did, but there were other things we did not laugh at for we knew they were sound.

'He had a unique approach which did wonders for us. He let everyone under his command see that he was responsible, from the very moment he arrived, that they understood not *only what* they were supposed to do, but *why* they had to do it.'[23]

McDavid took with him the nose of the shell that had wrecked Laurence Farm, the lamp that was damaged in the blast – and which in all probability had saved Winston from serious injury or even death – and some photographs of Churchill, to Clementine. When he had departed from Ploegsteert, Churchill was at headquarters and the news that McDavid carried with him was that Winston was in command of the 27th Brigade.

Clementine was, of course, excited at the news of his possible promotion, not least because it meant that he was likely to be far removed from the fighting. She expressed these feelings to him, pointing out a fact that Winston had himself also considered, that the Germans might have heard that the former First Lord of the Admiralty, who was well known to the Germans, was close to the front at Ploegsteert and would concentrate their artillery on that sector in a bid to score a hit upon such a famous person.

As it happened, Winston had already decided that the Hospice was too exposed to the enemy artillery and he sought another building for his rear headquarters. The place he settled upon was one of his company's billets at Soyer Farm as this was a further 800 yards from the front line. His move came only just in time, for on 9 February the Germans once again targeted the village, as Winston described in a letter to Clementine on the 10th:

'The shells hitting the church made enormous clouds of red brick dust wh mingled gaily with their white smoke. Other black and white shrapnel burst over the street and struck the houses. Three of our men who were strolling in the town were hit – one fatally, and another sustained a shock from being near a shell from wh he immediately died.'

This was the eighth man the battalion had lost since returning to the reserve billets – more than was lost in the six days it had spent in the trenches. The 6th RSF was now even more reduced in number.

It is worth a brief explanation of Winston's relationship with his second-in-command before relating further their adventures together with the 6th RSF. Sinclair was, according to Violet Bonham Carter, 'a romantic figure, gay gallant and good-looking, the owner of 100,000 acres of Caithness in the northernmost tip of Scotland'. He was, Bonham Carter wrote, 'in every sense the king of that wild and beautiful domain – great tracts of hill and moorland, spangled with lochs, through which the Thurso river runs from its source to the sea'.

She was scarcely exaggerating in describing him as the king of his realm, as not only the principal land owner, Sinclair was also the county's Lord Lieutenant and was soon to become its Member of Parliament. This was on the recommendation of Winston, who had met Sinclair some years before the war at a social gathering and had persuaded him to go into politics. They had an instantaneous rapport, with both being passionate polo players and great talkers.

This Scottish laird would later swap the salmon-filled rivers and the heather-topped moors for gilded corridors of the Palace of Westminster, becoming the Leader of the Liberal Party and holding the post of Secretary of State for Air from 1940 onwards throughout the Second World War. He was the ideal companion for Winston at the front.

During this period out of the trenches Churchill and Sinclair spent some time travelling around and on 10 February they went to observe a battery carrying out an artillery bombardment. They were conducted around by the general commanding the 9th Division's artillery, Brigadier-General Henry Hugh Tudor, which Winston later wrote about, describing how two points of the German trenches were selected as the targets and the three officers went to the front trenches, just 100 yards from the enemy positions that were to be shelled. The barrage lasted for exactly one hour, with 12-inch, 9.2-inch and field guns all concentrating on the two enemy points.

Of course shortly after the British guns started, the Germans replied. The British artillery made so much noise that Churchill could not hear the whistle of the German shells, 'but they burst all round, striking the parapet, or just skimming over, or bursting in the air with loud explosions and covering us with dirt and debris,' he told Clementine. 'It was very exciting, especially as our own 9.2s put two shells *behind* us by mistake.'

This was the first really 'sharp' artillery bombardment Winston had been under in the trenches and what he noticed was how well the earthen parapets withstood the shelling. He declared that he could understand how even the heaviest bombardments could be endured for days. This was not understood by the senior officers of the BEF. The next great battle for the British Army was that of the Somme which began less than five months later. Generals Haig and Rawlinson placed great faith in the artillery, fully expecting the German trenches to have been utterly destroyed by an intense and prolonged bombardment. When the attack was delivered the men were told merely to walk across No Man's Land and occupy the enemy trenches. They were slaughtered on an unprecedented scale because the German dugouts withstood the bombardment, as Winston had seen at first hand.

Once again, Winston expressed how much he actually enjoyed being under fire. As well as the shelling from the artillery, trench mortars were used, explained Winston: 'These you can see in the air; and after they fall there is an appreciable interval in which to decide what you will do. I liked these best of all. I found my nerves in excellent order and I do not think my pulse quickened at any time.'

On the evening of 10 February 1916, Winston went to have dinner with Arthur Holland[24] at the 9th Division's Headquarters at Nieppe in what he told Clementine was a pretentious château surrounded by a moat. Though three miles from the front, Nieppe was still within range of the enemy's artillery. 'It was dusk. Suddenly a loud bang. A shell coming from miles away had fallen in the moat, just outside our window. Presently came 1 more. No one paid the slightest attention to them. It is pure chance, and a shell may come anywhere at any time.'

This 'chance' element to the fortunes of life was a recurring theme of Churchill's, and perhaps explains why he showed so little fear in the face of often extreme danger. He had convinced himself that there was little he could do to avoid a chance shell or bullet and that there was, therefore, no point in worrying about it. What appeared to others to be foolhardy fearlessness was in fact the outcome of a logical thought process.

Whilst he had a little time on his hands before the next tour of duty in the trenches, Winston and Sinclair went over the border into France on 12 February to the town of Armentières which was frequently under bombardment: 'The debris of several hits that had occurred half an hour before was scattered in the streets,' he told Clementine, 'And every now and again a shell passed overhead. But there were a fair number of shops open, with women serving in them: and a lot of factories smoking away as if nothing was going on.'

The next day Winston and Sinclair went up to the front line to see if there had been any significant change whilst the 6th RSF had been resting. They were taken round the trenches by Lieutenant Colonel Alan Greenhill-Gardyne during which time a German aeroplane flew overhead.

The British artillery fired up at the aircraft, doing no harm to the aeroplane but putting the men on the ground in danger as the shell fragments fell to earth. They returned to Ploegsteert over ground in broad daylight with the bullets from German machine-guns 'zipping' around their path.

Churchill's actions this day demonstrate that his evident courage was well-considered and not merely a defiant refusal to be cowed by the enemy. As they walked back across the open ground they were seen by the enemy, who opened fire at no great distance. Greenhill-Gardyne continued to walk on regardless, which Winston regarded as being 'very foolish'. Winston immediately sought cover in a nearby trench, whilst Sinclair and other officers that had accompanied them 'scampered about'.

On 13 February the 6th RSF relieved the 8th Gordons and was back in the trenches for another six-day tour of duty.[25] As Winston had seen the day before there had been no change in the general dispositions. Again a German aircraft passed over the front line and Winston was 'disgusted' to see an enemy aeroplane 'sailing about scornfully' in the midst of fourteen British aircraft, none of which seemed willing or able to engage the enemy machine. 'Ours seemed to sheer off time after time, and he went where he pleased for at least half an hour.' As before, the British artillery fired hundreds of shells into the sky 'without lifting a feather of this hostile bird'.

During this period, a number of officers returned from leave and were 'homesick'. This moved Winston who decided that he would take eight days leave in March which he was entitled to. He told his wife that that he would undertake one more tour of duty in the trenches after the current one and then return home. That way he would be away for the six days' rest period, missing only two days that the battalion was in the trenches.

IN THE LINE

Urged on by Winston, patrols into No Man's Land were conducted on the battalion's first full night at the front. Two of these patrols went right up to the German wire, the men cut some of the wire and took it back as trophies. One of the men took a Union Flag with him and tied it to the wire to demonstrate to the Germans that the Scots had crept so close to their trenches in the night. Winston was annoyed at this 'silly' act because he knew that it would make the Germans far more vigilant and put future patrols at greater risk.

That first evening back at Laurence Farm Winston wrote as usual to his wife, this time painting a vivid picture of life as a lieutenant colonel in the forward lines: 'Another long day in the trenches has closed, and I sit in a battered wicker chair within this shot-scarred dwelling by the glowing coals of a brazier in the light of an acetylene lamp. At 6 [a.m.] I went round my trenches, just as day was breaking and was saluted on my doorstep by a vy sulky bullet. All morning I laboured in the small business of the battalion and dealt with my Company Commanders and sent off the numerous reports for wh our superiors clamour – patrols, operations, situations, wind, work, fighting strength, enemy's shelling, intelligence etc.'

The quiet of the first day was not to continue. General Furse wanted to turn the comparatively passive defensive stance of the division into a more aggressive approach, the start of which was to be a heavy bombardment of the German positions – and the 6th RSF's front was the one chosen for the beginning of this new operation. Brigadier-General Tudor went to Churchill's headquarters at Laurence Farm to explain what was going to happen. The idea was to undertake sudden heavy bombardments at different points in the line. This would take the enemy by surprise and they could not prepare for it as they would not know where or when the bombardment would begin.

Winston was told to withdraw his troops from those parts of the line and its approaches where it was thought most likely that the enemy's 'certain' retaliation would be delivered. Churchill, of course, wanted to watch the action from a location that was as close as possible. He duly accompanied Tudor to a ruined farmhouse and climbed onto the wrecked building's roof where they were completely exposed but from where they had an excellent view of the enemy's positions.

At 14.30 hours the British guns opened fire and, as predicted, the Germans responded almost immediately to Brigadier-General Tudor's 'strafe'. As planned the Germans were unable to bring as many guns to bear as the British, who threw around three times more shells. Because the trenches had been evacuated, there were no casualties amongst the 6th RSF.

Furse's plan therefore worked very well. It was felt that there could be no doubt that the British bombardment would have inflicted casualties amongst the Germans, with no corresponding loss to the Scots, other than damage to some of the trenches. Obviously this tactic could only work well a few times before the Germans realised what the British were doing and they adopted the same policy – and that would only lead to increased casualties.

That night Winston, along with Sinclair, went out into No Man's Land, and 'prowled about' inspecting the condition of the barbed-wire and visiting the battalion's listening posts. 'This is always exciting,' he told a despairing Clementine. The War Diary states, for the night of 14/15 February, that 'successful patrols explored No Man's Land and brought back good examples of German wire'.

One of these nocturnal inspections by Churchill was witnessed by Private Reginald Hurt. 'I was on sentry duty that night, which meant standing on the fire steps of the front line trench, and looking out towards the enemy lines. It was a bitterly cold, wet night and very quiet as regards action, and in a weak moment I stood my rifle up against the parapet; in a corner of the trench. I then marched up and down on the fire step trying to get some warmth into my arms and legs, when suddenly some-one jumped down behind me from the top of the parapet.

'Fortunately for me and my sleeping colleagues, it was Sir Winston Churchill and his Adjutant, Sir Archibald Sinclair and not a German patrol. The next five or ten minutes were amongst the unhappiest of my life, all because my rifle *was not* in my possession. I received, and deservedly, the most severe reprimand I can recall. Finally he asked me my age, and on learning that I was one of the youngest soldiers in the Battalion, and had been in the trenches at the age of eighteen, his anger evaporated and he became almost paternal.'[26]

On the morning of 16 February the German artillery was active once again, and this time it was the enemy's 4.2-inch howitzers that delivered some thirty to forty shells upon the trenches and area around Laurence Farm. Winston had yet to move into the Conning Tower, which was still being prepared for him, and he was having breakfast with his second-in-command, Sinclair, when the shells began to fall.

'Archie and I persevered in our breakfast,' he later recounted, 'till a tremendous bang, clouds of debris and the whizzing of splinters proclaimed our house hit again – this time our dining room was pierced on the other side, and our joint bedroom penetrated in 5 or 6 places … we hastily seized our eggs and bacon, bread and marmalade and took refuge in our dugout. Here we remained while perhaps 20 shells were devoted to our farm and its curtilage … It was odd gobbling bacon and marmalade in the dugout, while the doctor bandaged the gt raw wounds of [a] poor officer a foot or two away!'

Winston and Sinclair took it all in their stride and when the 'strafe' ended, they emerged from the shelter of the dugout and went about their business. The signal room which adjoined Winston's room, however, was completely shattered and the signals officer, Lieutenant Kemp, the poor officer Winston referred to, was wounded in five places and one other man was hit.

Winston remained convinced that his headquarters were being specifically targeted but he did not want to relocate as he found Laurence Farm convenient and, as far as was possible in the circumstances, comfortable. It is surprising how someone in his forties, brought up in the lap of luxury and who had spent the previous decade in the gilded corridors and oak-panels rooms of the Palace of Westminster, adapted so well to the harsh conditions of the Western Front and who was content with so little.

The attention continued and the following day Laurence Farm was again targeted[27]: 'We were shelled again at 9, at 11, and at 1 today. Two batteries now take an interest in us – one tries 30 lb and the other 15 pr shells and they shot from different sides so that they search our weak points vy disagreeably. Th house is much better sandbagged and by tomorrow morning shd be still more so. We were very punctilious about going into the dugout whenever the bombardment began and waiting for ten minutes without a shell before coming out. No other part of my line has been touched, and no casualties have occurred in the trenches.'

Despite his conviction that his headquarters was being specifically targeted, he told Clementine that, 'other farms in rear of the line are also being made a target – so there is no reason to suppose there is anything personal in the enemy's intentions'.

Nevertheless, Winston was stung into retaliation and the men soon saw two naval officers with Churchill in the front line. Special observers in the trenches located a concrete German mortar (*minenwerfer*) emplacement and a number of sniper posts. Winston arranged for 12-inch naval guns which were mounted on an armoured train some six miles away to hit these positions, and, as the two front lines were only about 100 yards or less apart, the RSF had to evacuate their trenches in case a shell or two dropped short. This clearly required careful timing and discretion so that the Germans did not take advantage of the empty British trenches.

With everything ready, the railway guns opened fire. 'With a noise like approaching express trains these huge missiles hurtled over our heads,' recalled Robert Fox, one of the battalion's Lewis gunners, 'and crashed into the German line. Each impact was like a miniature earthquake.'

Winston had to remain at Laurence Farm on the telephone in contact with the artillery during the bombardment and therefore did not get the chance to watch the bombardment – much to his disappointment. But he declared that his little piece of revenge worked well, and mist and rain the next day, the 18th meant that the German artillery could not respond.

On the 19th the battalion was relieved by the 8th Gordons and went back to Ploegsteert, and once again the village came under heavy enemy artillery fire. Archibald Sinclair maintained that their quarters were unsafe and said that when the village came under bombardment they should retire downstairs. The fearless Churchill did not like this.

As can already be gleaned, Winston was not one to be always diving for cover when under fire and he did not like the idea of having to consider when to retire to the cellar nearby. This would have meant giving too much attention to what the enemy was doing rather than his usual dismissive approach to the enemy's gunfire. It was not Winston's way to be dodging and diving from the enemy. Nevertheless, when the shelling became 'disagreeable' Winston agreed to go along to the cellar.

After a few near misses, Winston declared that the cellar was no safer than the rooms on ground level and that if the cellar suffered a direct hit it would kill them just as swiftly as if they were sat in their far more comfortable room in the house. The two men agreed to differ.

The next morning Sinclair went to inspect the troops whilst Winston remained to write up his latest thoughts on the war. At around 11.00 hours the Germans again targeted Ploegsteert.

When the bombardment began Winston was writing in his room in the Hospice. The room was favoured by Winston as its main feature was a large bay-window – hardly the place to be during an artillery bombardment. The old lady and her daughter who lived in the Hospice retreated into the cellar along with two of the battalion's telegraphists. Winston saw the wisdom in seeking shelter, but the little cellar was far too crowded for his liking and its roof looked disturbingly weak.

So Winston went into the adjoining building which was used as the battalion office. There, at least, were two brick walls between the Lieutenant Colonel and the flying shells. If struck, the first wall would take the initial impact and the second, hopefully, would stop the fragments and splinters. The bombardment was recorded by Winston in his book *Thoughts and Adventures:*

'And now "Plugstreet" Village began to endure one of the first of those methodical bombardments which gradually reduced it to ruins. Every minute or two came shells, some bursting on the fronts of houses, some piercing their roofs, others exploding in the courtyards and offices behind. The shriek of approaching projectiles, their explosions and the crash and rattle of falling brickwork, became almost continuous. My Adjutant soon joined me in our back room, and there we sat and smoked, at first not unpleasantly excited, but gradually becoming silent and sulky.

'From time to time tremendous explosions close at hand told us that the neighbouring buildings were struck. The soot came down the chimney in clouds, and the yard at the back, onto which we now looked, was strewn with fragments of brick and masonry. One shell burst on the face of the opposite building before our eyes, making a gaping hole. We continued to sit in our chairs, putting our faith rather doubtfully in our two brick walls [such] … were the commonplaces of the life of millions in those strange times.'[28]

After about an hour and thirty minutes the bombardment ceased and Sinclair joined Winston in 'the highest spirits'. On his tour of inspection of the men's billets beyond Ploegsteert he had been able to watch the whole episode quite safely from about 100 yards away. Together Churchill and Sinclair walked across to the Hospice. As they entered the back door, a scene of 'utter devastation' met their eyes. 'The room in which I had been writing was wrecked and shattered. Daylight streamed through a large hole in the brickwork above the bay-window. The table, the furniture, papers, objects of all kinds, had been hurled into confusion. Everything was covered with thick, fine, red brick-dust. Then, from the back of the house, appeared the old woman and her daughter, completely terrified; behind them came one of the signallers, grinning.'

The agitated woman demanded that Winston should look in the cellar. There he saw that a 30lb shell had penetrated his bedroom (this was for the third time) and had carried on through the building into the cellar where the two staff and the two Belgian females had been huddled. As it transpired the shell failed to explode, otherwise most likely they would all have been killed. Winston's point had been emphatically made.

The shelling continued over the next few days, with the village gradually being reduced to rubble. Sinclair told Winston that it was the most concentrated and prolonged bombardment he had experienced. In Churchill's mind this was confirmation that the Germans knew that he was stationed at Ploegsteert. 'One lives calmly on the brink of the abyss,' Winston told his wife who can hardly have been enamoured with his phlegmatic approach to danger. 'But I can understand how tired people get of it if it goes on month after month. All the excitement dies away and there is only dull resentment.'

Even the steeple of Ploegsteert's church, which had stood proudly over the village throughout sixteen months of intermittent bombardment, finally crumbled to the ground after being hit by a large shell. 'So this evening we are smashing up one of their steeples,' Winston wrote, 'and they are retaliating by scattering their shells in twos and threes on various points. Meanwhile the German aeroplanes sail about unmolested overhead watching the shooting, and scorning our anti-aircraft guns.'

The anger he felt at what he saw as British inferiority in the air was a frequent theme in his letters to his wife. On 17 January he had written: 'Air fights have been going on overhead this morning, and I think there has been an air raid on some of the neighbouring townships, as a lot of our machines are up. There is no excuse for our not having command of the air.'

After reading a report in *The Times* quoting Harold Tennant, the Under-Secretary of State for War, who said in the House of Commons that 'nearly every fight in the air takes place on the German side of the trenches,' he wrote to Clementine on 26 January: 'I saw one [a German aeroplane] flaunting himself 20 miles behind the line yesterday; and 4 of them threw bombs within 50 yards of the party of men I sent on to prepare these billets for our reception.'

Winston's bedroom at the Hospice was so badly damaged by the shelling that he went to Soyer Farm to sleep. As it happened, there was a heavy fall of snow which considerably reduced visibility, and the German guns fell silent for two days, which was a great relief to all the men of the battalion.

Snow still covered the ground when the 6th RSF returned to the trenches on 25 February. For their scouting patrols into No Man's Land the men wore white calico gowns which covered most of their body and made them all but invisible from as close as around 200 yards. 'I was up till 1.30 in the trenches,' Winston wrote to Clementine the following day, 'as the night was so dark and the price of safety is eternal vigilance. The artillery cooperation was vy loose last night and we took a vy long time to get a response from them.'

Winston told her how much he preferred Laurence Farm to Soyer Farm. 'Archie and I have a nice little square room together – the ceiling is propped up by timber, and there are 3 layers of sandbags and brick bags on the top, and all the sides are heavily protected. There are a good many things to burst a shell before it actually hits us, and then the sandbags may be counted on to stop the splinters and keep out the blast. Inside we have a glowing brazier and two comfortable canvas beds … we sleep warm and peaceful.'

The day after the battalion had returned into the front line, there was a burst of artillery activity, as the War Diary reveals: 'At 11.30 pm our guns fired in the trenches opposite T103-112 with 20 rounds deliberate and 20 rapid. At the same time the enemy's line was bombarded with trench mortars & rifle grenades & the companies fired 50 rounds rapid. Cease fire was at 11.40 pm. The enemy retaliated with a few 7.7cms which did no damage. Some of our shells burst short on the left (T.110) wounding 4 men & killing two. 2nd Lieut. A.E. Buchan was slightly wounded also.' The two men killed in this 'friendly-fire' incident were Private John Borland and Private David Cuthbert. Both were buried in Lancashire Cottage Cemetery.

The Germans appear to have sought some retribution the following day, the 27th, as Laurence Farm was shelled at noon, between twenty and thirty 7.7cm shells falling on the area. Three signallers working outside were caught in the barrage and were severely wounded. All three later died of wounds.

There was little change on the 28th, though this time the battalion headquarters was shelled on two separate occasions – once at 13.00 hours and again at 15.00 hours. The War Diary states that the 'cupola dugouts offered complete protection', though an 'orderly who was standing at the mouth of one, however, was severely wounded in the head'.

The following two days were a complete reversal with the artillery on both sides remaining silent. The only event of any note in the War Diary was the death of one soldier on 1 March, presumably having been shot by a sniper.[29]

Returning to Gibb's narrative, we gain a further insight into a future British Prime Minister:

It always struck me that Colonel Churchill achieved in a remarkable measure success in dealing with the rank and file of his battalion. His attitude towards the men was ideally sympathetic and was not marred by that condescending *hauteur* which goes so far to frustrate the efforts of a number of our regular officers. He found that the sentries were not as wholehearted and enthusiastic in the performance of their watch as he desired and for many nights he made a particular point of explaining their duties to them, going along the front line and selecting positions for the men which at once gave a maximum of shelter and enabled them to keep a perfect look-out.

To the young boys among them, especially, it seemed an

unpleasant thing to stand up for an hour and expose oneself to the all too frequent bullets that came over to us from the German sentries. Winston used to get up on to the firestep[30] and encourage them, demonstrating to them what a small chance, after all, there was of being hit and pointing out too how vital were the duties which they were performing. In all this there was such a complete absence of the "superior person" that the men welcomed his presence and his advice, and responded most loyally to his orders. He held very strong views about the crime of "sleeping on his post" and was always at the utmost pains, in fairness to the men, to prevent the possibility of such a thing occurring.

No commanding officer ever was more interested in or more attentive to his wounded. On the one hand he was utterly impervious to all feelings of aversion from the unpleasant sights of war and I have seen him several times sitting calmly discussing questions of state with "Archie" in blood-saturated surroundings: but on the other he was always first on the scene of misfortune and did all in his power to help and comfort and cheer. It did not matter where he was or what he was doing, if he heard that a man was wounded he set off at once to see him.

He would also discuss the various cases in a learned fashion with the Doctor. Winston had a *flair* for a good man of science. He used to take a delight in getting the Doctor to talk on his own subjects, and nobody was better pleased or more enthusiastic if the Doctor acquitted himself well. We had several M.O.s while Winston was with us and he used to discuss them and compare and contrast their points as enthusiastically as though they had been specimens of some wild animal which he collected.

> Winston's concern for the welfare of his men was exemplified by an incident recalled by Private Hurt: 'On one occasion, whilst acting as a company runner, I was walking along what had been Plugstreet's main road,

when I saw the OC coming along in the opposite direction. I gave him the usual smart salute, and had passed along about a dozen paces when he called me back and asked me why I was limping.'[31]

Hurt explained that he was limping because of the poor condition of his boots. When he had gone to the quartermaster to ask for a new pair he was told to go away as the shoes were good enough to last for another three months. That was simply not acceptable to Winston who immediately pulled an envelope out of his pocket, took out the letter, which he returned to his jacket, and on the envelope wrote, 'Quarter-master Sgt. B Company, supply bearer with one pair of boots *immediately*'. Winston signed it and handed it to Private Hurt.

There was one topic on which we all differed from the C.O. at first. It was very noticeable that whenever we were in the trenches we had a lot of shelling, whereas our relieving battalion had things very quiet. For example we had no sooner occupied the convent in Plugstreet than it was rendered uninhabitable. The same thing had happened at Lawrence Farm with the most distressing consequences to Ramsey's peace of mind, as already narrated. This was in our view evidence, circumstantial certainly, yet cogent enough to prove that the Hun knew Winston was there. But he would have none of this.

"I am just as well known in Germany as Tirpitz is in England and they don't like me there: they hate me. If they knew I was in the line here they wouldn't send over a few shells like this. They would turn on all their guns and blot the place out. They would love to do that."

I feel quite sure now that he was right, and yet the Germans must have known that Churchill had come out to Flanders. It was evidently not considered a fact of sufficient military importance to be censored in the newspapers, and knowing that he was out, it is curious that they didn't find out, assuming they wanted to, exactly what part of the line he was in. It would be amusing to learn as a fact whether they did know, and whether they did try to "blot him out."

> There was, though, the situation noted earlier, that Winston brought a lot of fire down upon himself and his men through his own actions. This was evident from an incident back on 26 January. The battalion was back in the front line and Churchill was ensconced, he believed, quite safely in a now heavily sandbagged Laurence Farm. He told Clementine that, 'Our farm is much protected, and it wd take 5.9-inch guns to smash it.'
> Feeling now quite secure, he decided to encourage the nearby artillery battery to 'strafe' the Germans again. This time it was not the inevitable German retaliation which saw his men hurt, it was the British guns. The British shells fell short, killing two men and wounding three others.

The subject of relationship with the men brings me to the only serious point of criticism which I am tempted to make with regard to Colonel Churchill's conception of the duties of a battalion commander. We considered him quite wrong about it and yet it may well be that it is the present system which is wrong, and that there is room for alteration in the stereotyped mode of thought regarding even such an important matter of discipline. The line which he took would be bound to shock the regular soldier, but a thoroughly good shaking-up of many of the ideas of the regular soldier has during the war had most salutary results, and it is not to be supposed that the healthful effect of the process is necessarily at an end. However, it is difficult to see how his ideas on this matter could receive sanction without serious detriment to the one essential of discipline, viz., prompt obedience to orders.

It used to happen that a soldier when ordered say, by a corporal, to perform some duty, did, through laziness or dislike of the corporal or distaste for the order given, refuse to obey that order, at the same time usually inviting the corporal to perform certain notoriously impossible physical feats or proceed to a certain non-existent destination, all in order to show his utter contempt of the corporal and emphasize his determination on no account to do as he was told. Now this is indiscipline in the highest degree, and a man is always "run in" at once for it, and on the facts being proved against him he is usually heavily punished. It was, however, impossible to get the C.O. to concur in the usual treatment of such offences. He considered that no man would wittingly incur the serious penalties inevitable in such a case, did he know that his conduct was in fact precisely such conduct as would render him liable to them. In any event, the Colonel used to say, whether or not the man knew, it was only fair to explain the position to him there and then, and there and then to give him a chance to depart from his insubordinate attitude.

It may be that this is strict justice, but even in civil life ignorance of the law is no excuse, and when, as in the Army, the consequences of such a crime are so serious, there seems to be all the less reason for admitting the principle that because a man sins in haste or through ignorance, he should on that account be afforded a second chance. We permanently differed on this matter, and I am afraid the men began to realize that they might at least once indulge themselves in the luxury of telling their sergeants to go to hell! I am not sure that the company orderly-room did not afford a way out of the *impasse*.

> This is the leniency that was mentioned earlier which Gibb felt undermined discipline in the battalion. The Lewis gunner Robert Fox, who became a journalist with the *New York Herald and the Chicago Tribune*, related one such incident, in a radio broadcast he made in 1964. 'Churchill was scrupulously fair to many men before him on a charge. I remember once, when acting as escort, I heard him cross-examine the NCO giving evidence against the man, with all the skill of a counsel at the Bar. The evidence did not satisfy him, so he dismissed the

WITH WINSTON CHURCHILL AT THE FRONT

BY CAPTAIN X.

Malbrook s'en va-t-en guerre

1/- NET.

LONDON & GLASGOW, GOWANS & GRAY, LTD.

The cover of the original edition of *With Winston Churchill at the Front* by Captain X. (Historic Military Press)

These pages and overleaf: A section of a trench map detailing some of the area around Ploegsteert. The British front line is indicated by the blue line, whilst the German trenches are marked in red and greater detail. A number of the locations described by Dewar Gibb and Churchill are marked on the map.

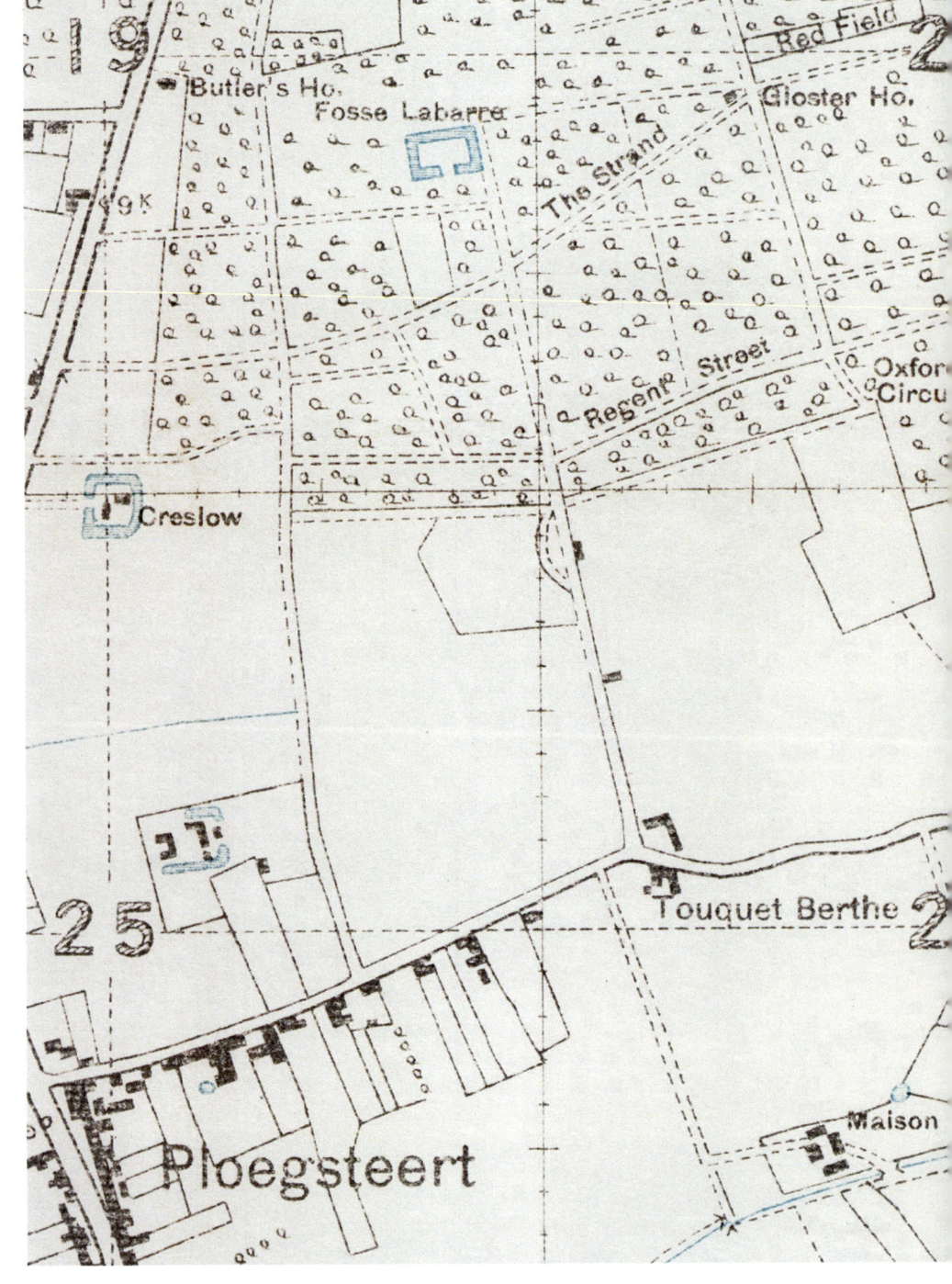

Ploegsteert

The Strand
Somerset Ho.
Spy Corner
German
Fleet Street
Piccadilly Circus
Rifle Ho.
Haymarket
Hampshire Lane
Essex Fm
Hants Fm
Lancashire Cottage
Laurence Farm
Red House
Mountain Gun Farm
La V

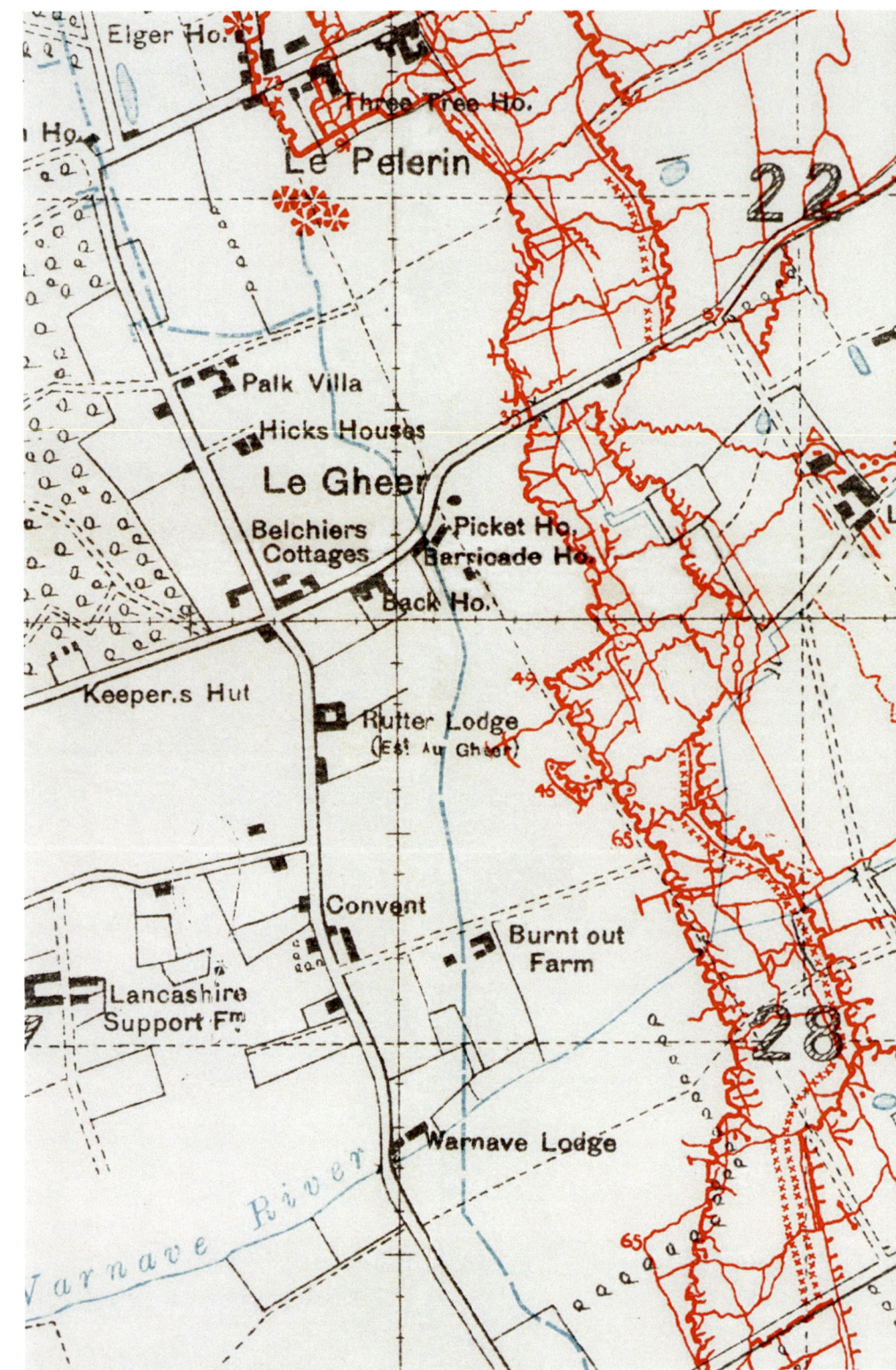

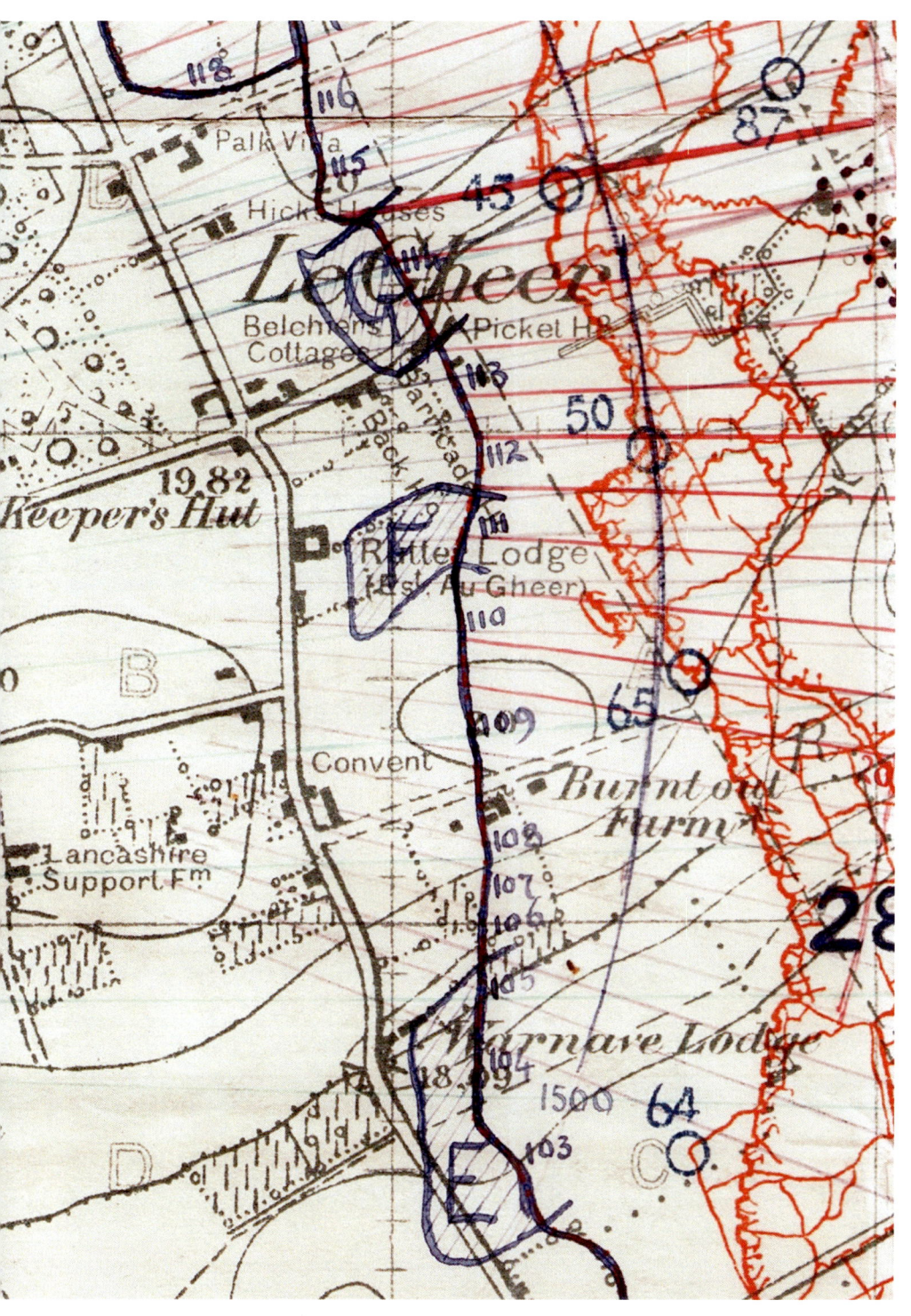

Above: An annotated section of trench map which shows the exact part of the line held by Churchill and his men – those sections of the blue line marked T103 through to T112.

Above: Winston Churchill's painting of Laurence Farm, entitled *Plug Street; Battalion Headquarters 1916*. The original caption states that it was 'presented by the Trustees of the 9th Scottish Division Fund to Queen Victoria School, July, 1948'. The school, at Dunblane in Perthshire, still has the painting on display. (Reproduced with permission of Anthea Morton-Saner on behalf of Churchill Heritage Ltd; © Churchill Heritage Ltd.)

Below: This painting by Churchill is entitled *Plug Street 1916*. It was painted in the area of the building known as Maison 1875 and London Support Farm. (Reproduced with permission of Anthea Morton-Saner on behalf of Churchill Heritage Ltd; © Churchill Heritage Ltd.)

Perhaps the objects most relevant to Winston's and Dewar Gibb's time together are those shown here. This is a splinter from a shell which exploded at Laurence Farm on 3 February 1916 whilst Churchill was partaking of coffee and port wine with Jock McDavid who was at the time the battalion's Adjutant. Winston told his wife about this in a letter the following day, declaring that 'the only serious loss is my milux lamp'. In reality Winston had a very narrow escape, as McDavid later revealed: 'A piece of shrapnel almost split the battery holder in two … It was less than two inches from his right wrist. If it had been any nearer it certainly would have taken off his wrist.' (Courtesy of the National Trust, Chartwell House)

This is the lamp which saved Churchill from serious injury (note damage tp left). McDavid was not as fortunate as his battalion commander, as he was hit on a finger and had to return to the UK for treatment. As a result, Winston invited Dewar Gibb to take over McDavid's role, and within days the new Adjutant resolved to write a memoir of his time with Winston Churchill at the front. (Courtesy of the National Trust, Chartwell House)

Above left; The plaque commemorating Churchill's time at Ploegsteert which can be seen on the Mairie in the Main Square. (Historic Military Press)

Below left: The site of Laurence Farm, which was through the gate on the right-hand side of the bend, in a view looking east towards what would have been the British front line (beyond the houses in the distance). The well-head, all that remains of the original farm, is the concrete structure to the right. (Historic Military Press)

charge and gave the NCO a homily on the virtues of exactitude.'

Gibb continued to butt heads with Churchill on the matter of indiscipline and one can only wonder if this would have had a detrimental effect on the battalion if Winston's period of time with the 6th RSF would have been longer.

This subject was one that Brigadier Walshe had also noted. One of his last acts with the 27th Brigade was to rebuke Churchill for 'undue leniency' in his punishments. Winston did not get the chance to respond before Walshe left the division.

The purely administrative side of his command, what is known as "A" work by the Staff, and the countless and somewhat formal "G" reports, the Colonel left as a rule to the Adjutant. He used, however, to see the companies' reports each morning, usually laconic and unenlightening save when Ramsey broke the monotony by introducing – well, conversational epithets into his "wind" or "operations" reports, which had in consequence to be bowdlerized by the Adjutant, before submission to the C.O.

Once, however, in the interests of literary form, the Colonel did interfere and issue a manifesto directing that "in company reports a blind shell should be referred to as such and not as a dud." He would, however, probably have intervened by way of retribution had the Adjutant not suppressed *in toto* Ramsey's persistent and brazen applications to have all *his* "duds" drafted into the corps which trained carrier-pigeons.

Correspondence on the following lines was of daily occurrence:

Adjutant to O's.C. Companies: "Report by noon any evidence of enemy activity on your front during last 24 hours."

O.C. B Coy. to Adjutant: "No evidence of enemy activity on my front. But No. 65437 Pte. Andrew Moore is stated to be an expert in the handling of 'doos'." (*anglicé*, doves).[32]

The arrival of reinforcements may or may not be a source of rejoicing to the reinforced, but it was apparently in the Colonel's opinion invariably an occasion to be improved, and I must say that the little speeches which he was wont to deliver to newly arrived drafts were a never-failing source of entertainment. It did not matter whether a draft arrived when we were in the line or not, that draft was duly harangued and so initiated into its Colonel's expectations regarding it.

I remember on one occasion about twenty scared mortals being led into the little courtyard of Lawrence Farm, our Battalion Headquarters in the line. It was a court-yard only in so far as it still by ruined buildings preserved the ground-plan of what no doubt had once been a playing-ground of hens and pigs. There was, however, a good deal more protection than appeared.

In the evening just after dark there was always a nice little concert of rifle and machine-gun bullets mewing and zipping among the splintered roofs and the thatch. The draft in question arrived that evening just in time for the concert, and were duly lined up to listen to the bullets, the first they had heard in most cases, *and* to the C.O. The latter gave a pretty eloquent address and, touching on the usual soldiers' temptations and failings, laid especial stress on drunkenness, the chief stumbling-block, in his opinion, of the Scottish soldier. It was a chilly welcome, but I think that most of those men would have let him say anything if only they could have been assured they had not really been lined up to be shot.

Chapter 12

Our Guests

We had a great many visitors, as was not unnatural. All battalions had a certain number, and I believe that later in the war the number increased, but undoubtedly we had more than most people. Most of us, however, saw but little of them.

One of the earliest was Lord Curzon, who came up one raw day in February, [this is the visit of 6 February referred to earlier] and did, I believe, go round the front-line trenches with the Colonel. I can only remember seeing him in a shocking soft cap, and, along with another fellow, following him down the duckboards to Plugstreet (where I came near my death by M.G. fire and he nearer to his than he knew) and finally making a gallant but quite abortive attempt to secure a lift in the admirable motor-car which awaited him at the end of the trolley line.

There was more of an incident attaching to the visit of Lord Birkenhead, then Sir F.E. Smith, who was a close friend of the Colonel's and who was at that time in some employment, I believe at G.H.Q. I think he was a Colonel on the Staff and had certain duties in connection with Courts-martial which he performed at G.H.Q. Naturally enough he conceived the idea of visiting the Colonel and he proceeded to carry out his idea. He came up of course by car, but, unfortunately, before leaving, he had omitted, to obtain the necessary passes. The result of the omission was rather startling, for this very considerable legal personage was given a practical introduction to a legal situation he must frequently have contemplated, though scarcely experienced, by being made the subject of an arrest.

During the initial warmth generated by this outrage the air was heavy with threats of vengeance against General Macready, the Adjutant-General, who it was supposed, had directly interested himself in its perpetration. It seems however that eventually, when taxed with it, the Adjutant-General pleaded ignorance of the whole transaction and said it was entirely the fault of some underling, name not vouchsafed. (This line of defence is occasionally adopted in the Army).

In any event it appears that the late Lord Chancellor is now the proud possessor of an affidavit or similar document made by General Macready to the effect that he was not the prime mover in the matter.

> What actually happened regarding the visit of Lord Birkenhead, is that late in January a number of Cabinet Ministers attended a conference in Paris, and passes were requested for some of these men to visit GHQ at St Omer. On the morning of 30 January information was received that Sir F.E Smith, the Attorney-General, a member of the Cabinet, intended to visit Winston. Smith, and one of the ministers did not have a pass but was still determined to journey to the front regardless. So the Provost-Marshal was informed who then warned all road posts to watch out for an individual passing through without the required documentation.
>
> Quite what went wrong has never been ascertained as no-one along the route saw Smith pass by. What was later discovered was that the Attorney-General, who was dressed in uniform, obtained a car without authority from the Mechanical Transport Department at St Omer, and drove on to find Winston. When, late in the afternoon, it was found that Smith had disappeared in the midst of the army, concerned telephone calls were made to try and find the missing minister. Sir Neville Macready, the BEF's Adjutant-Genera explained what happened next:
>
> 'At 10 p.m. Sir Frederick was discovered in Lieut. Col. Winston Churchill's dugout, and was conducted to G.H.Q.

by the Assistant Provost-Marshal of the 2nd Corps, not arriving, however, until 4 a.m., owing to an unfortunate breakdown of the car. An officer of the Provost branch at G.H.Q. who had arranged accommodation for Sir Frederick at the local inn was waiting for his arrival, and at the inn asked for his assurance that he would not disturb the Commander-in-Chief, or the Cabinet Ministers then in St Omer, until he had seen the Adjutant-General in the morning. There was some difficulty over this, which, however, was overcome, and at 9 a.m. the next morning I saw Sir Frederick. He was annoyed, perhaps naturally, that he had been technically 'arrested', a step that was not intended, the original order from G.H.Q. being that he should be escorted back to G.H.Q.

'It was I think, the fear of ridicule more than anything else that disturbed the equilibrium of the Attorney-General, but, as I pointed out to him, the Commander-in-Chief's order in regard to passes had evidently not been unwittingly evaded, because the other members of his party had arranged for the necessary permits, and further, in view of the fact that he himself had been on the Staff of the Indian Corps earlier in the war, it was a matter of greater surprise that he should have placed himself in such a position. In addition, I explained that had an application been made for him to visit Lieut. Col. Winston Churchill, I should have been glad to arrange it with the 2nd Army …

'Personally, I was sorry the incident should have occurred to anyone in a public position, but none the less it was a satisfaction to know that throughout the Army orders would be enforced without regard to persons or position, and I hope this may continue to be the case in our Army in future wars.'

The afternoon following Sir Frederick Smith's arrest, Winston went to see Macready, and they had a 'friendly chat' but Winston wanted to take the matter further. As Attorney-General Frederick Smith was the man to whom final appeals were sent in the case of serious courts-marital. Yet here he was being arrested. It was a matter, Winston wrote to Bonar Law, 'which cannot and will not end here in France. It will become public knowledge and will draw with it many other things.'

In fact, Bonar Law stepped in quickly and contacted Field Marshal Haig, just in time to stop the Attorney-General the added indignity of being sent under escort to Boulogne and deported from France for having no pass.

No such cavalier treatment however was meted out to any other guests of Winston's by the local military authorities. Canadian Generals especially were thickly with us throughout. On one occasion indeed we had to put up with a couple of Canadian Scouts or Scoutmasters lent to us by a Canadian General for the purpose of teaching us how to carry out efficient night patrols. This created great indignation, which on the *prima facie* ground of wounded martial pride was not remarkable, but which later was proved on all grounds to be fully justified by the utter mediocrity of the "instructors."

They ate and slept all day: towards evening they emerged and came down to drink, according to the manner of wild things, and when darkness had fallen (and there was no question of the moon's rising) they ventured to show a few incensed Jocks how to climb over the parapet and the wire, lie on their bellies in a dip in No Man's Land for a scanty interval and then return to the trenches, the men to their nightly sentry duties, and they themselves to their usual batlike existence in the most comfortable dug-out in the line.

To speak of Canadians is to recall another person who was a very frequent visitor, General Seely[1]. He was in command of a Canadian formation, which happened to be near us from time to time. He attended a Battalion concert on one occasion and was impressed to sing a song, which he did very nicely, playing his own accompaniment. The men were very pleased with this performance, and not a little surprised at finding a General from whose society it was possible to derive some slight pleasure.

But the most notable Canadian of them all was MacDonald – Foghorn MacDonald.[2] Whatever pretension this most gallant warrior had to direct descent from the ancient and honourable Scottish Clan whose name he bore, let not the Chief of that Clan disturb himself lest this scion of his house should ever or in any place depart from the precepts of vigour and robustness traditional among the MacDonalds. He was the embodiment or incarnation of that rude hustling force both in word and action which by a long tract of experience we have come to associate with persons bred in America. He was the perfect type of this form of manhood: never failing, always consistent. His sobriquet of course sufficiently indicated the force with which he was wont at least to speak. He sang of his deeds as the old Norse poets sang of their heroes' deeds: all his converse was in Sagas, and not Sancho Panza himself was more greatly master of the proverbs of his land than Foghorn MacDonald.

It is a matter of regret that I can in no way reproduce any of his narratives. To begin with, his own nice phrasing would be lost in the process and in such rococo master-pieces the exact adjustment of the parts is essential if the whole is not to be a mere mass of good things spoilt. An additional reason is that even in these days it would be impossible to get a type-setter to set up his *ipsissima verba*, assuming that the daring publisher of this book would consent to their remaining in the MS. I have never in all my life heard anything to rival his fluent impassive flowery profanity. And [I] recollect that his narratives were really interesting in themselves, and that never in all his life did Foghorn do an ordinary thing or take part in an ordinary adventure.

He was then an officer, but had at an earlier stage been a private soldier, in which capacity he appeared to have been a sort of official referee of grievances to the Canadian Forces. Armed with a grievance, he apparently never hesitated to point out to the officer concerned his wishes as to its immediate removal, with suitable monition of the penalties that awaited disobedience to his, Foghorn's, orders:

"And of *course* the b ——- man saw I b ——- well meant it and the thing was b ——- sharp done" was the conclusion of the typical Foghornian story. He knew every country in the world, but had evidently of late been concentrating on Mexico. We gleaned the idea that he would probably be King of Mexico as soon as he had got Carranza's affairs settled up, and Villa quietened. His opinion of Villa was that he hadn't a ——- of use for the ——- son of a ——- but by the ——- his ——-. His opinion of Carranza on the other hand was to the effect that — ——————.

They should have had Foghorn at the Peace Conference. He would have bellowed the delegates all into submission, ordered all the Germans to be shot, and made himself Emperor of Germany as Foghorn the First with Mexico as a sphere of interest. Politically and economically it would have been a great success and the Court memoirs of his reign would have been worth the most profound study.

We never saw the C.O. take a second place in conversation to anyone save Foghorn, who treated with noisy scorn such of Winston's ideas as differed from his own, and who when he found that they were in agreement would suffer no other person than himself to expound their common views. The C.O. merely sat and laughed at his sallies: he had heard him before. The rest of us, who had not heard him were not left strength enough even to giggle; we had, however, become Foghorn-worshippers. I hope he is still alive and will read these words; they are written in a spirit of the purest appreciation. There was never anyone quite like him.

General Tudor, the General Officer Commanding the Divisional Artillery, was often in the Mess, and was exceedingly popular with everybody, as he was not afraid of compromising his dignity by speaking to quite junior and quite temporary officers. He ultimately commanded the 9th Division and added greatly to his own reputation and that of the Division in the late stages of the war.

Such officers of other units in the Brigade as had to come often to Battalion Headquarters in the course of their duties were always very kindly received by the Colonel and, indeed, if they showed a disposition to make themselves agreeable, they were made much of by him. Two young R.E officers in particular had a *succès fou* which seriously upset the Bomb-boy and MacDavid, who by their long wearing of the cap and bells considered themselves privileged persons, alone to be fussed over.

Famous airmen also came and went, motoring all the way from the Calais coast to see their old chief. Notwithstanding their eminence and their special knowledge I could not avoid feeling always that they departed wiser than they had arrived. There was nothing of the back-number about Winston, even as regards the technical minutiae of flying.

Not long before we left Plugstreet there was a dinner-party in the line such as cannot have had many parallels during the war. The guests included the Divisional General, the Brigadier General on the General Staff of the Corps, two very distinguished flying-officers, and the Divisional General's A.D.C.

These people in addition to the usual members of the Mess made a pretty tight fit, but all went well and the mess-waiters managed to spill the minimum of soup on the General's lap, and the sulphurous parleyings in the outer darkness between the various functionaries interested, were for once conducted in an undertone. But Winston was too good a host to give his guests merely a good dinner and leave it at that. There must be entertainment beyond the merely gastric. And so with his blandest manner he turned to the General and said:

"I'm sure you'd like to see my trenches, General."

"Yes," said the General.

"Very well: you'd like to come too?" to another General.

"Oh yes, rather," said he, not to be outdone.

"We'll all go up then," said Winston "it's a lovely night, though very quiet. We might go out in front."

There was a picture in "Punch" about the time when our C.O. went to France, and in it he was shown as leading a string of Generals to victory, at a most rapid pace and on foot. Not otherwise did he on this very night in fulfilment of the prophecy lead his red-throated guests, not by way of the communication trench, but "over the ground," by the route which he used himself of nights when visiting the trenches. By this route one passed close to a little wayside shrine where stood a crucifix under a penthouse of wood, which remained untouched during our stay. And so the gallant company came into the front line, to the great consternation and bewilderment of the dwellers in that part.

The scene in front I did not witness but I can imagine it. Winston in his element, pointing out the sights – the scarcely stifled giggling of the Bomb-boy, swelling with a self-esteem engendered by the near presence of such very regular officers – the warm effect of the Very lights upon the unwonted red and gold – the polite "after you's" of the visitors – the hugging of mother earth and proximity to the cooling swamp – and over all, the savour wafted softly on the breeze from the age-old carcase of the loyal cow, killed in front of Burnt-out Farm.

The Battalion was delighted with this performance. I think the invitation to go forth was made in all good faith by the Colonel, but it was a first-rate joke to the jaded infantry to see them all out there tearing breeches and thumbs on the wire; wallowing in mud and cursing over clothes that had never been grovelled in before. That was certainly how the scene presented itself to the Battalion.

The infantry did not like the Staff, chiefly because in their opinion (which it is only fair to say was really quite wrong) the Staff did not like the trenches, and we were delighted, justifiably as we thought, at seeing them in the trenches, and even having their noses, so to speak, rubbed in them. The criticism was wholly wrong, although inevitable on this unique occasion. The Battalion, however, was no stranger to the sight of General Furse, the Divisional Commander, walking on the top at night for an hour or two at a time.

Chapter 13

The Mess

Nobody who was entertained there ever forgot it. And who was not entertained! Certainly all the officers of the Battalion – some of them frequently: certainly every poor stray who blew past looking for an O.P. site, or a site for the newest trench engine to be tried and to explode in, or spying out the land against the joyless day when *his* battalion should relieve us. Let his business be what it might be he was certain to be haled [*sic*] in and entertained in a way which made him glad, and if he left without a large cigar lighting up his mollified countenance that was because he was a non-smoker and through no fault of Colonel Churchill.

Animosity towards the distinguished intruder ceased in most cases after the first dinner party given by the Colonel at Battalion Headquarters. That was in the Outersteene [*sic*] region. Hazebrouck had, in defiance of all rules, yielded up its entire content of peach and apricot brandy, which undoubtedly is a powerful corrective of the acid and sub-acid humours in even thoroughly cantankerous constitutions. In conjunction with tobacco administered in its most attractive form, the least hopeful cases yielded. And thus the flesh being rendered more willing, the spirit became receptive of the extraordinary influence of an outstanding personality, and so the first difficulty which Churchill had to face, the danger of domestic unpleasantness, was happily overcome.

This triumph over his own subjects was only the forerunner of many won over outsiders, all of which signally helped in the fostering of harmonious and therefore efficient relationships with those whom it was essential to work in harmony with. Their first shyness over, the companies opened their doors in turn, and I well recollect a gala-night at Ramsey's company mess in their workman's dwelling opposite well-shelled Delennelle, at which the Colonel was the guest of honour. Not in vain had Armentières and the Divisional Canteen been scoured for lobster, or tinned fruits of all hues and flavours, for wine and gin and strawberry brandy, and for cigars. Not in vain were the efforts of Kelly the cook – of Clough with moist but willing hands and burnished brow – not in vain had Ramsey's Baxter oiled his locks and caused his face to shine a welcome through its polish bred of honest yellow soap. The dinner was a great success and so the hospitable tradition yielded its further useful crop of that good-will without which in armies, as in other joint efforts, failure must ensue.

There was absolutely no reticence about Churchill during ordinary social intercourse with his officers in the Mess. If he were asked a question about even the most delicate-seeming subjects he gave always a frank and honest reply. He would sit and discourse of Antwerp and the Dardanelles with perfect freedom, and after listening to his account of the Dardanelles affair I for my part was quite won over and believed, as I believe to this hour, in the justness of the decision he then took.

He amused us much by his frequent stories of Lord Fisher, for whom he seemed to have the greatest admiration. He regarded Fisher as the type of man that was needed to win the war. Probably he was entirely correct in that view. There was certainly no lack of sting about the man who warned a crowd of great shipbuilding magnates against tardy delivery of the ships they were building by assuring them that in the event of their being late he would make all their wives widows, their children orphans and their homes dunghills. I believe Churchill corroborated this story. Fisher was to him an unscrupulously whole-hearted fighter for his country's good – a ferocious "brute," he called him *à propos* of his conduct of war. There was never any trace of hostility or animosity towards him – nothing save the most profound admiration.

Regarding Lord Kitchener, on the other hand, he was less enthusiastic. He did not regard him as the awe-inspiring, relentless, terrifying being which the country thought him. He told us that on his first going to meet him in conference he, Churchill, was rather nervous and subdued, thinking that Kitchener would be as awe-inspiring as he was painted, but he assured us that he got on well with him and found him to be a "very nice old cup of tea." But withal not the slightest disrespect.

Undoubtedly the story that most delighted his audiences was the story of the old Dartmoor shepherd who had been sentenced to fourteen years penal servitude for stealing a few shillings from an offertory box. This episode occurred while Churchill was at the Home Office, and it was the excuse for many a round dozen columns of "sob-stuff" in newspapers throughout the land. Churchill admitted that it was an exceedingly good point for the Tories, and that his side undoubtedly were made to look very silly over it; he found it very good fun himself. "Bah," he would say "after all what *is* sacrilege? – it's all one, rob a parson or a poacher – the stealing is the crime."

Having recently removed an ornamented hassock from Plugstreet Church to make my evening rest sweeter, I applauded this observation with some sincerity. He was never afraid to tell of the times when the tables were turned on him and I remember his laughing most heartily over a *rencontre* he had with Joe Chamberlain in early days in the House, when Chamberlain found him out and brought his crime home to him.

Regarding Mr. Asquith at that time he was somewhat bitter: it was in no way surprising to anyone in the line in 1916: it was merely endorsement by an insider of the feelings of most of us.

Had he not been so decent about it we should have been annoyed by that tin bath of the Colonel's. A private bath in billets! – unheard of – a breach of custom – of war etiquette – all but a military offence. Still there it was. It was a thing like a greatly magnified soap-dish, but it was possible to have a very good bath in it. Many a one I had, as had most of us.

It was in charge of the Colonel's bâtman, a man named Watt, who came from the Oxford and Bucks Hussars. I don't think Watt liked the bath much. It took a lot of hot water to fill it, besides it was always being "borrowed" by other people. But the harassed Watt was a pale figure compared to certain others of the officers' servants. Sinclair had a colossal servant, one Martin, who came from the Life Guards. He and MacDavid's servant, a pigmy called Blackwood, assiduously watched for Watt's dozing moments in order to filch the bath.

Martin and Blackwood were the knockabout comedians of the place. It is unfortunate that no approximation to a report of one of their turns can be given. The language was too horrifying. Martin was a cockney about 6 ft. 6 inches in height and Blackwood, a Lowland Scots lad of about 5 ft. 2 inches. The staple and commonplace of Blackwood's converse with Martin was none the less a constant assurance that if he, Blackwood, had any more of Martin's "impidence" he, Blackwood would – well "land him wi' a hell thump on his ——— " They would sit outside the mess for hours indulging in variants on this theme in the best of good humour while waiting to steal the bath, as soon as the distressed Watt was summoned by his master.

The Colonel, as I have already said, always amused me by his peculiar *flair* for a good doctor. We had several during his short time with us and he never wearied of summing them up, extolling this quality – criticising that and generally descanting on their characters and qualifications. The doctor was usually mess-president and this was an office that led directly to great personal responsibility to the Colonel.

Some of the doctors didn't do much good at it, and usually received very sharp reminders of their negligence. There was one James, an Englishman, to whom the Colonel took a great fancy and he certainly was an able man – a brain-specialist, I believe. To another again he conceived an antipathy and he became a member of a company mess. This marooning in a company's billet was a normal penalty for unpopularity at Battalion Headquarters. I recollect having an outcast from the Battalion mess so thrust upon our company. He was a nuisance of a fellow and, strange to say, was a Padre. As surely as we came out of the line feeling utterly done up and weary and sick, there he sat in our best chair, looking smug and clean as though fresh from a bien pulpit in Aberdeen. He had all his meals with us and lived elsewhere.

Once when he went sick and sent to the mess, as though to a circulating library, for something to read, we attempted to indicate our views in an indirect fashion, and for literature we collected an *Aberdeen Free Press* (a month old), a *Paisley Daily Express* (two months old – lately used by Kelly for wrapping round our best Canadian butter) and a more than ordinarily audacious number of *La Vie Parisienne*, and sent them with kind thoughts. I regret to say that we tried to choke him off eventually by telling exceedingly improper stories at mess, which, I now admit, was blameworthy conduct.

Delafons was a pathetic and unrestful figure. He presided over a trench-mortar unit which was supposed to work with our battalion. It was certainly no fault of this zealous officer that his wretched tubes wouldn't burst except in our own lines, for those were earlyish days. He was out and about night and day, begging, borrowing and stealing.

It is always the fate of the luckless attached officer. He was to obtain what he wants by indirect and often humiliating means: he has no rights and no friends and no orders except of the vaguest kind. The poor devil had no rations even. But his was a rather unhappy nature and he certainly didn't quite make the best of it. At about 1.30 a.m. he would glide into the Mess, serious, war-like, efficient. Always he wore his tin-hat, then new and considered very ludicrous and not quite "the thing" (a fatal etiquette). With anxious look and voice he would ask the Colonel for 100 men – a fatigue party – a carrying party to transport his deadly ammunition to the front line; with equally grave voice the Colonel would refuse his request. Expostulations followed. The Colonel began to pull his leg in his effective yet kindly way. Delafons never saw it and blundered into more requests, usually for rations. Finally, however, he withdrew, sighing, and retired into the darkness to make his unbusinesslike yet necessary requests elsewhere.

Truth to say, we didn't like this particular form of warfare and cared little if his perilous cargo of ammonal or T.N.T. never got itself a yard nearer to the front line. The Colonel's words did not lack point when he summed him up – *Delafons et origo malorum*. But Delafons was efficient, though somewhat open to be ragged, and this is what cannot be said of another youth of long and oily locks who was once our guest as representing an 18-pounder battery of the illustrious corps of the Royal Field Artillery. It can hardly be that he didn't really know, but I heard him solemnly assure the Colonel at the conclusion of a searching cross-examination by the latter that the shells fired by his battery weighed 12 pounds! I believe that consequent upon this dreadful *gaffe*, he was told that his Corps' proud motto of "*Ubique*" would for the future in his case be construed strictly with reference to the waggon-lines!

It is noteworthy, if it be true, that Mr. Churchill has always been rather noted for his hats, that he always wore in the line, not the ordinary tin-hat, but a specimen of the much more ornamental French helmet. A photo of him, thus equipped, is reproduced in this book. The Glengarry he never took to, though he did his best to like it, I am sure. Truth to say it did not become him. I am told that on putting it on first and observing himself in the mirror, he gave his characteristic chuckle, uttered piously and monosyllabically, "———," and took it off again in haste.

Like every other mess in France we had a gramophone and we had a great many records good and bad. I thought the Colonel's taste in music a trifle robust, but he was probably quite right. What was needed in France was an exhalation of the Hippodrome rather than of the Aeolian Hall. There were many absurd songs such as "Chinatown," "Dear old Dublin," "Chalk Farm to Camberwell Green," which are to most of us now, I daresay, very much more than the stupid concatenation of cheap harmonies warrants.

An undying recollection will be of a lovely spring day in the courtyard of Laurence Farm. The Colonel sat tilted on a rickety chair reading his pocket Shakespeare and beating time to the gramophone which was being assiduously fed by one of the servants. The Adjutant was cursing and tearing his hair at a table in the open, over wind and weather and intelligence reports. The sergeant-major was preening himself in the sun. The other officers were lying about reading or sleeping and Blackwood was persistently lending Martin *sotto voce* assurances of his undying intention of "landing" him ultimately on his posterior. Democracy and domesticity! There was something to be learned from the picture. The feudal army may not always carry the day.

> On 2 March 1916, the battalion was relieved by the 8th Gordons in what must well have started to become a well-oiled routine. The relief took place at 07.00 hours and was completed without any casualties being suffered.[1]
>
> It was also on this day that Winston sailed back across the Channel for a spell of leave, with Archie Sinclair being left in charge of the battalion. When he reached London Winston learnt that the Naval Estimates were to be introduced in the Commons five days later. He immediately decided that he would use the debate that would follow to tackle the man who had taken over at the Admiralty, Arthur Balfour.
>
> Winston had not spoken in the House as a critic of the Government for twelve years. During that time he had been a part of the decision-making process of the incumbent administration. Now he owed no allegiance to the Prime Minister or the Cabinet. So Winston was going on the offensive. It would be a role for which Churchill would become renowned in the years before the Second

World War when his was a lone voice arguing against a policy of appeasement towards the Nazi regime in Germany.

Winston criticized all aspects of the direction in which the Royal Navy was being taken by Balfour. 'A strategic policy for the Navy, purely negative in character, by no means necessarily implies that the path of greatest prudence is being followed.' Winston said. 'I wish to place on record that the late Board would certainly not have been content with an attitude of pure passivity during the whole of the year 1916 ... we cannot afford to allow any delay to creep into the execution of our [warship building] programme ... To lose momentum is not merely to stop, but to fall ... Blood and money, however lavishly poured out, would never repair the consequences of what might be even an unconscious relaxation of effort.'[2]

Winston might have received much support for his condemnation of the apparent lack of progress at the Admiralty since he had left the previous year. But he then went on to propose that Sir Henry Jackson, the First Sea Lord, should be dismissed and his place taken once again by Lord Fisher – the man who had been instrumental in Winston's downfall!

Winston's speech met with disbelief and derision, and was heavily condemned by the Press the following day. Proposing the return of Fisher, who had repeatedly threatened to resign in the past and who was now considered a man of the past, was a terrible mistake. There was also no identifiable or known reason why Henry Jackson should be dismissed. His attack on the Government, which he hoped would lead to its collapse and Churchill's return to power and influence, failed. 'You will one day discover,' commented Lloyd George, 'why you do not win trust even where you command admiration ... national interests are completely overshadowed by your personal concern.'

On the 9th Asquith asked Winston to see him at 10 Downing Street. He told Winston that his father, Lord Randolph Churchill, had committed political suicide through one impulsive action and he urged Winston not to follow the same path. He told Winston that, at the present time, he had few political friends either inside or outside Cabinet and that there was no office that he could offer him. He told Winston that one day he would come back, indeed, must come back, to a position within government – 'If only he isn't killed,' Asquith told his daughter Violet Bonham Carter. Supposing that he were killed – what should *we* feel, those of us who have urged him to go back? I could only advise him to do what I am sure is right – right above all for his own sake.'[3]

Others wanted Churchill to continue his assault upon the Government and a by-election on 10 March in East Hertfordshire saw the Coalition candidate heavily defeated. Winston was told that there was 'seething discontent throughout the masses', and he was encouraged to believe that if he persisted he could bring the Government down, with the tempting prospect that he could lead the next administration. Asquith, however, advised Winston that 'As you are returning [to France] with my full approval to your military function at the front, I wish to assure you that hereafter you should find that your sense of public duty called upon you to return to political life here, no obstacle will be put in your way.'

Winston was far from reassured, and a number of his friends urged him to lead the parliamentary opposition in the Commons. Winston, though, was due back with his battalion and so, on 13 March, Colonel Churchill set off for Dover.

Before leaving the UK he sent a letter to Asquith asking to be relieved of his command. Whilst his demand for the return of Fisher had been unwise, there was a strong anti-government sentiment in the country and Winston felt that he could take advantage of that. But he was convinced that if he was to make his mark once again in politics he had to act now.

Churchill returned to Ploegsteert and discussed the situation with Archie Sinclair, who, as some had also done, advised Winston not to make a precipitate return to Westminster without being able to claim a justifiable reason for leaving his battalion. The battalion, meanwhile, had come out of the line at 06.30 hours on the morning of 14 March, being relieved as ever by the 8th Gordons.

It is interesting to note that Winston was now convinced that his true stage was in the debating chamber and not the muddy trenches of Flanders. In his first week back in reserve the unpopular General Walshe was relieved of his command and fresh hopes arose of Winston being offered command of the brigade. Just a few weeks earlier this was a position Churchill would have treasured, now it was of little interest to him.

When it was dark on the evening of Winston's return to Ploegsteert he and Sinclair took a walk along the front line to the right of the ground held by the 6th RSF, and visited the headquarters of the battalion.

There had been a number of incidents of note whilst Winston had been away. For example, on the 10th it was recorded that during the hours of darkness there had been 'much more rifle fire from the enemy than usual. Our patrols reported that at every point the enemy is much more vigilant than before'. It was surmised that a German 'relief had probably occurred'.[4] Then, at around 10.00 hours on 11 March, three men of 'B' Company had been severely wounded by what the battalion War Diary describes as 'a new German front line bomb' while sitting in the mouth of a dugout. Two of the men died from their wounds. At 14.30 hours, the Scots responded by firing fifty rifle-grenades at the German line and fired twenty rounds from their trench mortars. They followed that up again the next day, with once again fifty rifle-grenades and eighteen mortar bombs.

The battalion was scheduled to return to the front on 20 March and Winston felt that by that time he would have made his decision to leave the Army. On 17 March he read of the Army debate which had taken place in the Commons and he saw how, with his first-hand experience, he could have materially influenced the course of the debate. This made him even more aware that in Flanders he could do nothing of any real importance, and that he had to return to Westminster. 'My conviction strengthens and deepens each day,' he told Clementine in a letter he wrote that night, 'and that I could fill it with credit and public advantage.'

In that same letter he also made an interesting, and salutary, observation: 'We are elated to have our little town [Ploegsteert] mentioned in Haig's daily report as a scene of artillery activity. The odd thing is that this mention occurs *the day before* the shelling took place! How history is written.'

With the passing of each day Winston became increasingly restless, despairing of every moment lost in which he was not speaking out in Parliament about the direction and management of the war. Even his letters home, which used to be so full of exciting anecdotes and amusing tales had taken a more solemn tone:

'This evening Archie and I took a stroll up the lines on our right and went to the HQrs of the battalion there. The same conditions and features reproduce themselves in every section – shattered buildings, sandbag habitations, trenches heavily wired, shell holes, frequent graveyards with thickets of little crosses, rank wild growing grass, muddy roads, khaki soldiers – and so on for hundreds and of miles – on both sides. Miserable Europe.'

This visit made him even more conscious of the fact that out on the front line he was just one of thousands of officers, little able to make any significant difference to the outcome of the war, which seemed to have no end. At any moment a lucky shell or a stray bullet could end his life altogether, and then, in his own mind, he would have achieved little in his life. But for Winston money was an almost constant concern, and the salary of a Brigadier-General was not to be dismissed out of hand. If promotion was offered to him, he told Clementine that he would consider accepting it.

It was not to be. Command of the 27th Brigade was handed to Colonel Gerald Trotter who had been in the British Army since 1885 and was a Major in the Grenadier Guards. Ranks in the Guards regiments were rated one step higher than in the line and county regiments, so his Army equivalent was the same as Winston's – though he could have few complaints at Trotter being given command of the brigade, as his service was continuous unlike Winston's, and his front line experience was greater. Nevertheless, it further reinforced his growing belief that he 'had no prospects' with the BEF and that his rightful place was in Parliament.

Yet he told Clementine that he 'did not mind a bit' being under Trotter's command. If I were to stay out here, I cd hardly be better suited than where I am. A Brigade wd give me no more scope and less personal interest. There is no doubt at all in my mind as to what I ought to do.' He did not elaborate further on that comment but it was clear that what he meant was he had decided to return to Westminster.

The 6th RSF moved into the trenches at 06.30 hours on 20 March and Winston was soon back at Laurence Farm. His mind, previously so focussed on matters military when at the front, was now more frequently preoccupied with his next political move. If he was to leave the government benches and lead the Opposition, it would be a major gamble. He would be setting himself against the major political figures in the country. He had earlier in his political career changed sides and in doing so had created many powerful enemies. Was he really prepared to risk alienating what few friends he still had left in the government?

What he was hoping for was some significant change in his circumstances that would provide him with a reason for resigning his command. He could then return to the House of Commons to save the nation from what was seen widely as the disastrous mismanagement of the war following the Dardanelles fiasco and the Shell Scandal and no apparent improvement in the situation of the Allies on the Western Front.

He marshalled his thoughts in a letter to Clementine on 22 March from Laurence Farm, justifying his decision to leave the Army. These crystallized into four headings:

- That he was not motivated by personal gain because he gave up a salary of £4,300 per annum with the Duchy of Lancaster to serve his country in the field.
- That he had served for almost five months on the Western Front, much of it in the front line not at GHQ.
- He was a long-established politician who had held senior cabinet posts and would be better employed in the Commons than in the trenches.
- That the country's fortunes were 'critical and grave' and he therefore could not 'exclude himself' or 'divest himself of responsibilities' by absenting himself from the House at this vital time.

Winston really does seem to have believed that he could return to Westminster and sweep all before him, oust

Asquith and lead the country. But the reality was that few MPs would fight against the Coalition. Before the end of the year Asquith would be forced from power with the resignations of Lloyd George and Balfour. That, though, was many months in the future, by which time the Battle of the Somme had been fought, with its shocking casualties, and the country was outraged at conscription being extended to married men.

Now, though, was not the time and Lord Curzon counselled caution. He reminded him that, having resigned from office only a few months before, to then resign from the Army might give the impression that he had 'acted spasmodically or without sound and deliberate judgement.' Similarly, Clementine warned him not to 'break' himself 'as an instrument by a premature return, and very succinctly said to him, 'Your motive for going to the Front was easy to understand. Your motive for coming back requires explanation.'

In another letter she told him that by remaining with the army he was in an 'honourable' position. 'You say you want to be where you can help the war most. If you come home and your return is not generally accepted as correct soldier-like conduct you will not be really able to help the war. You *are* helping it now by example.'

Others also suggested that Winston should bide his time, pointing out that he was only forty-one and could wait even a year or two and it would not diminish his standing in the country.

Winston would not listen to these wise words. He stated that, 'nothing will now turn me from my intention.' He was encouraged in this by a letter from C.P. Scott, the Editor of the *Manchester Guardian*, who told him that the Opposition was leaderless 'and waits for you to lead it'.

Winston also argued that even if a strong Opposition movement developed the MPs were hardly likely to write to an officer in the field to ask him to come back and lead them. It would be a case of out of sight, out of mind, and the longer he stayed away from Westminster, the more his influence would wane. 'If I wait for a Ministerial crisis,' he explained to Clementine, 'will it not look as if I had come back like a sultan hastening unbidden to a feast'.

Though he was steadfast in his resolve, he had a particularly black moment on 24 March 1916 when he was walking up to the trenches, remarking that he would not mind 'very much' if he stopped living, declaring, in a moment of bleak honesty, 'I am so devoured by egotism'.

He could hear shells falling on his left, with each shot coming closer, 'as the gun travelled round searching for prey. One cd calculate more or less where the next would come. Our road led naturally past the ruined convent (where I have made the "Conning Tower") and I said "the next will hit the convent". Sure enough just as we got abreast of it, the shell arrived with a screech and a roar and tremendous bang and showers of bricks and clouds of smoke and all the soldiers jumped and scurried, and peeped out of their holes and corners. It did not make me jump a bit – not a pulse quickened … But I felt – 20 yards more to the left and no more tangles to unravel, no more anxieties to face, no more hatreds and injustices to encounter: joy of all my foes … a good ending to a chequered life, a final gift – unvalued – to an ungrateful country – an impoverishment of the war-making power of Britain which no one wd ever know or measure or mourn.'

In later life Winston would become seriously affected by depression, which he referred to as his 'Black Dog,' and already Clementine had witnessed how he could be thrown into bouts of deep despair when things went badly for him. She did not want him to return to Parliament, expecting great things only for him to be snubbed again. She knew that he would take it very badly.

Yet, for every word of caution, there followed one of incitement to action. Sir Arthur Markham wrote that it was clear, in his opinion, that he could be more effective commanding the House than commanding a battalion. 'All that I want is to see effective opposition for the good of the country.'

There was now little in Winston's letters about the 6th RSF, their content being directed towards seeking the advice of friends, and of paving the way for his return (describing the latter as the equivalent of having to cut through the barbed-wire before he could launch his assault). He learnt all he could about which issues were likely to bring down Asquith's administration and what alliances he might be able to form.

His letters of early April demonstrate to what extent he was plotting the Government's downfall and it was the question of universal conscription that clearly offered the best chance of bringing down Asquith. Anti-conscription organisations had grown up around the UK and a number of people had been arrested for producing anti-conscription literature. The debates in the Commons were very heated with both sides accusing each other of betraying the country.

Asquith was consequently very reluctant to introduce universal conscription though it was seen by most people to be not just inevitable but essential. The Prime Minister was regarded as the main obstacle to the introduction of the bill and this, Winston believed, offered him the opportunity he sought. He could return from the battlefield to lead the fight for universal conscription on behalf of the men in the trenches. It would play very well.

Clementine continued to try to dissuade him, saying that he was 'deluded' if he thought that he could bring down the government. This did not dissuade Churchill in any measure, particularly as on 9 April he received a letter from Lord Carson who held a Cabinet post as leader of the Irish Unionists telling him how severely divided the administration really was and that he did not see how it could hold together much longer.

Winston fired off letters to Lloyd George and C.P. Scott telling them that he was going to return to Westminster very shortly to gauge their reaction. He also wrote to the Attorney General, F.E. Smith, putting forward his opposition to the persistent idea that the Allies should always be mounting offensive operations against well-prepared enemy defences with the resultant high casualties. 'Let the Germans attack if they will', he wrote, whilst stating that probably the exact opposite will happen. He was proved quite right, of course, as only a few months later, on 1 July, Haig mounted the BEF's largest offensive of the war on the Somme which led to the highest number of casualties the British Army had ever experienced.

Winston's hopes of leading the Opposition received a severe blow when Lord Milner declared openly that universal compulsory military service was essential for the survival of the country and received widespread support. The Opposition now had a prominent and well-respected leader. It did not need Winston Churchill.

What made the situation even worse for Winston was that he and Lord Milner had history. Milner was Governor of Cape Colony and High Commissioner for Southern Africa during the Boer War. Winston had publicly criticized Milner's handling of the war and the two men had become bitter enemies. So not only did the Opposition have a leader, its leader would never allow Churchill a position of any standing within that group.

Winston was now in a situation where he was not wanted by either the Government or the Opposition. His only hope, he believed, lay in Asquith being forced to stand down due to pressure from within the Coalition Government. Alternatively, if the Coalition broke up, he might stand a chance, once again, of claiming a position within any reformed administration. This, though, was supposed to be a time of national unity and such a division within the Cabinet was hard to contemplate. Though this would come later, when Asquith resigned under pressure from his ministers, but in the early months of 1916 it was a step too far.

Milner's move, however, did oblige Asquith to seek to explain his position on conscription at a Secret Session of Parliament and when he learnt of this Winston applied for leave to attend. This, it might seem surprising, was granted and on 19 April 1916 he returned to London – but on the strict understanding that as soon as the session was over he would return to his battalion.

The session was a disappointment for Churchill as he was without party and without influence. He saw his career as a leading politician fading rapidly and it confirmed his belief that the longer he remained away from Westminster, the weaker his position would become. He therefore asked for a further two week's extension of his leave.

Whilst Haig had no objection to Winston remaining in Britain a little longer, Major General Furse certainly did and Winston had no choice but to return to Ploegsteert.

On 27 April Parliament met in open session to discuss conscription but to his utter frustration Winston could not be there. It proved to be a decisive debate and Asquith finally succumbed. A week later, on 3 May, a new Bill was put before the House of Commons extending compulsory military service to all men between the ages of eighteen and forty-one. The one subject that Winston had advocated before any other, and the one that offered him the greatest platform from which he could launch attacks upon the current administration, was no longer a subject of debate. The Bill was passed and Asquith remained as Prime Minister.

Winston, true to his oft-stated motto of 'Never give in', saw this as only a temporary setback. He was firmly of the opinion that the war was being run badly and that whilst this particular crisis had passed, others would soon follow – and when the next one came along he could not afford to be on the other side of the Channel. Churchill had made up his mind; he was going to end his long military career and resign his commission.

As it transpired, a favourable opportunity to leave the Army with dignity and his reputation intact was about to present itself. There were discussions at GHQ about the possibility of amalgamating the weakened 6th RSF with its sister 7th Battalion, both of which were below average strength. This would mean that either Winston or the commander of the 7th Battalion would not be required. Lieutenant Colonel Edward Ian Drumearn Gordon, who commanded the 7th Battalion was a regular officer who had been with the Royal Scots Fusiliers since 1899, and was therefore senior to the part-time solder Churchill. He told Clementine on 29 April that the battalion was likely to be broken up within ten days and that after the completion of its present tour, it would not return to the trenches.

Winston discussed the situation with Haig, whom, one source claimed, offered Churchill command of a brigade but had said that he would do more for the Army and the country by using his energies to drive the conscription Bill through Parliament. As Violet Bonham Carter once recalled, Churchill 'wanted above all things to be back on his old battlefield in Parliament'![5]

Churchill, Violet Bonham Carter, added, 'wrote to Lord Kitchener asking to be released from the Army. Lord Kitchener, knowing that he faced criticism whatever his reply, accepted Winston's resignation on condition that he undertook not to apply for military service again during the war.'[6]

Haig may have welcomed the opportunity to be rid of a potentially meddlesome politician and his offer of a brigade was most probably spurious. Winston, with just as much political acumen, declared that to his regret he saw the wisdom in Haig's words and that he accepted that he could be of greater service to the BEF in Westminster than Flanders.

On 3 May Winston led the 6th Battalion, Royal Scots Fusiliers out of the trenches for the last time. He also then wrote to his Corps Commander, General Sir Charles Fergusson, stating that he did not want further employment with the BEF preferring instead to return to his Parliamentary duties.

Three days later Winston took leave of his battalion with a farewell lunch with his officers at Armentières. After the meal, that afternoon, 6 May, the 6th RSF left by train for Béthune. The following day the battalion was inspected by the General Officer Commanding the 15th Division. It was also on the 7th, notes the War Diary, that 'Colonel W.S. Churchill left the battalion'. The 6th RSF's new CO, albeit only temporarily, was Captain A.D. Gibb.

A week later the battalion was amalgamated with the 7th Battalion to form the 6th/7th Royal Scots Fusiliers.

This was not quite the end for the battalion as an independent entity. Though the 6th/7th RSF was disbanded at the end of the First World War, it resurfaced in the Second World War, serving, this time, with the 15th (Scottish) Division. It was, though, the end of Winston's military career, and ahead were political battles which he never seemed to enjoy quite as much as those he fought in Flanders.

Chapter 14

Finale

In early 1916 evil days came to the Scottish regiments. No Scotsman, who remembers a little that Scotland is not England, can fail to be moved by the contemplation of his own little country's efforts in the war. Speaking in Glasgow in 1915 Mr. Lloyd George told his audience that so far Scotland had contributed the greatest number of men to the Army proportionately to her population.

Whether or not this could be said at the end of things I know not, but certain it is that in 1916 it became increasingly difficult to find enough Scotsmen to fill the gaps in the Scottish regiments. A process of amalgamating battalions set in, and our battalion was eventually marked down for amalgamation with the 7th (Service) Battalion of the Regiment, then serving in the 15th Division. This was a very bitter pill to us, and we thought the shoe was on the other foot and that the battalions of the 15th Division should have been incorporated with the battalions of the 9th Division and served with us. The change also meant that some of us at least would be cast upon the world, as a battalion cadre could not contain the entire strength of the two existing battalions. It was soon decided who was to go to the new battalion, and in the first place our Colonel, as the junior, had to give way to the C.O. of the 7th Battalion.

We went into billets with the 9th Division for the last time at a place called Papôt, near Le Romarin. We were all very sick about the business, but a change is always interesting, so we managed to be interested as well. There was a large farewell luncheon party: there were farewell visits by the Staff: there were farewell parades: there were even farewell "drunks." The General allowed us to have our photographs taken, and thus it is that with the aid of an unwashed and Semitic artist of Armentières, the monstrous souvenir which forms a frontispiece to many war albums was "secured." The Colonel, as may be seen, played the man and wore his Glengarry bonnet. The perfidy of Sinclair, false Scot, is recorded for all time!

During our stay at Papôt the Colonel and the Adjutant paid a visit to the 7th Battalion, then at Vermelles. They were patronised by all ranks from the G.O.C. downwards. The G.O.C. was McCracken, a distinguished laconic soldier. He once came to lecture to the Reserve Battalions at Fort Matilda and warned us against doing various acts which he stigmatised as being "bad for" various things, and wound up by solemnly cautioning us against leaving lamps on the road, as if mechanical transport passed over them it would be "bad for lamps."

He entertained the Colonel and the Adjutant to luncheon in his magnificent country seat outside Béthune. The chief entertainment provided by the battalion authorities was a recitation by one member after another, of the usual daily number of killed, wounded, and missing in that sector. The amalgamation seemed more impolitic than ever.

But at last the way having been made smooth by those emissaries, the battalion did entrain, at Steenwerck, for Béthune. There was a great deal of handshaking and saluting and well-wishing: a great deal of lung-inflation by the pipers: a great deal of confusion in the staff-arrangements and the usual amount of cursing by the troops. The train started late in the afternoon, and I found myself with the acting-doctor and the Colonel in possession of a compartment. I had realized earlier that while the doctor, as a doctor, was doubtless all that was most accomplished, as a mess-president he scarcely appreciated his responsibilities. I had accordingly seen fit to fill a large hamper with every variety of food and drink which I could find in the Mess. My plans were appreciated and the Colonel, in one of those amusingly naif confessions of his, said when an altogether unexpected bottle of whisky was produced, "Whatever else they may say of me, my dear X———, at least nobody can say I have failed to display a meet and proper appreciation of the virtues of alcohol."[1]

Arrived at Béthune the Battalion proceeded to wander about and lose itself in the town as a result of the excellent arrangements made for us by the Divisional Staff. However, we did eventually get settled down and had a somewhat noisy supper at the restaurant then opposite the station. Winston was in splendid form, and was much gaped at by the astonished soldiery as also by the demoiselles of the eating-house. That was the last evening he spent with the Battalion.

On the following day there was an inspection by the General Officer Commanding the Division, and to our great amusement he invited the Colonel's attention to the case of a private soldier who was manifestly unshaven. If the General's own face enjoyed the ministrations of a razor that morning, it was a razor of a surprising benignity and inefficiency. Winston took what was probably his last telling off with his usual sang-froid.

At 2 p.m. there was an orderly-room, to which all officers were summoned. The Adjutant had been going about looking worried: he was taciturn and at lunch he drank both whisky and brandy, though he usually drank neither. As we were going into the orderly-room he said to me, "I'm going to make a speech: Winston's been devilish decent to us and he'd like to hear that the officers appreciate him. All the same it's a ticklish job."

The Colonel said a few words, a few very kind words, of farewell. He told us, I remember, that he had come to regard the young Scot as a most "formidable fighting animal," and he touched on his other connections with Scotland in the most appreciative fashion. As he rose to shake hands, the Adjutant spoke up and told him what we were all thinking, and what it had been to us to serve under him. Certainly he was sincere and I believe every man in the room felt Winston Churchill's leaving us as a real personal loss.

Gibb's final entry in his diary provides us with possibly the most endearing picture of Winston at the front: '1 May: WSC brought gramophone into the yard @ 6pm and all the men came out and sat around with WSC in the middle reading Shakespeare - funny, surreal scene.'

It has been very difficult to avoid being fulsome in writing these few scrappy notes about Churchill. I am firmly convinced that no more popular officer ever commanded troops. As a soldier he was hard-working, persevering and thorough. The expected fireworks never came off. He was out to work hard at tiresome but indispensable detail and to make his unit efficient in the very highest possible degree. I say nothing of his tactical and strategic ability – these were not tested in our time, but I cannot conceive that exceptionally creative and fertile brain failing in any sphere of human activity to which it was applied. And moreover, he loved soldiering: it lay very near his heart and I think he could have been a very great soldier. How often have we heard him say by way of encouragement in difficult circumstances, "War is a game to be played with a smiling face." And never was precept more consistently practised than this.

I speak with all possible warmth and affection of him as the friend of his officers. This was most strikingly demonstrated in the last days of his command when he was anxious to find employment, congenial employment, for those who were to be thrown out into the cold when the battalions amalgamated. He took endless trouble: he borrowed motor-cars and *scoured* France, interviewing Generals and Staff-officers great and small, in the effort to do something to help those who had served under him. Needless to say, the orderly-room was seething with applications of all sorts, possible and impossible, but he treated them all with the utmost patience and good humour. No man was ever kinder to his subordinates and no commanding officer I have ever known was half so kind.

There is little more to be said. The early months of 1916 are by far my most treasured war-memory. It was my happiest time and it was my most interesting time. For work in intimate association with Winston Churchill was the last experience in the world any of us expected – our course did not lie that way. At first the prospect frightened us, but those feelings did not survive the first week. We came to realize, to realize at first hand, his transcendent ability. He came to be looked on as really a possession of our own, and one of which we were intensely proud. And much more, he became our friend. He is a man who apparently is always to have enemies. He made none in his old regiment, but left behind him there men who will always be his loyal partizans and admirers, and who are proud of having served in the Great War under the leadership of one who is beyond question a great man.

> Lieutenant McDavid also had fond memories of Winston's time with the RSF: 'No detail of our daily life was too small for him to ignore. He overlooked nothing ... Instead of a quick glance at what was being done he would stop and talk with everyone and probe to the bottom of every activity. I have never known an officer take such pains to inspire confidence or gain confidence; indeed he inspired confidence in gaining it.'
>
> The author Frank Brennand once described Winston as 'a soldier's soldier': 'That is most of his time was spent among the ranks who had to carry out his orders and suffer their consequences. He was not above sharing his sentry's guard and talking the situation over with him. He consulted N.C.O.s almost as often as he consulted officers. He made war on lice and dirt as well as on Germans and by the time he left the 6th Royal Scots had an *esprit de corps* rivalling that of some crack regiment.'[2]
>
> The Official History of the Royal Scots Fusiliers summarised Winston's period with the regiment: 'The 6th Battalion, in the 27th Brigade of the Ninth Division, spent three months of 1916 in the Ploegsteert section of the front. Few incidents marked these months, the last of its

existence as a separate unit, but it served under a most distinguished commander.

'Mr Winston Churchill had ceased to be First Lord of the Admiralty on the reconstruction of the Ministry in the early summer of 1915, and his energy of mind could not long be content with the nominal duties of the Chancellor of the Duchy of Lancaster. A soldier by profession, and a profound student of the military art, he went to France in the early winter of 1915, and at the close of the year was put in command of the 6th Royal Scots Fusiliers. The advent of so famous and controversial a figure was awaited with a certain trepidation, but a week's experience of Colonel Churchill sufficed to convince doubters, and when the 6th Battalion was united with the 7th one of the chief matters of regret to its officers was that they must lose their commanding officer.'

Writing on 4 April 1916, Churchill expressed similar views: 'I can assure you that I shall always regard this period when I have had the honour to command a battalion of this prestigious regiment in the field, one of the most memorable in my life.'[3]

Part III

Chapter 15

Back From The Front

If Churchill expected to be welcomed back into Westminster as the saviour of the nation, he was to be sorely disappointed. The revolt by those demanding universal conscription, which Winston could have led, was quashed when Asquith finally agreed to accept the bill. The Prime Minister, though, was not willing to extend conscription to Ireland where the political temperature was very hot, following the suppression of the Easter Rising in Dublin the previous month. A debate on this subject was scheduled for 9 May, just two days after his return from Flanders.

Churchill spoke against the Irish exclusion clause but without being able to garner the support he sought. All he achieved by opposing the Government was further isolation. Winston continued to argue against Government policy from the Opposition benches.

With conscription still a highly contentious issue, Winston spoke out about the wastefulness of manpower he had witnessed during his time at the front:

> From all the sources of the population not now in uniform, and the sources of this country, it would appear that there are several important sources from which we may draw supplies of men for the fighting line. I shall proceed to examine five large reservoirs of men which are capable of being drawn upon scientifically and systematically to feed the necessities of our fighting lines. I say our fighting lines advisedly, because the first part of

the argument which I am asking the indulgence of the House to be allowed to unfold to them is that our fighting troops do not bear any due or any sufficient proportion to the total numbers of our Army. That is the first proposition with which I start, and therefore I select as the first of our reservoirs for examination this afternoon our armies already in the field.

The first thing that strikes a visitor to our Armies in France or in Flanders – and I make no doubt that our armies in the East exhibit a similar condition – is the very large number of officers and men in the prime of their military manhood who never, or only very rarely, go under the fire of the enemy. In fact, you perceive one of the clearest and grimmest class distinctions ever drawn in this world – the distinction between the trench and the non-trench population.

All our soldiers, all our officers, are brave and honest men. All are doing their duty, a necessary duty, and are ready to do any other duty which they may be asked to perform. But the fact remains that the trench population lives almost continuously under the fire of the enemy. It returns again and again, after being wounded twice and sometimes three times, to the front and to the trenches, and it is continually subject, without respite, to the hardest of tests that men have ever been called upon to bear, while all the time the non-trench population scarcely suffers at all, and has good food and good wages, higher wages in a great many cases than are drawn by the men under fire every day, and their share of the decorations and rewards is so disproportionate that it has passed into a byword.

I wish to point out to the House this afternoon that the part of the Army that really counts for ending the War is this killing, fighting, suffering part.[1]

All those who had ever served at the front would have cheered this speech by Winston, but he had more to say. He pointed out that keeping battalions under-strength resulted in disproportionately fewer actual fighting men. This was because in every battalion there are between around 200 and 250 who are employed on the transport, signalling, and orderly services, and as stretcher bearers, clerks, servants, cooks, musicians, road wardens, and brigade and divisional employees. Whether the battalion is 800 strong or 1,200 strong, the same subtraction of around 200 or so men is made. The more battalions means more non-fighting men. Winston had experienced this with the 6th RSF which had wisely been amalgamated with the 7th Battalion, and he advocated an extension of this.

He continued to argue against the Government, long and hard, from the Opposition benches, but it was from the back benches that he spoke for he had no official position. His opposition angered many who still saw Winston as the architect of the Gallipoli campaign and he repeatedly found himself under attack. Other aspects of his time at the Admiralty also came under scrutiny. This was particularly the case regarding the establishment of an Air Department which the Government was intent on forming. This new body would coordinate the operations and policy of the Royal Naval Air Service and the Royal Flying Corps. As much of the early aviation had been led by the Royal Navy, Winston felt he was the man to take charge of such a body. His opponents believed that whilst he had been at the Admiralty he should have concentrated on boats and ships and left the air service to develop under its own leaders.

Many of Churchill's speeches at this time were in defence of his own record, which he was happy to do, as each one was an opportunity for him to speak his mind and for him to explain his conduct before the House. To some Churchill's persistent wrangling was nothing more than an attempt to make headlines for the journalists, and to keep him in the news. His proposed policies certainly had great popular appeal. He attacked the Government for not making use of the large numbers of African and Indian men who had volunteered for service in the Imperial Army and had not yet been allocated a posting. He persisted in his arguments against what he saw as futile and appallingly costly offensives which Haig, and the Government, continued to promote. 'Do not let us be drawn into any course of action not justified by purely military considerations,' he argued. The argument which is used that 'it is our turn now' has no place in military thought.'

Winston did not believe that victory could be achieved by throwing men at the German defences, and the events of 1 July on the Somme, just a few weeks after this speech demonstrated just how right Churchill had been. He continued to attack Government policy, but his lone offensive did him no good, though his words were eagerly consumed by the Press, and he received many supportive letters from the general public.

Winston also demanded the publication of all the minutes and decisions of the Government concerning the Dardanelles campaign. This, he knew, would show that it was not just his decision to attack the Dardanelles and that from an early stage he had advocated the employment of ground forces which had been withheld by Kitchener. When the truth was known, Winston believed, his policies would be vindicated and another bar to his return to high office would have been removed. It was not to be. Asquith refused to present the Dardanelles papers on the grounds of national security.

The turbulence in the Government, that Winston so dearly sought to exploit for his own ends finally surfaced. It was agreed that the management of the war should be delegated to a three-man War Committee which Lloyd George, as Secretary of State for War, insisted should be chaired by him. Asquith agreed to this, on the basis that he could step in whenever he chose. However, a newspaper article suggested that Asquith was being sidelined and called for Lloyd George to become Prime Minister. At this Asquith said that he was going to take back chairmanship of the War Committee. Lloyd George then resigned as did Arthur Balfour the First Lord of the Admiralty.

Facing this rebellion, Asquith received King George's permission to demand his ministers' resignations and reconstruct his government, believing that this would bring everyone into line under his authority – but he misjudged the situation. The following day, 6 December 1916, the Leader of the Conservatives, Bonar Law, Lloyd George, Arthur Balfour, and the Leader of the Labour Party, met at Buckingham Palace. In the resultant discussions it was made clear to Asquith that he could no longer expect the support of either the leading Conservatives or Liberals. After being in power for more than eight years, H.H. Asquith resigned and Lloyd George became Prime Minster.

This was a disaster for Winston who had seen himself as leading the next administration. His only hope lay in being offered a position in the new Cabinet But it was not to be. The Conservatives still refused to sit in the same Government as Churchill.

Though it seemed that Winston's political career was at an end, his banishment from power was only temporary and in 1917 he was appointed Minister of Munitions. At the time he was one of two MPs for the constituency of Dundee. Under the Parliamentary rules applying at the time, Members of Parliament appointed to ministerial posts had to resign their seats and fight a by-election, though since the start of the war an electoral truce had existed between the main political parties by which it was agreed that all by-election vacancies would be filled unopposed by the party holding the seat. Churchill, however, was not to face an uncontested election.

During the campaign leading up to the by-election, Churchill's service on the Western Front was often to bring him much support. For example, five days before polling day, which was on 30 July 1917, Bandmaster W. Robertson, serving with the Royal Scots Fusiliers at Fort Matilda, Greenock, wrote to the *Daily Record*:

> 'I see that a candidate is opposing the re-election of Mr. Winston Churchill as a member of Parliament for Dundee, and that he is being supported by the Discharged Soldiers' Association.
>
> 'As is well known, the 6th Battalion of my regiment was commanded by Col. Winston Churchill for some time, and, if you think it necessary, I am prepared to come to

Dundee at my own expense and let the people know how highly he was esteemed by all under his command, how well he cared for the comfort and welfare of the men, and the great reputation he has with the rank and file who served with him.

'Personally, I did not have the honour of serving with him, but as the oldest in service of the Royal Scots Fusiliers, I made it a point of seeing all those who have been wounded and invalided on their arrival here, and all the 6th Battalion lads have been unanimous in their expressions – "One of the very best." "He would do everything for us, and we would do anything for him," and so on. Not one man could find any hole to pick with their C.O.'s methods, and there were men who had served under many other officers of the best type.

'We Fusiliers think that our old C.O. of the 6th Battalion deserves the very best position in which his power of initiative and forethought can be utilised for the benefit of the country, and if it lay in our power we would see him back in the House of Commons without a contest.

'I am only voicing the opinion of the 6th Battalion lads here when I say that our best wishes are with Mr. Winston Churchill in the election and in his work as Minister of Munitions. Do not forget to command my services if you consider it necessary, and I will be honoured at being permitted to help people realise that his old regiment regard their old colonel, Winston Churchill, as one of the bravest and best of the many splendid colonels the old regiment has been blessed with.'[2]

No doubt helped by supporters such as Bandmaster Robertson, Churchill won a resounding victory during the by-election. The result was a hold for the government party with Winston taking nearly 80% of the poll and a majority 5,266 votes.

Over the years that followed, Churchill's political fortunes continued to fluctuate until 10 May 1940 when at last he became

Prime Minister and led his country through the Second World War.

Despite all his fame and his achievements, Winston's brief spell in the trenches showed the true nature of the man – brave, kind and generous, possibly not the image usually associated with this renowned British bulldog. It was on 12 April 1916 that Clementine wrote these words to Winston at Ploegsteert when he was planning on returning to Westminster: 'I could not bear you to lose your military halo. I have had cause during the 8 years we have lived together to be proud and glad for you so often, but it is this I cherish most of all. And it is this phase which, when all is known, will strike the imagination of the people: The man who prepared and mobilized the Fleet, who really won the war for England – in the trenches as a simple Colonel. It would be a great romance.'

How right she was.

When Winston's old battalion was merged with the 7th Battalion to form the 6th/7th Royal Scots Fusiliers, Dewar Gibb was given command of a company in the regiment's 1st Battalion. At Winston's instigation he was sent on a Staff Course at Cambridge, following which he was appointed Staff Captain, Northern Command, at Lichfield. Shortly thereafter he was transferred to the War Office, although he repeatedly requested a return to the front line, and sought Winston's help in this. Eventually his transfer was accepted and an appointment came through, only for it to coincide with the Armistice in November 1918, and the posting was cancelled. Captain Gibb remained at the War Office until the spring of 1919 when he was demobbed.

Winston never forgot his brief spell with the Royal Scots Fusiliers nor did those that served under him. There are letters in the Churchill Archives that show Winston used what influence he had to help former members of the battalion that appealed to him to find employment during the difficult years of the early 1930s.

In particular, Winston maintained contact with his former adjutant, and at various times over the years after the First World War they corresponded. Winston congratulated Gibb on being called to the Bar, stating that his wartime experience would help him face the battleground of the courtroom.

Equally, Dewar Gibb remembered his old lieutenant-colonel with great pride and affection, as his recollections of their time together show so well. When he decided to write his brief memoir of Winston with the 6th RSF he sent the manuscript to his old colonel before publication. After viewing it for the first time Winston had second thoughts and asked to see it again, 'as there may be one or two expressions attributed to me which ought not to appear in print'. Winston was ever the cautious politician.

When Dewar Gibb failed to win the seat for Hamilton when he stood for the Unionist Party in the 1924 general election, Winston was quick to send his condolences, saying that he believed that 'the Conservative Party ought to get some young fellows like you with good war records to settle down as Candidates in some of those seats where there has been so much rowdyism.'

When Winston lost the 1945 election, Dewar Gibb likewise sent a message of sympathy to his former commander, whom he always referred to as 'Colonel Churchill'. Then, when Winston resigned his leadership of the Conservative Party on 6 April 1955, Dewar Gibb wrote the following:

'I would like to write a line or two to say how sorry I am to hear that you are giving up the Premiership which you have so richly adorned. But no man has ever deserved leisure as you do ... It is small wonder that no statesman has ever gained the affection and gratitude of his country as you have done.'

Gibb signed himself off in this last letter to Winston as a 'most grateful admirer'.[3]

Chapter 16

Following in Churchill's Footsteps: A Visitor's Guide to Plugstreet

Most visitors to Ploegsteert will visit Ieper or be based in or around that lovely Belgian city. The French spelling, Ypres, is no longer used and local people are keen to emphasise their Flemish identity. It is from Ieper that the N336, the Rijselseweg, travels the nine miles south to Ploegsteert. At Sint-Elooi the road branches, and it is the right-hand fork, the N365 (which becomes the Iperstraat), that continues on to Wijtschate, Mesen (Messines), Ploegsteert and then beyond to Armentières.

It was in 1914 that Ploegsteert was first occupied by British troops, in the form of the 1st Cavalry Division, a position that was retained by the Allies for most of the war. The adjacent wood, which can be seen on the left-hand side of the N365 before reaching Ploegsteert, was partially recovered by the Germans in 1914 and then completely overrun in the German Spring Offensive of 1918, albeit only temporarily.

As there is much to see in and around Ploegsteert Wood, the description that follows – and which is spilt into two parts, north of Ploegsteert and then south – will not concentrate solely on the locations and events relating to Churchill's time at this sector of the front. There is no better place to begin the tour than the town's main square. It is that the rebuilt church, which Winston mentioned so often during his spell in Ploegsteert, and a commemorative plaque, with a carving of Churchill looking out over trenches to a heavily-shelled church, on the Mairie can both be seen. The latter was unveiled on 11 November 1991.

From the main square head north out of Ploegsteert on the N365 in the direction of St Yvon (St Yves). Almost as soon as you start to leave the built-up area you will encounter the first of many of the Commonwealth War Graves Commission (CWGC) cemeteries in the area. Located on the right-hand side, the Strand Military Cemetery was started in October 1914 when two burials were made at this spot, close to an Advanced Dressing Station. The cemetery's name was derived from the fact that it was this site that The Strand trench led off into Ploegsteert Wood. It was mainly used from April 1917, whilst, after the Armistice, at least eight small cemeteries were concentrated here and now it now holds the remains of more than 1,100 British and Commonwealth soldiers.

As you head north up the road, look out for a set of surviving concrete bunkers on the right-hand side – they are positioned behind a house a very short distance from the cemetery. In fact, it is stated that these structures, built later in the war, were part of the Advanced Dressing Station, known as Charing Cross, which was based there.

Continuing north away from Ploegsteert, and visible from some distance, is the imposing Ploegsteert Memorial with the two stone lions sitting proudly at its entrance. The names of the 11,447 men of the United Kingdom and South African forces who died in this sector during the war and have no known grave are commemorated here. The memorial serves the area from the line Caestre-Dranoutre-Warneton to the north, to Haverskerque-Estaires-Fournes to the south, including the towns of Hazebrouck, Merville, Bailleul and Armentières, the Forest of Nieppe, and Ploegsteert Wood. The original intention had been to erect the memorial in Lille. Amongst the names on the Memorial are three Victoria Cross recipients.

The Memorial is set within the CWGC's Berks Cemetery Extension. This burial ground was first used in June 1916 and remained in service until September 1917. At the Armistice, the extension comprised only what is now known as Plot I; plots II and III were added in 1930 when graves were brought in from Rosenberg Chateau Military Cemetery and Extension, about half-a-mile to the north-west, when it was established that these sites could not be acquired in perpetuity. This came about because the Château's owner, whilst he was rebuilding his property, felt that the cemetery would stand too close to it. Despite pleas from the British and Belgian authorities, he remained intransigent, and eventually the 475 men interred there were exhumed and moved the half mile distance to their final resting place. In March 1930, *The Times* reported that 'each body, as it was reverently taken from the earth, was placed in a coffin draped with the Union Jack and removed by motor ambulance to the Royal Berkshire Cemetery Extension'.

On the opposite side of the road is the smaller Hyde Park Corner (Royal Berks) Cemetery, which was begun in April 1915 by the 1st/4th Battalion, Royal Berkshire Regiment and was used at intervals until November 1917. It contains eighty-three Commonwealth burials of the First World War and four German war graves. Among the former is the grave of Rifleman Albert French of the 18th (Service) Battalion (Arts & Crafts), Kings Royal Rifle Corps, who died in July 1916 aged just 16. Grave 1A, meanwhile, is that of Rifleman Samuel McBride, of the 2nd Battalion, Royal Irish Rifles, who was executed for desertion not far from the cemetery at Hope Farm (which was on the northern edge of Ploegsteert Wood near where Prowse Point Cemetery, see below, is today) on 7 December 1916.

Many people will be aware of the Last Post ceremony held each evening in Ieper. A similar ceremony, though necessarily smaller in scale, is held at the Memorial on the first Friday of each month at 19.00 hours.

Adjacent to the Royal Berkshire Cemetery is l'Auberge restaurant, the owner of which, Claude Verhaeghe, organises tours of the area at 09.00 hours and 14.30 each day, though l'Auberge itself does not open until 11.00 hours.

Nestling in the woods behind the Ploegsteert Memorial is the Plugstreet 14-18 Experience. The pyramidal building, which opened in November 2013, provides an overview of the First World War and the fighting in the Ploegsteert sector. The Plugstreet 14-18

Experience opens throughout the year from 10.00 hours Monday, Tuesday, Thursday and Friday, and at 13.00 hours on Wednesday.

From the Memorial, the N365 sweeps round to the right, the bend ending at the staggered crossroads at what was known to the troops as Hyde Park Corner. This is identified by a CWGC sign to Underhill Farm Cemetery (on the left), as well as an information board concerning the Catacombs dug in the adjacent hill. These deep shelters, constructed and extended by Australian engineers, were capable of housing two entire battalions and were used from November 1916 onwards.

On the opposite side of the junction is a narrow, but well-kept road. This is Mud Lane. A signpost indicates that the road is for the use of local traffic only.

It was whilst stationed off Mud Lane that Lieutenant R.B. Talbot Kelly, of the 52nd Brigade, wrote the following in his book, *A Subaltern's Odyssey*: 'My section had a forward gun on the edge of the wood near Mud Lane. The pit lay in a verdant thicket of little willows and Blackberry bushes. Ten yards away, a cross marked the grave of Ronnie Poulton, prince of Rugby players.'

Ronald Poulton Palmer, known to many as RPP (he officially changed his surname to Palmer by Royal Licence as a condition of inheriting a fortune from his uncle, George Palmer of the famous Huntley and Palmer biscuit company, in 1914), was an England captain and regarded as possibly one of the best attacking threequarters the game has ever seen. In 1914, just before the outbreak of war, he led England to what would be called today the Grand Slam. Having enlisted, Palmer was commissioned into the 1st/4th Battalion, Royal Berkshire Regiment.

By early 1915, Palmer's battalion had been posted to the Western Front. On 15 April 1915, Ronald's Company moved back into the line in Plugstreet Wood itself, pushing up to reserve breastworks called 'The Tourist Lines', so called as reporters and other dignitaries were taken into them to observe the German lines through the trees beyond the edge of the wood itself. Four days later, the men moved again, this time into a sector north of Ploegsteert Wood. They were to hold two stretches of front line trenches, called 'Sutherland' and 'Oxford', astride a track on which was situated a collection of shell-battered buildings called Anton's Farm. Ronald's No.13 Platoon held the farm.

The historian and author Jon Cooksey describes what happened on the night of 4/5 May 1915: 'Lieutenant Palmer was in charge of a working party out strengthening dugouts in Trench 40 just north of Anton's Farm. It was exceptionally dark, the moon had not risen and a slight fog brushed its back against the British breastworks and rolled over No Man's Land.

'Ronald, moving along the trench, had a word with Sergeant Perrin and then moved along to supervise another small party working on a new officers' mess dugout. Why he did what he did next we will never know ... at twenty minutes past midnight Ronald heaved himself up onto the roof of Captain Thorne's dugout to better oversee the work on another in front of the offices' mess. At that moment a single rifle shot pierced the silence in the valley of the River Douve. The single bullet struck and entered Ronald's body on his right side at the level of the third rib and knocked the air out of him. As he fell backwards into the arms of Sergeant Brant, all he was heard to say was "Oh!". RPP was dead before the Sergeant could put him on the ground.'

Ronald Poulton Palmer was the first officer of 1/4th Royal Berks to fall on the Western Front. His body was taken down by stretcher party through the lines of the 1st/7th Battalion, Royal Warwickshire Regiment to the Field Ambulance that had been established in the Convent in Ploegsteert – a building that Churchill would come to know well just a few months later.

At 18.30 hours on the evening of 6 May 1915, Palmer was buried in Berks Cemetery Extension (which is described above). Just eighteen minutes earlier a telegram had been delivered to his parents' house in Oxford: 'Regret your son killed last night. Death instantaneous.'

Mud Lane itself skirts along the northern edge of Ploegsteert Wood. A number of information boards can be found in it; one of these includes a map of the interior of the wood during the war. By Mud Corner Cemetery, a smaller road branches off to the right.

This leads through the wood down to Toronto Avenue Cemetery and, further into the wood, Ploegsteert Wood Military Cemetery. Both of these cemeteries can generally only be reached on foot. The CWGC website has the following warning: 'Access is only possible via a track in the woods to which motor vehicles are not allowed – a post is in position preventing vehicle access.' Whilst Toronto Avenue Cemetery was named after one of the paths used by troops in Ploegsteert Wood, Ploegsteert Wood Military Cemetery was made by the enclosure of a number of small regimental cemeteries.

Mud Lane itself continues to a road junction with a public road that runs east out of the village of St Yvon. For those who opted not to take a vehicle along Mud Lane, this junction can be reached by heading a short distance north back up the N365 from Hyde Park Corner and then taking the right-hand turn in St Yvon – Chemin du Mont de la Hutte. We will pick up our description from this turning.

A few hundred yards down the lane is Prowse Point Cemetery. This cemetery is unique on the Salient for being named after an individual. It is the site of the stand made by men of the 1st Battalion, Hampshire Regiment and the 1st Battalion, Somerset Light Infantry in October 1914, which featured the heroism of a Major Charles Prowse. Later, as Brigadier-General C.B. Prowse, DSO (Somerset Light Infantry), he would be killed on the first day of the Battle of the Somme, whilst commanding the 11th Infantry Brigade. Whilst at Prowse Point, if you stand with your back to the main cemetery gates and look north, Anton's Farm, as known to Ronald Poulton Palmer, was directly on the opposite side of the field in front of you.

Beside the cemetery, a mock-up of a small, and rather pristine, trench has recently been constructed close to an original First World War British bunker. Also there is a new monument to the famous football match between British troops and the German 133rd Saxon Regiment during the Christmas Truce of 1914. To reach the field that was the site of this impromptu game, head a short distance further east along the road – passing, almost immediately, the north end of Mud Lane – until you encounter a wooden cross, erected by the 'Khaki Chums' in 1999, and an accompanying information panel on the left-hand verge.

During Thursday, 24 December 1914, the weather across the Western Front turned cold but dry. A hard frost fell across the trenches. As the day wore on, in some areas of the front British soldiers were astonished to see Christmas trees with candles and paper lanterns appearing on enemy parapets. Later that evening, and through the night, the singing of carols, hymns and popular songs added to the atmosphere.

By the following day, the first Christmas of the Great War, a number of British and German soldiers found themselves in No Man's Land in an act of fraternisation that has since given rise to the legend that is 'The Christmas Truce'. One of those present that day was Major John Hawksley who was serving with 135 Battery, Royal Field Artillery, near Ploegsteert Wood. On 27 December 1914, Hawksley wrote to his sister:

'Christmas day in our immediate front was quite extraordinary. I was at my observation post just a few yards behind the infantry advanced trenches on the afternoon of Xmas Eve. After dark our men & the Germans whose trenches were only 1 to 2 hundred yards apart sang in English Home sweet Home together. Then God save the King was sung by both. I don't know what words the Germans sang to this tune. Then late on a German shouted out to the Warwicks – "We won't fire tomorrow if tomorrow if you don't". Our men shouted back "All right".

'When it was light on Xmas day, each side showed itself above the trenches. First head & shoulders then seeing they were not shot at – Showed a little more – until a German got out of his trench & then an Englishman did. Finally about 100 Germans & 60 Englishmen including officers on both sides stepped out & fraternized with each other!!'

The Truce often ended just as it had begun; by mutual agreement. Captain C.I. Stockwell, of the Royal Welch Fusiliers, also in trenches near Ploegsteert Wood, recalled how, after a truly 'Silent Night', he fired three shots into the air at 08.30 hours on Boxing Day. He then climbed onto the parapet. A German officer who had given him some beer the previous day also appeared on the German side of No Man's Land. Both men bowed, saluted, and climbed back into their trenches. A few moments afterwards, Stockwell heard the German fire two shots into the air. Then, in his words, 'the war was on again'.

At this point, there is an extra location that is worth a visit if you have time – though it is to the south of Ploegsteert. We mention it here because of its relevance to the Christmas Truce. If you head immediately south out of the centre of Ploegsteert on the N365, just over a mile later there is a turning on the left – Chemin de la Blanche. After about a mile, this road becomes the Witteweg. At about this point you will come across, on the right, Calvaire (Essex) Military Cemetery. Started in November 1914, this burial ground was established beside a building known as Essex House and is an example of a regimental cemetery, many of which were made in 1914 and 1915. Two of the 218 First World War burials in the cemetery stand testimony to the fact that the Truce on Christmas Day was far from universal.

In the belief that a truce was 'supposed to be prevailing', Private Ernest Palfrey, a 21-year-old former miner, had been out into No Man's Land with a group burying their dead comrades. As he returned to the Monmouthshires' trenches he was hit by a bullet in the back of his neck which killed him instantly. Similar circumstances surrounded the death of one of the Sergeants in Palfrey's battalion. Frank Collins, who hailed from Monmouth and had already received a Mention in Despatches, had made his way across No Man's Land with tobacco and jam to present to the Germans opposite. During the return journey he was shot through the back and died almost immediately. It was reported in a South Wales paper that the Germans later sent over an apology.

Returning to our narrative, continue east along the road from the Khaki Chums' wooden cross. After a sharp bend to the right the lane then quickly bends to the left. Facing you on the south side of the road is the site of the cottage where Lieutenant Bruce Bairnsfather of the 1st Battalion, Royal Warwickshire Regiment, first brought to life his famous cartoon character 'Old Bill' – as pointed out by a large bronze plaque mounted on the wall. His dugout was located beneath the house that once stood on this spot.

Bairnsfather's humorous cartoons, depicting life in the trenches and entitled 'Fragments from France', were published weekly in *The Bystander* magazine during the war. Acting as a machine-gun officer, he was with his battalion in Ploegsteert Wood from November 1914, and he took part in the Christmas Truce. Bairnsfather later gave this account of his part in that momentous event:

'Walking about the trench a little later, discussing the curious affair of the night before, we suddenly became aware of the fact that we were seeing a lot of evidences of Germans. Heads were bobbing about and showing over their parapet in a most reckless way, and, as we looked, this phenomenon became more and more pronounced.

'A complete Boche figure suddenly appeared on the parapet, and looked about itself. This complaint became infectious. It didn't take "Our Bert" … long to be up on the skyline. This was the signal for more Boche anatomy to be disclosed, and this was replied to by our men, until in less time than it takes to tell, half a dozen or so of each of the belligerents were outside their trenches and were advancing towards each other in No Man's Land. I clambered up and over our parapet, and moved out across the field to look. Clad in a muddy suit of khaki and wearing a sheepskin coat and Balaclava helmet, I joined the throng about half-way across to the German trenches.'

Continue east along the road until you come to a T-junction. The bank facing you on the opposite side of the road you are about to turn right on to, is the remains of what was, in the war, a far more pronounced sunken lane. This bank also marks the line of what was the British firing trench in this part of the front line for much of the war. No Man's Land was also narrower here than at any point for some distance north or south.

Having turned right into Chemin de St Yvon, head south down the gentle slope – for the next half a mile or so the road continues to follow the British front line, with No Man's Land to your left. As you drive down this stretch of road look out for a white memorial marker on the field's edge on your right. It commemorates Private Harry Wilkinson, 2nd Battalion, Lancashire Fusiliers, who was killed in action on 10 November 1914.

The 29-year-old former cotton mill fire-beater had headed to the Western Front on 23 August 1914. He left behind his pregnant wife, Eva, and his six-year-old son, Harry, at their Lord Street home in Bury. Wilkinson was then involved in almost non-stop fighting, including at Le Cateau, Marne and on the Aisne. His battalion eventually moved to the Ypres Salient. Private Wilkinson met his death, along with two other soldiers, during a raid on German-held trenches at a farm house in Ploegsteert Wood on 10 November 1914. His body was buried in a shallow shell crater near where he fell. His remains lay in the Flanders' earth until they were uncovered by Belgian amateur war historian Patrick Roelens after the ground had been ploughed for the first time in eighty-five years. His identity was confirmed by his metal identity tag, and other artefacts (including his Lancashire Fusiliers cap badge), that were uncovered with his body.

On 31 October 2001, Private Wilkinson was reburied in Prowse Point Cemetery. His coffin was borne by six members of the 1st Battalion, Royal Regiment of Fusiliers, to music from the Minden Band of the Queen's Division, which was based in Germany. Private Wilkinson's great-great-grandson and the Duke of Kent were among those who gathered for the interment.

At the end of the straight stretch of road that you are travelling down, the road turns sharply to your right, though there is a lane leading off to the left. At this spot, the road marks the course of the German firing trench – the British line having swung west back towards the wood. It was here that the fortified enemy strongpoint known as the 'Birdcage', and which Captain X described as being 'a beastly place', was located. The 'Birdcage' gained its name from the amount of barbed wire that the Germans had laid around the position. The information panel located on this bend also points out that nearby was the site of a massive explosion in 1955 when an underground mine, unfired and abandoned after the Armistice, detonated following a lighting strike. The resulting crater no longer exists.

Continue to head south along the lane until you reach the crossroads in the hamlet of Le Gheer. An information panel at this spot details two notable events in the fighting around Ploegsteert. At 05.15 hours on 21 October 1914, the Germans attacked the British line, driving the 2nd Battalion, Inniskilling Fusiliers back about a quarter of a mile towards Ploegsteert. The Germans then began to consolidate the ground they had won. At 09.00 hours a counter-attack was mounted by men of the 1st Battalion, East Lancashire Regiment, the 1st Battalion, Somerset Light Infantry, the 2nd Battalion, Inniskilling Fusiliers and the 2nd Battalion, Essex Regiment, and the lost ground was recovered. German losses in the fighting were estimated at around 1,000 men; over the course of the following days more than 300 of their dead were buried in and around Le Gheer.

The other incident occurred less than two weeks later. On the morning of 3 November the trenches occupied by the 1st Battalion, East Lancashire Regiment came under heavy enemy fire. A Private McNulty had left the trenches and was hit in the pit of his stomach, falling to the ground some thirty yards away. The Germans were trying to hit him again and the men of his battalion could see the earth flying up around McNulty as the bullets struck the ground.

Despite the very real danger that he exposed himself to, Drummer Spencer John 'Joe' Bent left the safety of the trenches and ran across the open ground, zigzagging to spoil the aim of the Germans. In an interview with his local paper, the *Suffolk Chronicle and Mercury*, shortly after the war, Bent recalled the incident: 'They did not snipe at me whilst I was advancing, but as soon as I got hold of McNulty's shoulder something seemed to take my feet from under me, and I slipped under McNulty. This took place close to the walls of a ruined convent, and just as I fell, several bullets struck the wall, sending a piece of plaster against my left eye. I thought I was wounded and started to rub the blood away, as I thought, but fortunately the skin was only grazed. I felt it was time to get out of it, and knowing it was impossible to stand up, I hooked my feet under McNulty's arms, and using my elbows I managed to drag myself and him back to the trenches about 25 yards away. When I got him there safely, I went for a doctor and stretcher-bearers. As far as I know he is still alive. At any rate, [he] was the last time I heard of him.'

For his actions that day Joe Bent was awarded the Victoria Cross. The announcement was published in *The London Gazette* on 9 December 1914, where his citation highlighted his 'conspicuous gallantry' and identified four separate acts of bravery. He also received £50, then a considerable sum, from an Ipswich resident who had offered it to the first local man to be awarded the VC. Bent was the first man from his regiment to be awarded the Victoria Cross in the Great War; he received his decoration from King George V at Buckingham Palace on 13 January 1915.

The ruined convent that Bent referred to is quite possibly the same building that Churchill mentions in his letters, as this was situated a short distance down the southern arm of the crossroads.

From Le Gheer, our route takes you back towards Ploegsteert on the N515. After little more than 200 yards you will come to a solitary house on the right-hand side of the road. Next to the building, beside another information panel, is a track heading north into the heart of the wood. This is the start of the track which was known as Hunter's Avenue. Approximately 100 yards along this path on the left is a narrow track which leads to a well-preserved machine-gun post and bunkers. Amongst these is the remains of a First Aid Post that was known to the troops as 'Blighty Hole'. A young Lieutenant Anthony Eden, who was to serve under Winston as Foreign Secretary during the Second World War, was based in Hunter's Avenue in April 1916 – the same time that Winston was just a few hundred yards to the south. Also in the 1st Battalion, Royal Warwickshire Regiment at the time was Second Lieutenant Alan Alexander Milne, the man who, better known by his initials A.A. Milne, became famous for his Winnie-the-Pooh books.

Heading a short distance further into Ploegsteert Wood brings you to Rifle House Cemetery – though this cannot be accessed easily by vehicle. Rifle House Cemetery was named after a strong point, of which no trace now exists. The earliest graves are those of men of the 1st Battalion, Rifle Brigade, their burials beginning in November 1914. Worthy of mention is the headstone commemorating the death, in action on 19 December 1914, of Rifleman Robert Barnett. The son of Phillip and Esther Barnett, of 95 Belgrade Road, Stoke Newington, London, Barnett is described by the Commonwealth War Graves Commission as 'one of the youngest battle casualties of the war'. He was just 15 years old.

Continuing along the N515 will bring the visitor to Lancashire Cottage Cemetery – from where there are good views of the southern edge of Ploegsteert Wood. Designed by Charles Holden, the cemetery was begun by the 1st Battalion, East Lancashire Regiment (which has eighty-four graves in it) and the 1st Battalion, Hampshire Regiment (which has fifty-six) in November 1914. It was used as a front line cemetery until March 1916 and occasionally later. The cemetery was in German hands from 10 April to 29 September 1918 and they made a few burials in it during that spring and summer. The cemetery contains 256 Commonwealth burials of the First World War – many of which, as the previous pages reveal, are from the period of Churchill's time in the sector. There are also thirteen German war graves.

The last stretch of the 'northern' part of the tour brings you back into Ploegsteert's main square. The 'southern' part of the tour, in effect the part that covers more of Churchill's time in the trenches in this area, heads south from the square towards Armentières, once again on the N365.

As you travel down the Rue d'Armentières take the first turning on the right – Rue Sainte-Marie (also known as Sinte-Mariastraat). Follow this for some three-quarters of a mile until you come to Soyer Farm. This can be identified by a barn with a large pig motif on the end, in front of which is a new information panel – due to be unveiled in April 2016.

Churchill's journey to the front at Ploegsteert involved him travelling from the village of Nieppe, which lies just over a mile to the south-east over the French border, to Soyer Farm. The farm itself was destroyed in the war, though the farmhouse and courtyard were rebuilt to an almost identical shape and style. The farm is still owned and worked by direct descendants of the wartime occupants. Even as late as 1948 Churchill was still in touch with them – on 16 October that year, for example, he had written to congratulate them on a wedding in the family!

To follow in Churchill's footsteps towards the front, turn around and retrace your route back along Rue Sainte-Marie to the N365. On reaching this, turn right and continue to head south.

Almost immediately you will need to keep an eye open on the right for the terraced property with No.121 on the wall. This building stands on the site of the former 'Hospice' where Winston stayed when not in the trenches – though it was often referred to by the British troops as a 'Hospice' or 'Convent', this was not in fact the case, it being a nunnery school for girls known as L'Ouvroir des Soeurs de Charité.

Not that much further on, and again on the right-hand side of the N365, is the London Rifle Brigade Cemetery. The cemetery was begun by units of the 4th Division in December 1914, and used by fighting units and field ambulances through until March 1918; some German burials were made in April and May. The cemetery owes its name to the twenty-two burials of the London Rifle Brigade (which then belonged to the 4th Division) in Plot III, made in January, February and March 1915. The cemetery now contains 335 Commonwealth and eighteen German burials of the First World War. One of Churchill's men, Private Andrew McLellan who was killed in action on 5 February 1916, is buried near the northern wall on the right hand side of the cemetery as you walk in. His grave reference is A.14 in Plot II.

Also of interest regarding London Rifle Brigade Cemetery is the fact that in June 1927 Lieutenant General Sir H.F.M. Wilson, former General Officer Commanding 4th Division, unveiled a tablet set in the wall at the north corner of the cemetery. It commemorates the dedication of the cemetery by the Bishop of London on Easter Day 1915.

London Support Farm, to where Churchill was summoned on 6 February 1916, for one example, can be seen across the field directly opposite on the other side of the N365. The former brewery which, at Churchill's instigation, was turned into a bath house was located further south down this main road.

Another 300 yards down Rue d'Armentières, on the left (eastern) side, is the Chemin Duhem (Duhemweg). Before you turn on to Chemin Duhem, this is the ideal point at which to make a visit to Calvaire (Essex) Military Cemetery should you wish to do so; the road to it is the next turning on the right off the N365.

Regardless of whether or not you opt to make this additional stop, you will need to make your way on to Chemin Duhem. When you reach the stretch of open road, stop and look north across the fields towards Ploegsteert and its Church. This is a similar view to that often seen by Churchill – and which features in at least one of his paintings completed in 1916.

After a few hundred yards, the road turns abruptly left, with another road, the Chemin du Crombion, heading off to the right. From this point, Chemin Duhem becomes increasingly rough, but not impassable, though it can be extremely muddy in wet weather. It must also be pointed out that at the junction with Chemin du Crombion there is a sign indicating that, like Mud Lane earlier, Chemin Duhem is for local traffic only.

Keep following Chemin Duhem. On the very next bend, which is to the right, the visitor is afforded another view of London Support Farm across the field in front of you. As with nearly every building in and around Ploegsteert, it was rebuilt following the war after the original had been destroyed. As one local historian put it, 'There are no buildings more than 100 years old here'!

As you continue along the track, closer to what was the front line, the next farm you will see to the north, roughly in a line due east from London Support Farm, is the building known as 'Maison 1875'. Named after a plaque built into its walls denoting the year it was constructed, Maison 1875 was used as a billeting and mustering point by British troops.

A short distance further on, the road crosses the Warnave river. One of the bridges here, over which Churchill and his men almost certainly crossed at one time or other whilst en route to or from the trenches, was known as McKenna's Bridge.

Halfway along this small road, almost directly opposite Lancashire Cottage Cemetery which is across the fields to the north, the road bends to the left. On the right can be seen a well-head situated in a field behind a metal gate. Though the head of the well is post-war grey concrete, the well itself is the original one. It is all that is left of Laurence Farm, the place where Winston and Gibb formed that bond, in the midst of death and destruction, which continued long after the war. A new information panel is scheduled to be unveiled here at the same time as that at Soyer Farm.

Continue along the road in the direction of Le Gheer. The only other buildings you pass are those of what was known as Lancashire Support Farm. The authors Tony Spagnoly and Ted Smith note that the farm was named by men of the 1st Battalion, East Lancashire Regiment when it was used by them as a collecting point for materials to support troops in the line just a few hundred yards to the east. 'While the troops did their stints in the front-line around Le Gheer,' they write, 'the whole length of this track would become a busy thoroughfare after dark, with men going about their business: sweating ration parties; jostling company messengers; and serious grim-faced men engaged in the relief of the front-line troops treading their way carefully towards the trenches, slipping and sliding in the mud, until the stark jagged ruins of the convent just south of Le Gheer crossroads would hove into view announcing that the front-line had been reached.' Churchill and Gibb must have walked the ground around here many times.

It is to the convent described by Spagnoly and Smith that our route now heads. After passing the site of Lancashire Support Farm, the track ends at the main road heading north towards Le Gheer. Turn right and a short distance on the left, just before Rue du Gheer (also on the left) is the site of the convent. Churchill had planned to use its cellars as a forward HQ, which he called the 'Conning Tower', as it was only 100 yards from the front line. Rebuilt, of course, it is now a chapel.

Your last direction of this tour of the Ploegsteert area is to turn left into Rue du Gheer, which is signposted as a dead-end. Only a couple of hundred yards in length drive down to the building at the end. This is on the site of what was known as Burnt Out Farm. Stop at the building. Its west-facing corner sits directly on the firing trench that formed the British front line, roughly in the very centre of the sector Churchill and his men manned. These trenches ran north to just this side of the main road through Le Gheer – an uninterrupted view of this area is available to you from Burnt Out Farm. Much of what had been No Man's Land directly in front of you, and the southern half of Churchill's front line domain, has been obliterated by the construction of the main N58 road.

Though much has changed since Churchill left the front for the last time, and indeed following the Armistice over two years later, it was in this area around Ploegsteert that Churchill and the men of the 6th Battalion, Royal Scots Fusiliers battled the enemy, dodging bullet, bomb and shell to try and survive. Some never succeeded and remain to this day in Belgian soil. There is no more fitting a place to end a tour of Plugstreet.

References and Notes

Chapter 1: Winston the Warrior
1. Winston S. Churchill, *My Early Life: A Roving Commission* (Leo Cooper, London, 1930), p.98.
2. Quoted in Lewis Broad, *Winston Churchill, 1874-1951* (Hutchinson, London, 1951), p.11.
3. Winston S., Churchill, *The River War, The Reconquest of the Sudan* (Four Square Books, London, 1964), pp.274-6.
4. Frank Brennand, *Winston S. Churchill* (New English Library, London, 1965), p.22.

Chapter 2: Winston at the Helm
1. Quoted in Michael Paterson, *Winston Churchill: His Military Life, 1895-1945* (David and Charles, Newton Abbot, 2006).pp.186-7.
2. Winston S. Churchill, *The World Crisis 1911-1918* (Barnes & Noble, New York, 1993), p.171.
3. Quoted in Douglas S. Russell, *Winston Churchill - Soldier: The Military Life of a Gentleman at War* (Conway, London, 2005), p.351.
4. Winston Churchill, 'Antwerp; The Story of its Siege and Fall', *The Collected Essays of Sir Winston Churchill* (Library of Imperial History, London, 1976), p.172.
5. J.E.B. Seely, *Adventure* (Heinemann, London, 1930), p.189.
6. *The World Crisis 1911-1918*, vol.1, p.470.
7. TNA CAB 42/1/4, War Council minutes 25/11/14.
8. Robin Prior, *Gallipoli: The End of the Myth* (Yale University Press, London, 2009), p.13.
9. Edward J. Erickson, *Gallipoli, The Ottoman Campaign* (Pen & Sword, Barnsley, 2010), p.16.
10. Martin Gilbert, *Winston S. Churchill*, Volume III 1914-1916 (Heinemann, London, 1971), p.446.
11. Helen Violet Bonham Carter, *Winston Churchill As I Knew Him* (Eyre & Spottiswoode and Collins, London, 1965).

Chapter 3: The Western Front 1915
1. Edward Underhill, *A Year on the Western Front* (London, 1988), p.18.

REFERENCES AND NOTES

Chapter 4: With the Grenadiers
1. Brennand, p.65.
2. Winston S. Churchill, *Thoughts and Adventures* (Butterworth, London, 1932), p.100.
3. ibid, p.69.
4. TNA, WO 95/1215/1.
5. This revolver, which he carried during his time in the trenches, and stayed with him throughout the Second Wold War, can be seen on display in the Churchill War Rooms in London.
6. *Yorkshire Post and Leeds Intelligencer*, Monday, 27 December 1915.
7. The announcement of the award was published in *The London Gazette* on 22 January 1916. It stated: 'For conspicuous gallantry and enterprise opposite Le Tilleloy on the night of 14th/15th December, 1915. He [Parnell] made his way through the German wire, entered their trench and surprised a post of the enemy, two of whom were killed, one taken prisoner and the remainder dispersed. On the previous night he had also got into the enemy's trenches and brought back valuable information.'
8. Violet Bonham Carter, *Winston Churchill As I Knew Him* (Eyre & Spottiswoode and Collins, London, 1965), pp.439-40.
9. Quoted in Walter Reid, *Douglas Haig, Architect of Victory* (Birlinn, Edinburgh, 2009), p.251.
10. ibid, p.252.

Chapter 6: The Thunderbolt
1. Quoted in Gerard J. De Groot, *Liberal Crusader: The Life of Sir Archibald Sinclair* (C. Hurst & Co., London, 1993), p.19.
2. Gilbert, p.632.

Chapter 7: The Arrival
1. The Argyll and Sutherland Highlanders. This was a line infantry regiment of the British Army that existed from 1881 until amalgamation into the Royal Regiment of Scotland in March 2006.

Chapter 8: The Battalion
1. The Battle of Drumclog was fought on 1 June 1679, between a group of Covenanters and the forces of John Graham of Claverhouse (later Viscount Dundee) at High Drumclog, in South Lanarkshire, Scotland.
2. National Library of Scotland, the papers of Professor Dewar Gibb,Dep.217, Box 7.

Chapter 10: Settling Down (Continued)
1. Croft W.D., *Three Years with the Ninth Division* (John Murray, London, 1919), p.19.
2. Arthur Holland was the son of Major General Butcher who changed his name to Holland in 1910. Holland was commissioned into the Royal Artillery in 1880, serving in the Boer War. He then became Assistant Military Secretary

REFERENCES AND NOTES

to the Governor and Commander-in-Chief of Malta before moving to the War Office in 1903. Nine years later he was appointed the Commandant of the Royal Military College Sandhurst. In the First World War he was the commander of the artillery of the 8th Division, rising to take command of artillery of VII Corps. In September 1915 he was appointed to the command of the 1st Division, later becoming Commanding Officer of the artillery of the Third Army. Holland survived the war, retiring from the Army in 1920.
3. National Library of Scotland, the papers of Professor Dewar Gibb, Dep.217, Box 7.
4. ibid.
5. Croft, p.27.
6. Lieutenant Colonel Norman McDonald Teacher DSO, was aged 39 when he died of wounds on 26 September 1917. The husband of Dorothy Teacher, of Newtown Hill, Leixlip, Co. Kildare, he was buried in Ypres Reservoir Cemetery.
7. Handwritten letter held by the Manuscript Division, US Library of Congress.
8. Gilbert, p.651.

Chapter 11: In the Line
1. This M1915 Adrian helmet, known to the French as the Casque Adrian, would become one of the most distinctive reminders of Churchill's time in the trenches of the Western Front. It had been presented to him by the French General Émile Fayolle. Churchill kept the helmet, stating it 'will perhaps protect my valuable cranium'. It has survived and is today on display at Chartwell which, now a National Trust property and open to the public, was Churchill's principal adult home.
2. The 'Birdcage' was a fortified German strongpoint located just to the east of Ploegsteert Wood. It gained its name from the amount of barbed wire that the enemy had laid around the position.
3. 'Old Bill' was the famous cartoon character created by Charles Bruce Bairnsfather. Born into a military family at Muree on India's North West Frontier (now Pakistan) on 9 July 1887, Bairnsfather is one of the best known of the UK's First World War artists and cartoonists. Educated at Rudyard Kipling's old school, Bairnsfather passed the Army entrance exam and enlisted in the Militia. He then studied at commercial art school but re-enlisted with the Royal Warwickshire Regiment when war broke out in 1914. It was as a Second Lieutenant in the 1st Battalion that he arrived on the Western Front, going on to experience the sights and sounds that ultimately led to him becoming a household name by the end of the war. It was whilst serving in the Ypres Salient that Bairnsfather soon began to use his skill as a cartoonist to depict life at the front, many of his drawings featuring the walrus-moustached character 'Old Bill'. These cartoons were soon published as the series that came to be known as 'Fragments from France'; they became an immediate success. Appearing in the weekly magazine *The Bystander* from March 1915, these cartoons inspired merchandise from playing cards to handkerchiefs as well as plays and films. A first compilation volume of his drawings, *Fragments from France*, was published in January

REFERENCES AND NOTES

1916. It went on to sell more than a million copies.
4. TNA, WO 95/1772. The casualty that day, the first member of the 6th Battalion, Royal Scots Fusiliers killed in action under Churchill's command, is believed to be Private 11934 John Marshall. Born and raised in Glasgow, Marshall was buried a short distance behind the line in Lancashire Cottage Cemetery.
5. The 8th Battalion, Gordon Highlanders was the next regiment to take over from the 6th RSF in the trenches and the two battalions would alternate over the coming weeks.
6. National Library of Scotland, the papers of Professor Dewar Gibb, Dep.217, Box 7.
7. This was a memorandum begun by Churchill in December 1915 and intended for submission to the Committee of Imperial Defence, amongst other institutions or individuals, on variants of the offensive. A copy is held by the Churchill Archives at Cambridge under the reference CHAR 2/73/1.
8. Perhaps at the instigation of his CO, Sinclair made the following observations in the battalion War Diary's entry for 28 January: 'Wind in SE direction; favourable for enemy gas attack' (TNA WO 95/1772).
9. Gilbert, pp.657-8.
10. ibid, p.658.
11. Gilbert, pp.658-9.
12. ibid, p.659.
13. Michael Paterson, pp.217-8.
14. Gilbert, footnote on p.660.
15. Like Winston's Adrian helmet, this torch has survived. It can also be seen at Chartwell in Kent.
16. Poor Bloody Infantry. This was a term that was widely used amongst infantry units at the time. The terms, as well as the initials P.B.I., appeared frequently in *The Wipers Times*, a trench magazine that was published by soldiers fighting in the Ypres Salient during the war.
17. In *Dictionary of Tommies' Songs and Slang, 1914-18* (John Brophy and Eric Partridge, Frontline Books, London, 2008), a 'Whizz-bang' is described thus: 'A light shell fired from one of the smaller field-artillery guns – the British 18-pounder, the French 75 (millimetres), the German 77 (millimetres). The term is onomatopoeic, and was applied to the explosion. Owing to the short range and low trajectory, whizz-bangs arrived as soon, if not sooner, than anyone heard them.'
18. Lord Beaverbrook, *Politicians and the War*, (Oldbourne, London, 1960), Volume II, p.76.
19. The 'Soldiers Died in the Great War' database lists three men from the 6th Battalion, Royal Scots Fusiliers who died during the period 1 February to 6 February 1916. Two are listed as having 'died of wounds', the third as being 'killed in action'. The former were Private 17533 Methven Clark (the son of Peter Anderson Clark of 'Calm Torrance', 213, Main Street, Gorbals, Glasgow – died on 3 February) and 20-year-old Private 11055 William Henry Kenny Ingram, who served as Kenny (the son of Samuel and Annie Ingram, of 62 Vernon Road, Aylestone Park, Leicester – died on 6 February). Both Clark

and Ingram were buried in Bailleul Communal Cemetery Extension, Nord – Bailleul being an important hospital centre at the time. The soldier killed in action, on 5 February, was Private 11934 Andrew McLellan, a native of Tradeston, Glasgow. McLellan was buried in London Rifle Brigade Cemetery, which is a short distance to the south of Ploegsteert.
20. There is no mention of the circumstances surrounding Rossell's death in the War Diary. Born and enlisted in Leicester, and a resident of Houghton-on-Hill, Rossell was buried in Lancashire Cottage Cemetery. He lies today beside his fellow battalion comrade John Marshall.
21. The new Act specified that men from 18 to 41 years old were liable to be called up for service in the army unless they were married, widowed with children, serving in the Royal Navy, a minister of religion, or working in one of a number of reserved occupations. An application for a certificate of exemption, usually temporary and issued with conditions attached, could be made, either by the individual concerned or his employer, through a series of Military Service Tribunals which were established across the country, under certain circumstances. These included instances where 'serious hardship would ensue owing to his exceptional financial or business obligations or domestic position' or 'ill health or infirmity'. Conscientious objectors – men who objected to fighting on moral grounds– were also exempted, and were in most cases given civilian jobs or non-fighting roles at the front.
22. *The Times*, 31 January 1916.
23. Gilbert, p.633.
24. Colonel Arthur Holland (see also Chapter 10).
25. TNA, WO 95/1772.
26. Gilbert, p.673.
27. The 17th also saw the battalion suffer two further casualties when, as the War Diary points out, 'two valuable NCOs [were] wounded when wiring'. The 'Soldiers Died in the Great War' database lists one Sergeant as having been killed in action on this date; Samuel Hart, a resident of Tollcross, Glasgow. A second NCO, Sergeant William James Quinn is shown as having died of wounds at Bailleul on the 20th.
28. *Thoughts and Adventures*, pp.82-3.
29. This casualty was 29-year-old Private 20138 Samuel Storah. The son of William and Mary Storah of Shaw, Lancashire, and the husband of Ellen Storah, of 5, Rushcroft Road, High Crompton, Shaw, Oldham, Samuel was also buried in Lancashire Cottage Cemetery.
30. A firestep is 'the step running along the forward side – the fire bay – of a trench on which soldiers stood to keep watch or fire, (see *Dictionary of Tommies' Songs and Slang, 1914-18*).
31. Gilbert, pp.673-4.
32. At this point, Gibb added the following footnote in his original publication: '*A propos* of reports: The Brigade hailed with delight the first "Intelligence Report" issued by the newly appointed Brigade Intelligence Officer, when he was good enough to inform his readers that "opposite Trench A 22 there were heard last night the sounds of girlish laughter."

REFERENCES AND NOTES

Chapter 12: Our Guests
1. General John Edward Bernard Seely, 1st Baron Mottistone. Despite being the Secretary of State of War in the two years preceding the First World War, Seeley spent almost the entirety of the war on the front line. Known to his soldiers as General Jack he became best known for leading his horse Warrior into a huge cavalry charge at Moreuil Wood in March 1918. Described as 'a great friend of Winston Churchill's', Seeley was the only former cabinet minister to go to the front in 1914 and still be there four years later.
2. Neil Roderick MacDonald (also spelt McDonald), often known as 'Foghorn', was born in the township of Lancaster, Ontario, though he once described himself 'as Scottish as oatmeal'. Aged 53 when he enlisted as a private following the outbreak of war in 1914, MacDonald had experienced a remarkably diverse life until that point. As well as a miner and explorer, he had even served for a time as an officer in the United States Army, more specifically the Third Volunteer Cavalry of the Spanish War. His nickname was derived from his deep bass voice. Standing over six foot tall, a fellow officer once said of him: 'Foghorn is the sort of officer whose men would follow him to the gates of hell itself and walk in laughing.'

Chapter 13: The Mess
1. The War Diary does go on to state that one individual was 'wounded [later] today near Le Romarin by shrapnel'.
2. Hansard, Volume 80 cc1401-46 (House of Commons debate, 7 March 1916).
3. Violet Bonham Carter, p.454-5.
4. TNA, WO 95/1772.
5. ibid, p.455.
6. ibid.

Chapter 14: Finale
1. In *The Irrepressible Churchill* (compiled by Kay Halle; Conway, London, 2010), this statement is given as: 'Whatever else they may say of me as a soldier, at least nobody can say that I have ever failed to display a ... proper appreciation of the virtues of alcohol.'
2. Brennand, p.67.
3. A handwritten letter from Winston S. Churchill to Field Marshal Sir William Robertson, Chief of the Imperial General Staff, dated 4 April 1916 and marked '6th Royal Scots Fusiliers ... In the field'; held in the archives of the Royal Highland Fusiliers Museum, Glasgow.

Chapter 15: Back From the Front
1. Hansard, Volume 82 cc2003-69 (House of Commons debate, 23 May 1916).
2. *Daily Record*, Saturday, 28 July 1917.
3. The National Library of Scotland, the papers of Professor Dewar Gibb, Acc.9188/1.

Bibliography & Source

THE CHURCHILL ARCHIVES
Char 1/118 Personal Correspondence of Clementine S. Churchill.
Char 1/124 Personal Correspondence of Winston S. Churchill.
Char 1/136/18 and 19 Correspondence between WSC and ADG.
Char 28/120 Miscellaneous Acquired Papers.
GBR/0014/THRS The Papers of Archibald Sinclair, 1st Viscount Thurso.

THE NATIONAL ARCHIVES
TNA CAB 42/1/4, War Council minutes 25/11/14.
TNA WO/95/1772 War Diary, 6th Battalion, Royal Scots Fusiliers.

PUBLISHED WORKS
Benn T., *et al*, Churchill Remembered: Recollections by Tony Benn MP, Lord Carrington, Lord Deedes and Mary Soames, *Transactions of the Royal Historical Society*, (Cambridge University Press, Vol. 11, 2001).
Beaverbrook, Max Aitken, Baron, *Politicians and the War*, (Oldbourne, 1960).
Brennand, Frank, *Winston S. Churchill* (New English Library, London, 1965).
Broad, Lewis, *Winston Churchill, 1874-1951* (Hutchinson, London, 1951).
Carter, Helen Violet Bonham, *Winston Churchill As I Knew Him* (Eyre & Spottiswoode and Collins, London, 1965).
Churchill, Winston S., *The Story of the Malakand Field Force: An Episode of Frontier War* (Longmans, Green & Co, London, 1898).
———, *My Early Life: A Roving Commission* (Leo Cooper, London, 1930).
———, *The Collected Essays of Sir Winston Churchill* (Library of Imperial History, London, 1976).
———, *The River War, The Reconquest of the Sudan* (Four Square Books, London, 1964).
———, *The World Crisis 1911-1918* (Barnes & Noble, New York, 1993).
———, *Thoughts and Adventures* (Butterworth, London, 1932).
Croft, Lieutenant Colonel W.D., CMG, DSO, *Three Years with the Ninth Division* (John Murray, London, 1919).
Erickson, Edward J., *Gallipoli, The Ottoman Campaign* (Pen & Sword, Barnsley, 2010).

Gilbert, Martin, *Winston S. Churchill*, Volume III 1914-1916 (Heinemann, London, 1971).
Groot, Gerard J., *Liberal Crusader, The Life of Sir Archibald Sinclair* (C. Hurst & Co., London, 1993).
Halle, Kay, *The Irrepressible Churchill* (Conway, London, 2010).
Holt, Major and Mrs, *Ypres Salient & Passchendaele* (Pen & Sword, Barnsley, 2008).
Paterson, Michael, *Winston Churchill: His Military Life, 1895-1945* (David and Charles, Newton Abbot, 2006).
Prior, Robin *Gallipoli The End of the Myth* (Yale University Press, London, 2009).
Reid, Walter, *Douglas Haig, Architect of Victory* (Birlinn, Edinburgh, 2009).
Russell, Douglas S. **Winston Churchill - Soldier: The Military Life of a Gentleman at War** (Brassey's, London, 2005).
Celia Sandys, *Chasing Churchill, The Travels of Winston Churchill by His Granddaugher* (Unicorn Press, London, 2014).
Seely, J. E. B., *Adventure* (Heinemann, London, 1930).
Soames, Mary, *Speaking for themselves, The Personal Letters of Winston and Clementine Churchill* (Doubleday, London, 1998).
Underhill, Edward, *A Year on the Western Front* (London, 1988).

Index

Aitken, William Maxwell, 1st Baron Beaverbrook, 29, 48, 120
Anton's Farm, 193, 194
Antwerp, Siege of, 18-20
Armentières, 84, 92, 93, 94, 102, 127, 154, 172, 174, 189, 190, 201
Ashcroft, Robert, 5, 6
Asquith, Herbert Henry, 1st Earl of Oxford and Asquith, 14, 19, 26, 28, 48, 119, 122, 155, 161, 166, 168, 169, 170, 181, 184, 185
Aubers Ridge, Battle of, 26
Ayr, 55, 63

Bailleul, 72, 190
Bairnsfather, Lieutenant Bruce, 196
  'Old Bill', 94, 196
  The Bystander, 197
Balfour, Arthur James, 1st Earl of Balfour, 11, 28, 159, 160, 166, 184, 185
Barnett, Rifleman Robert, 201
Bent, Drummer Spencer John 'Jo', 199-200
Berks Cemetery Extension, 190-1, 193
Béthune, 172, 174, 175
Birdcage, The, 94, 198
Bléquin, 35
Blighty Hole (First Aid Post), 200
Boer War, 6-9, 35, 169
Bologne, 19, 35, 148
Bonar Law, Andrew, 26, 120, 148, 185
Bonham Carter, Helen Violet, Baroness Asquith of Yarnbury, 125, 161, 171
Borland, Private John, 137
Brennand, Frank, 35, 177
British Army, 4
  British Expeditionary Force, 18, 20, 30, 31, 34, 35, 39, 48, 61, 62, 123, 172
  XI Corps, 42
  Guards Division, 36, 37
  1st Cavalry Division, 189
  9th (Scottish) Division, 33, 34, 50, 55, 72, 89, 108, 113, 126, 127, 150, 173, 177
  15th (Scottish) Division, 173
  19th (Western) Division, 46
  27th Brigade, 55, 74, 122, 124, 143, 164, 177
  52nd Brigade, 192
  56th Brigade, 46
  Dublin Fusiliers, 6
  Durham Light Infantry, 6
  Queen's Own Oxfordshire Hussars, 15, 28, 35, 38, 48
  1st Battalion East Lancashire Regiment, 199, 204
  1st Battalion Hampshire Regiment, 194
  1st Battalion Rifle Brigade, 201
  1st Battalion Somerset Light Infantry, 194, 199
  1st/4th Battalion Royal Berkshire Regiment, 191, 192
  1st Battalion Royal Warwickshire Regiment, 196, 200

215

INDEX

1st/7th Battalion Royal Warwickshire Regiment, 193
2nd Battalion Essex Regiment, 199
2nd Battalion Grenadier Guards, 37, 38, 39, 40, 41, 42, 46, 47, 49, 51, 56, 91
2nd Battalion Inniskilling Fusiliers, 199
2nd Battalion Lancashire Fusiliers, 198
2nd Battalion Royal Irish Rifles, 191
4th Queen's Own Hussars, 1, 3
6th (Service) Battalion Royal Scots Fusiliers, 51, 52 *et seq*
6th/7th (Service) Battalion Royal Scots Fusiliers, 172, 187
7th (Service) Battalion Royal Scots Fusiliers, 171, 173, 187
8th Battalion Border Regiment, 89, 94, 96
8th Battalion Gordon Highlanders, 101, 102, 103, 105, 120, 128, 133, 139, 162
9th Battalion King's Royal Rifle Corps, 50
11th Battalion Royal Scots, 98
18th (Service) Battalion (Arts & Crafts), King's Royal Rifle Corps, 191
21st Lancers, 3
135 Battery, Royal Field Artillery, 195
64th Field Company RE, 113
Buchan, Second Lieutenant A.E., 137-8
Buller, General Sir Redvers Henry VC, 6
Burnt Out Farm, 205

Calvaire (Essex) Military Cemetery, 196
Campbell, Lieutenant General Sir William, 28
Captain X, 57, 111, 198 *et seq, see also Dewar Gibb, Major Andrew*
Carden, Admiral Sir Sackville Hamilton, 23, 24, 25, 26
Cavan, Field Marshal Frederick Rudolph Lambart, 10th Earl of Cavan, 36, 37, 45, 46, 49
Cecil, Mr. E., 48
Champagne, First Battle of, 30
Charring Cross Advanced Dressing Station, 190
Christmas Truce, The, 194-6, 197
Churchill, Clementine Ogilvy Spencer-Churchill, Baroness Spencer-Churchill (née Hozier), 11, 35, 36, 37, 40, 41, 42, 43, 46, 61, 72, 73, 90, 91, 96, 97, 98, 105, 110, 120, 122, 124, 127, 129, 130, 132, 136, 137, 141, 164, 165, 166, 167, 168, 171, 187
Churchill, Jeanette, Lady Randolph (née Jerome), 3, 104
Churchill, Lord Randolph Henry Spencer-Churchill, 1, 5
Churchill, Major John Strange 'Jack' Spencer-Churchill, 15
Churchill, Randolph Frederick Edward Spencer-Churchill, 88
Churchill, Winston,
  Amalgamation of 6th (Service) Battalion, Royal Scots Fusiliers, 171
  Antwerp, defence of, 18-20
  Arrives at the 6th (Service) Battalion, Royal Scots Fusiliers, 55
  Artillery Barrage, 117-9
  Being under fire, 126-7
  Body-guard suggestion, 99
  Captured in Boer War, 7
  Childhood, 1
  Command of 6th (Service) Battalion, Royal Scots Fusiliers, 51

INDEX

Command of battalion, 48, 49 *et seq*
Command of brigade vetoed, 48
Conning Tower, the, 114, 131, 167, 204
Conservative Party, 5, 6
Dardanelles Committee, 27-8
Departure for Western Front, 35
Departure from the Admiralty, 27
Deserted brewery baths, 72
Dinner party in Hazebrouck, 85, 86-7
Drill instructions, 76-7
Duchy of Lancaster, 27, 28, 165, 178
Dundee by-election, 185-6
Dugout hit by shell, 42-3
Elected as MP for Dundee, 11
Elected as MP for Oldham, 9
Escape from Boers, 8-9
First Lord of the Admiralty, 13-15
First Patrol in No Man's Land, 105-6
Gallipoli Campaign, 20-26
German aircraft overhead, 127-8, 136
Hit by shell fragment, 110-1
Home Secretary, 12
In Boer War, 6-9
In Cuba, 1-2
In India, 2-5
Initial reception by battalion, 60
Joining the Grenadier Guards, 36-51
Joining the Liberals, 10
Kaiser's birthday, 96-7
Leaving the Army, 161-5
Miner strikes, 12
Minister of Munitions, 185
Nearly arrested as spy, 109-10
Oldham by-election, 5, 6
Painting, 108

Queen's Own Oxfordshire Hussars, 15
Resignation from the Army, 171-2
Resignation Speech, 28-9
Resigns commission, 5
Return to Oldham, 9
Senior officers' visit to No Man's Land, 151-2
Sentry asleep at Post, 44
Silesia, German army manoeuvres, 16
Singing, 73-5
Sudan Expedition, 3-5
The Malakand Field Force, 3
The River War, 5, 10
Thoughts and Adventures, 134
Thoughts on the Battle of Loos, 74
Variants of the Offensive, 45, 103
Views on alcohol, 91
War on lice, 68-9, 72, 177
Writing for the *Morning Post*, 4, 6, 9, 10
Würzburg, German army manoeuvres, 16
Collins, Sergeant Frank, 196
Conning Tower, The, 114, 131, 167, 204
Convent, The, 114, 116, 167, 199, 200, 204
Cuthbert, Private David, 138
Curzon, George Nathaniel, 1st Marquess Curzon of Kedleston, 47, 58, 120, 145, 166

Daily Graphic, 2
Daily Record, 185
Daily Telegraph, 2, 11, 40
Deedes, William Francis, Baron Deedes, 40
Delennelle Farm, 84, 95, 154
Dewar Gibb, Major Andrew, 56, 57, 65 *et seq*
    Made Adjutant, 111
Dunbar, Jo, 65

INDEX

Dunottar Castle, 6

Ebenezer Farm, 39, 40
Eden, Captain Robert Anthony, 1st Earl of Avon, 200
Estcourt, 6, 7
Essex House, 196

Fergusson, General Sir Charles, 7th Baronet, 83, 84, 172
Fisher, Admiral of the Fleet John Arbuthnot, 1st Baron Fisher, 15, 22, 24, 25, 26, 27, 154, 160, 161
Foulkes, Captain, 65, 81, 82
Fox, Robert, 133, 142
French, Field Marshal John Denton Pinkstone, 1st Earl of Ypres, 32, 33, 34, 35, 36, 46, 47, 48
French, Rifleman Albert, 191
Fulton, Lance Corporal Robert, 108
Furse, Lieutenant General Sir William Thomas, 55, 85, 120, 129, 130, 152, 170

Gallipoli Campaign, 20-26, 47, 121, 154, 165, 183, 184
Gilbert, Sir Martin, 60, 106, 111
Gilliland, Corporal Walter, 44
Gordon, Lieutenant Colonel Edward Ian Drumearn, 171
Greenhill-Gardyne, Lieutenant Colonel Alan David, 127, 128
Greenok, 185
Grigg, Edward William Macleay, 1st Baron Altringham, 40, 41

Haig, Field Marshal Douglas, 1st Earl Haig, 48, 49, 119, 126, 148, 163, 169, 170, 171, 172, 184
Hakewill Smith, Lieutenant Edmund 'Bomb-boy', 60, 64, 72, 87, 106, 108, 112, 151, 152
Haking, General Sir Richard Cyril Byrne, 42
Haldane, General Sir James Aylmer Lowthorp, 6-7
Hankey, Colonel Morris Pascal Alers, 1st Baron Hankey, 22
Harvey, Captain, 65, 71, 81
Hawksley, Major John, 195
Hazebrouck, 85, 86, 87, 153, 190
   Station Hotel, 85, 86, 87
Hearn, Major Gordon Risley RE, 113
Herzog, Lieutenant Emile, 72
Hohenzollern Redoubt, 33
Holland, Lieutenant General Sir Arthur Edward Aveling, 74, 85, 127
Hope Farm, 191
Hospice The, 84, 90, 95, 97, 103, 104, 116, 124, 134, 135, 137, 202
Hunter, Sir Charles Roderick, 3rd Baronet, 47, 48
Hunter's Avenue, 200
Hurt, Private Reginald, 130, 139, 140
Hyde Park Corner, 192, 194
Hyde Park Corner (Royal Berks) Cemetery, 191

Jackson, Admiral of the Fleet Sir Henry Bradwardine, 23, 160
Jeffreys, General George Darell, 1st Baron Jeffreys, 37, 39, 40, 41
Joffre, *Marechal* Joseph Jacques Césaire, 30

Kemp, Lieutenant Lawrence, 64, 132
   wounded, 132
Khaki Election, 9
Kitchener, Field Marshal Horatio Herbert, 1st Earl Kitchener, 3, 5, 18, 22, 23, 24, 25, 26, 28, 33, 55, 64, 155, 171, 184

La Crèche, 89
La Gorgue, 37, 45

Lancashire Cottage Cemetery, 201, 204
Laurence Farm (Lawrence Farm), 84, 96, 108, 114, 115, 123, 124, 129, 131, 132, 133, 137, 138, 140, 141, 144, 159, 164, 165, 204
Le Gheer, 90, 98, 199, 200, 204, 205
Le Romarin, 95, 173
Lichfield, 187
Lille, 31, 190
Lloyd George, David, 1st Earl Lloyd-George of Dwyfor, 11, 24, 120, 160, 166, 169, 173, 184, 185
London Rifle Brigade Cemetery, 202
London Support Farm, 119, 120, 202, 203
Loos, Battle of, 32, 34, 55, 56, 63, 71, 74, 89, 137
Lyne, C.E., 109, 110

MacDonald, Major Neil Roderick 'Foghorn', 149, 150
Macready, General Sir Cecil Frederick Nevil, 1st Baronet, 12, 146, 147
Maison 1875, 84, 94, 95, 203
Markham, Sir Arthur Basil, 1st Baronet, 168
Marlborough, Duke of, 1, 15, 37, 88
McBride, Rifleman Samuel, 191
McCracken, Lieutenant General Sir Frederick William Nicholas, 174
McDavid (MacDavid), Lieutenant Jock, 72, 79, 82, 105, 106, 111, 112, 123, 124, 151, 156, 177
wounded, 111-2, 123
McGuire, Corporal John, 73, 107
McKenna's Bridge, 203
McLellan, Private Andrew, 202
McNulty, Private, 199
Merris, 55, 62, 75
Merville, 42, 192
Mesen (Messines), 189

Meteren, 55, 88
Military Service Bill, 121
Milne, Captain Alan Alexander 'A.A.', 200
Milner, Alfred, 1st Viscount Milner, 169
Moolenacker, 55, 61, 83, 84, 89, 95
Moolenacker Farm, 59
Moore, Private Andrew, 143
Morning Post, 4, 6, 9, 10
Mud Corner Cemetery, 193
Mud Lane, 192, 193, 194

Napier-Clavering, Lieutenant Francis Donald, 113-4
Neuve Chapelle, 37
Neuve Chapelle, Battle of, 31
Nieppe, 93, 102, 120, 127, 190, 201
North-West Frontier, 2
Notre Dame de Lorette, 50

'Old Bill', *see Bairnsfather, Lieutenant Bruce*
Oldham, 5, 6, 8, 9
Oliver, Admiral of the Fleet Sir Henry Francis, 23
Omdurman, 5
Oswald, James, 5, 6
Outtersteene, 87, 153

Palfrey, Private Ernest, 196
Palmer, Lieutenant Ronald William Poulton, 192-3, 194
Papôt, 173, 174
Paris, 31, 56, 146
Parnell, Second Lieutenant The Honourable William Alastair Darner, 46-7
Pioneer, 2
Ploegsteert, 34, 83, 85, 94, *et seq*
Ploegsteert Memorial, 190-1
Ploegsteert Wood, 189, 190, 191, 192, 193, 194, 195, 197, 198, 200

INDEX

Ploegsteert Wood Military Cemetery, 194
Plugstreet, *see Ploegsteert*
Plugstreet 14-18 Experience, 191-2
Pretoria, 7
Prowse, Brigadier General C.B., 194
Prowse Point Cemetery, 191, 194, 198

Ramsey, Captain Bryce, 65, 78, 79, 81, 95, 99, 100, 112, 117, 140, 143, 154
Rifle House Cemetery, 200
Robertson, Bandmaster W., 185-6
Robertson, Sir C. Scott, 48
Rosenberg Chateau Military Cemetery Extension, 190-1
Rossell, Private William, 120
Royal Military College Sandhurst, 1, 64, 72
Royal Navy, 13-27
    Royal Fleet Reserve, 18
    Royal Naval Division, 18-20
    Warships,
        Agamemnon, 17
        Cornwallis, 25
        Dreadnought, 16

Salisbury, Lord, Robert Gascoyne-Cecil, 3rd Marquess of Salisbury, 3, 5
Sanctuary Wood, 64
Scott, C.P., 166, 169
Scott, F.G., 59
Seely, Major-General John Edward Bernard, 1st Baron Mottistone, 19, 148
Sevastopol, Siege of, 78
Shell Scandal, 26, 32-3, 165
Sidney Street, Siege of, 13
Simon, John Allesbrook, 1st Viscount Simon, 122
Sinclair, Major Archibald Henry Macdonald, 1st Viscount Thurso, 55, 59, 65, 72, 81, 82, 89, 98, 110, 125, 127, 128, 130, 131, 132, 133, 134, 135, 136, 156, 159, 162, 174
Sint-Elooi, 189
Smith, Frederick Edwin, 1st Earl of Birkenhead, 145, 146, 169
    arrest, 146-8
Somme, Battle of, 126, 166, 169, 184, 194
Soyer Farm, 84, 95, 124, 137, 201, 204
Spencer-Churchill, Charles Richard John, 9th Duke of Marlborough, 88
Spiers, Captain Edward, 50, 55
St. Omer, 35, 36, 37, 46, 48, 49, 50, 59, 119, 146, 147
St. Yvon (St. Yves), 190, 194, 197
Steenwerck, 95, 174
Stockwell, Captain C.I., 195-6
Strand Military Cemetery, 190
Strazeele, 88

Talbot Kelly, Lieutenant Richard Barrett, 192
Teacher, Lieutenant Colonel Norman McDonald, 87
Tennant, Harold John, Under-Secretary of State for War, 47, 136
The Strand trench, 190
The Bystander, see Bairnsfather, Lieutenant Bruce
The Times, 26, 28, 40, 136, 191
Toronto Avenue Cemetery, 194
Trotter, Colonel Gerald, 116, 164
Tudor, Lieutenant General Sir Henry Hugh, 118, 119, 126, 129, 130, 150

Underhill Farm Cemetery, 192
Underhill, Second Lieutenant Edward, 34

Victoria Cross, 200

Vimy Ridge, 50

Walshe, Brigadier General Henry Ernest, 120, 122, 143, 162
Warnave river, 90, 94, 203
Waterloo, Battle of, 4
Wilkinson, Private Harry, 198
Wilson, Lieutenant General Sir H.F.M., 202

Wolseley, Sir Garnet, 1

Ypres (Ieper), 31, 32, 34, 55, 56, 64, 83, 93, 189, 191, 198
Ypres, First Battle of, 31
Ypres, Second Battle of, 32
Ypres Salient, 32, 34, 55, 56, 194, 198